The Peace Script

Rhetoric, Culture, and Social Critique

Series Editor
John Louis Lucaites

Editorial Board
Jeffrey A. Bennett

Carole Blair

Joshua Gunn

Robert Hariman

Debra Hawhee

Claire Sisco King

Steven Mailloux

Raymie E. McKerrow

Toby Miller

Phaedra C. Pezzullo

Austin Sarat

Janet Staiger

Barbie Zelizer

THE PEACE *Script*

Framing Violence in US Anti-War Dissent

DOMINIC J. MANTHEY

THE UNIVERSITY OF ALABAMA PRESS
Tuscaloosa

The University of Alabama Press
Tuscaloosa, Alabama 35487-0380
uapress.ua.edu

Copyright © 2025 by the University of Alabama Press
All rights reserved.

Inquiries about reproducing material from this work should
be addressed to the University of Alabama Press.

Typeface: Adobe Caslon Pro

Cover image: stock.adobe.com
Cover design: Sandy Turner Jr.

Cataloging-in-Publication data is available from the Library
of Congress.
ISBN: 978-0-8173-2246-5 (cloth)
ISBN: 978-0-8173-6218-8 (paper)
E-ISBN: 978-0-8173-9574-2

To Sarah and Isaac

Contents

List of Figures   ix

Acknowledgments   **xi**

Introduction: Fighting War by Scripting Peace   1

1. Rehearsing a Masculine Peace in the Copperhead Movement   26

2. Violent Compassion in the Anti-Imperialist League   47

3. Scripting a Spectacle in Henry Ford's Peace Expedition   75

4. Maternal Peace and Memory in the Mothers' Movement   100

5. Rewriting the National Script: Vietnam Veterans against the War   122

Conclusion: The Remnants of "Negative" Peace and the Future of War   143

Notes   153

Bibliography   195

Index   219

Figures

1. Advertisement for the Greater American Exposition in Omaha, Nebraska, 1899   51

2. Clifford Berryman's *Washington Post* comic showing a small Emilio Aguinaldo trying to pry Uncle Sam's massive boot off from the Philippines   55

3. Advertisement for Ford Model T with Henry Ford's face below the caption "Buy a Ford—and Spend the Difference"   80

4. "First Photographs Made Aboard Ford Peace Ship," *Philadelphia Inquirer*, December 28, 1915   88

5. An advertisement for Vietnam Veterans against the War in *Playboy* magazine, February 1971   123

Acknowledgments

I would like to thank Stephen H. Browne for the motivation, support, friendship, and intellectual engagement he offered me, combining his vast knowledge with genuine curiosity about what I had to say, even if it did not quite make sense at first. I thank him for always pushing me to refine my thinking without ever telling me what to think.

Kirt Wilson, Anne Demo, Bradford Vivian, and John McCarthy also helped me tremendously and inspired me to rise to the challenge of their own creative and critical thinking. Rosa Eberly and Michele Kennerly were formative for my development as a scholar during these years. Thomas Benson, Jeremy Engels, William Blair, Lior Sternfeld, Ekaterina Haskins, Mary Stuckey, and Pamela VanHaitsma helped me at various phases of this project, for which I am very grateful. Barbara Biesecker, Allison Prasch, and Sara McKinnon offered useful advice to elements of this project at conferences. Anthony Irizarry, Keren Wang, Jeremy Cox, Brandon Johnosn, Matthew Parnell, Michael Delayo, and John Rountree also helped me think through this project.

I thank the Department of Communication Arts and Sciences at Penn State University for funding my travel over the years on trips that spurred my exploration of anti-war protest. Special thanks to Daniel Waterman and the entire editorial staff at UAP, as well as my two peer reviewers, for their professional and timely assistance in sharpening my thinking. My colleagues at the University of South Dakota also gave me a supportive environment to wrap up the manuscript. Finally, I want to thank my family for all they have done for me. To my wife, Sarah, and son, Isaac, thank you for always being there.

The Peace Script

Introduction

Fighting War by Scripting Peace

"I have almost reached the regrettable conclusion that the Negro's great stumbling block in his stride toward freedom is not the White Citizen's Counciler or the Ku Klux Klanner, but the white moderate, who is more devoted to 'order' than to justice; who prefers a *negative peace* which is the absence of tension to a positive peace which is the presence of justice."
—Martin Luther King Jr. "Letter from a Birmingham Jail"

The greatest obstacle facing peace may not be war but peace itself. Consider the fallout from Secretary of State Colin Powell's address on Iraq's alleged possession of weapons of mass destruction. In its wake, citizens around the world united for one of the largest mobilizations of dissent in recorded history.[1] From Catherine Verrall, a seventy-two-year old Canadian grandmother armed with a sign that read "Bombs Kill Kids" to hundreds of thousands of New Yorkers shouting "Earth to [US President George W.] Bush[!] No war!," these global demonstrations revealed the power and potential of peace.[2] The massive turnout was undeniably diverse: Christians, Buddhists, and Muslims joined together to protest the war across nations from Japan to Thailand to Brazil.[3] If the health of a democracy depends on its degree of civic engagement, then maybe it wasn't naive to feel optimistic about the future in 2003. Listening closely, one could faintly hear a unifying chord of peace calling for harmonious coexistence beyond borders, race, and creed.

These protests, however, also illustrated the vulnerability of peaceful, democratic dissent to violent rhetoric. While most protesters were nonaggressive and inclusive, some displayed more divisive and extreme tendencies. In Greece, for instance, dozens of disguised activists threw "gasoline bombs" at police.[4] In South Africa, a group of activists reportedly yelled "Viva Osama," in honor of Bin Laden.[5] In the United States, accusations of "authoritarianism and anti-Semitism" arose within the ranks of protesters.[6] For all its promise, which is indeed great, peace rhetoric is not immune to the temptations of anger and hostility it opposes. This book is predicated on the idea that such proximity of violence to nonviolence is no historical oddity; nor is it mere discursive quirk. In fact, the history of US anti-war dissent testifies to a frequent exchange between the language of war and the language of peace. Determining what counts as "peaceful" in US history repeatedly involves other judgments, such as who counts as a proper citizen. Often, these judgments are acts of cultural exclusion. Of particular concern in this book is the extent to which such peace rhetoric reflects and reframes long-standing inequalities related to race, gender, and class.

My criticism of violent peace rhetoric should not evoke a dismissal of peace advocates or an indictment of the goal of peace. Quite the opposite. Those who foster a democratic, inclusive, and equitable culture of peace are doing enormously difficult work that inspires this book. By considering the shortfalls of several prominent peace arguments in US history, which is my narrow focus, we can better understand when someone argues for peace well. This project strives to appreciate such rhetorical work—not to mention the social, political, and financial sacrifices required to persuade people not simply to oppose the overt violence typical of warfare but also to unite and build a sustainable future free from needless conflict and inequality.

To best show the nature of this discursive labor, I propose the "peace script," a partly rhetorical, partly historical concept to interpret and compare the symbolic construction of anti-war discourse. The peace script acts as a sort of topos, or rhetorical theme, across time and place that is present whenever people communicate opposition to violence, real or perceived, with others. As public texts, these scripts often help fellow citizens rehearse a version of peace because they tend to dramatize society through protagonists, antagonists, motives, themes, and a plot, all designed to end violence and, presumably, bring harmony to the world.[7] Many peace scripts are admirable and not riddled with violent implications, as seen throughout the tradition of Quaker pacificism or the work of the Woman's Peace Party during World War I.[8] Nevertheless, a rhetorical approach to peace scripts exposes how easily people can co-opt and distort the ideals, assumptions, and values of peace—what we might call the "myths of peace"—to justify shockingly unequal worldviews. While professing to offer a nonviolent alternative to war, the scripts I focus on use the occasion to strengthen cultural hierarchies, often based on race, gender, and class. To be clear, the five social movements under consideration here do not represent the totality of peace activism or even come close to expressing the best arguments for peace available. Nevertheless, each movement marks a well-publicized voice against war at a critical moment in US history when competing visions of peace were drowned out by cultural assumptions about who does and does not belong in a supposedly peaceful America.

The history of these scripts serves as a cautionary tale about the prospects for democracy and dissent during the "perilous time" of war when governments threaten civil liberties.[9] In fact, we repeatedly see that the presence of volatile peace scripts coincides with periods of governmental repression targeting protesters. As long as countries wage wars, the quality of peace rhetoric will greatly depend on grassroots activists who go against national policy to imagine a better future. These anti-war activists face tremendous obstacles, ranging from social pressure to draconian law to the threat of bodily harm or even death.[10] In each war covered in this book, to varying degrees, we see the government crack down on First Amendment rights to stifle public opposition, often labeling activism "disloyal."[11] Robert Ivie, a renowned scholar of war rhetoric, reminds us that in such periods lacking robust democratic dissent, we risk undemocratic rhetoric taking the stage along with acts of scapegoating and dehumanization.[12]

While many have addressed this pro-war demagoguery, my research highlights such tendencies specifically in anti-war movements during key military conflicts in US history.[13] We frequently see that when the government declares war and dissent is stigmatized, activism dries up and lacks diversity. The few who retain the privilege and power to speak out in the face of adversity drown out other voices and often offer the public a highly charged, reactionary peace script. This book details how such dissenters employ "warlike practices of reverse recrimination" that illustrate how the language of peace can be used to reframe racial, gendered, and class-based inequalities, now ensconced in a sacred—though superficial—aura of harmony, civility, and decorum. Like a war hawk might justify the need for violence by framing the enemy as a "savage other," peace protesters also might vilify a group, advocating for a vision of society that perpetuates systems of exclusion.[14]

In each chapter, we learn something about social movement failure, as I excavate the argumentative remains of peace movements that did not achieve their goal of immediately ending warfare. Such failure is rich in significance, giving us insight into what kind of peace rhetoric was permitted, even embraced, while other types were heavily repressed; what combination of race, gender, and class made for an acceptable, even popular, anti-war script; and, most shockingly, how citizens can mimic the language of a progressive and sustainable peace while publicizing a deeply exclusionary vision of society. Although not all peace movements employ such rhetoric, studying those prone to violence offers a fresh perspective on the pitfalls of peace talk, as well as the utility of rhetorical analysis for any sustainable peace-building project. To better write a peace script, we must study the ones that miss the mark and perpetuate inequalities. In the twenty-first century, as polarization and aggression show few signs of waning, Martin Luther King Jr.'s diagnosis of America's peace problem seems spot on: one group's vision of peace may be another group's worst nightmare. In his anti-war address at Riverside Church, King implored his audience to counter militarism by thinking more fully about peace. We must not fixate on one aspect of war but examine the connections among warfare, racism, poverty, and sexism that are too often shrouded under dubious overtures to civility and nonviolence.[15] Such is the goal of this book.

But why do we so easily miss these connections? Why do some protests fail to address larger systems of inequality and cultural violence? Why do voices of peace sometimes sound as aggressive as those of war? To answer these questions, I draw on Johan Galtung's ethical standard of "positive" peace.[16] This concept refers not simply to the absence of war but to a nuanced approach that addresses myriad forms of violence to create a sustainable future where all humans may flourish. Strictly speaking, none of the movements in this book achieve a "positive" peace. Such a goal, to be fair, is an open-ended process rather than a zero-sum, "all-or-nothing" task.[17] Instead of labeling these scripts as instances of "negative" peace and moving on, I inquire *how* these scripts arrived at their ethical shortcomings while achieving a degree of popularity. Some came close to a "positive" peace, but none avoided rescripting deep-seated assumptions of race, gender, and class into their anti-war appeals. Even if the violence sanctioned is old, its justifications are new, marked by their historical moment and, as anti-war scripts, are written with the symbols of harmony, nonviolence, and civility. This book contributes to the work of "positive" peace by showing how slippery it is as an objective. Nevertheless, there is no other target worth pursuing if we wish to end war without sowing the seeds of further conflict.

The Fog of Peace: Demystifying Anti-War Rhetoric

To better glimpse how easily one can shift from a "positive" to a "negative" peace script, consider the career of US politician Ernest Gruening. As a young man, Gruening wrote acclaimed essays opposing President Woodrow Wilson's intervention in Haiti, eventually becoming a leading voice of peace for the Anti-Imperialist League. In arguing for the self-determination of other countries, Gruening advocated something resembling a "positive" peace. Rather than just opposing conflict—the realm of "negative" peace—Gruening considered the conditions for a sustainable peace among nations.[18] However, the plot of Gruening's peace script thickens and reveals just how elusive "positive" peace is as a goal for activism. Years later, acting as head of the Division of Territories and Island Possessions for President Franklin Delano Roosevelt, Gruening reversed course and squared off against Puerto Ricans fighting for independence.[19] In pursuing what has been called a "cross-national" peace (one dictated by the United States and its allies), the erstwhile anti-imperialist now sounded like a champion of colonialism and a proponent of the violence he once repudiated. To his critics, Gruening's defense of the officers responsible for the "Ponce Massacre," a March 1937 tragedy where police fired on pro-national activists and killed nineteen Puerto Rican civilians, was the final straw.[20] The former dove of peace now circled his prey as a war hawk. He replaced his plea for a global, "positive" peace with a curt call to end the conflict on unilateral terms. Clearly, Gruening abandoned his morals to embrace a "negative" peace. Or was it so simple? For Gruening, as for many of his colleagues occupying positions of power, the task was less to choose between war and peace, or even a "positive" or "negative" peace, than it was to find the path of least resistance for a specific policy objective—one that some might call "peace," but many would not.

Gruening's tacking back and forth from a "positive" to a "negative" peace position does not mean we must be distrustful of peace activism or hold it to an impossible standard. On the contrary, Galtung's ethical ideal of "positive" peace is a generative concept that invites conversation rather than ending it. As peace scholar David Barash states, "The movement toward peace is not an all-or-nothing phenomenon . . . [it] is likely to be halting and fragmentary, with substantial success along certain dimensions and likely failures along others."[21] We do not need to deem a peace movement or script as irredeemably "negative" but instead can inquire how it comes up short and, most significant for rhetorical critics, why certain groups find it persuasive. Galtung's distinction helps us learn from previous scripts by giving rhetorical studies a standard by which to interpret and compare peace discourse, considering how it may have both "positive" and "negative" elements. Frequently, such tension arises when a movement opposes a direct form of violence, such as a war, while embracing a less obvious, more structural form of violence. With this in mind, this book examines major peace movements' arguments to bring attention to the various rhetorical strategies that stifle the work toward "positive" peace. As Barash describes, this involves not only dealing with the physical realities of war and inequality but also "redrawing of the 'conceptual cartography' through which most people structure their view of the world and their place in it."[22]

How better to do this than through the peace appeals that circulate during times of war? Consider the dramatic discursive shifts in response to the Afghanistan War, the longest war in US history. For decades, the United States dedicated an astonishing number of lives and resources toward an objective many argued was impossible to achieve through force and occupation. Was the goal "peace"? Depending on who you listened to, it certainly was. Still, it could symbolize so much more: "civilization," "progress," "pluralism," "tolerance," "freedom," "democratic aspirations," and "safety."[23] The uses of war and peace appear endless—and this makes the task of peace-building all the more complex.[24] The flexibility and slipperiness of peace rhetoric again becomes apparent when new global opportunities arise to oppose human rights violations, such as Syria in 2011 and Ukraine in 2022. Suddenly, some of the same actors who supported the wars in Afghanistan and Iraq now advocated against direct involvement, embracing an isolationist position.[25] This "halting," zigzag pattern of rejecting violence of one kind to allow violence of another, all while borrowing from the language of peace to justify clashing policy positions, describes many peace scripts written by foreign policymakers. The buzzwords, motives, and values tied to these arguments chart the "conceptual cartography" that illustrates the rhetorical history of war and peace.[26] Seeing this map is requisite for building a lasting peace.

In all this, we cannot lose sight of a crucial observation: the consequences of peace discourse are not evenly distributed across society but tend to disproportionately harm marginalized communities. Analyzing peace scripts according to Galtung's distinction can help address the disparities of peace by asking how, in the formulation of anti-war rhetoric, are certain symbols, identities, and values, no matter how peaceful and harmonious they may sound, possibly working to justify future violence whether based on race, gender, and class. Let us go back to Gruening, whose tenure as governor of Alaska demonstrates the need for this focus. At this time, he again exhibited both "positive" and "negative" peace dimensions by seeking enhanced rights and statehood for the territory while overseeing the forced detention of its indigenous population during World War II. He would later confess, as a sort of apology, that he made the wrong decision because he "did not know what resentment might lurk behind their smiling faces."[27] Years later, as senator of Alaska, he was one of only two Congress members to vote against the Gulf of Tonkin Resolution—a bold, albeit futile, attempt to stymie the Vietnam conflict.[28] Once again, violence and nonviolence blur as policymakers rarely consider the harm done by their decisions to marginalized communities.

These tales of "positive" and "negative" peace can also teach us about a tension between war and democracy: the delicate and often volatile balance between persuasion, volition, and freedom on one side and coercion, force, and repression on the other. We see the susceptibility of peace discourse to violence, of democratic people to undemocratic acts, when we analyze the rhetorical dynamics of anti-war movements rather than focus solely on generalizations and abstract ideals. Therefore, we must become as sensitive to the myths of peace as we are to the myths of war. When understood this way, Gruening is the proverbial canary in the coal mine, warning us of the harm we may indirectly sanction in even our most self-assured moments of nonviolence. In his words, and in all those who fill the pages of this book, are lessons about the discursive ecosystem of the United States and the sacrifices believed necessary to sustain it, often voiced by the privileged few. To be clear, not all peace discourse is equally toxic, and few are irreparably corrupt. The value of Galtung's theory is that it allows us to identify and critique "negative" peace with an eye toward more "positive" ends.

Though not all appeals to peace fall prey to the trappings of war, we find that peace dissent, like most protest, tends to be as robust as the democratic culture surrounding it. Especially in times of war, the purview of this book, we find undemocratic climates abound, typified by extreme government pressure on citizens to conform. I join other scholars in calling this period the "emergency context" from which a unique script is composed: the war script. In opposition to the peace script, the war script narrates current events through the language of uniformity, obedience, and even repression, often damaging the vitality of peace discourse by reducing the diversity of voices available to the public. Before we can see this process, we must first dispel the myths of peace and their relationship to democratic dissent.

The Myths That Make the Script

The myths of peace refer to the deeply ingrained cultural attitudes and assumptions regarding nonviolence and anti-war advocacy. These beliefs frequently appear in peace scripts and help explain how even the most well-intentioned pursuit of a "positive" peace might go astray and veer toward a "negative" worldview. These myths cloud our ability to take peace seriously—to see it as not just the absence of war but a call to rethink the terms of human coexistence; a challenge to create a sustainable world that offers everyone the chance to thrive. The goal of identifying these myths and their presence in peace scripts is to foster a nuanced analysis of failed peace or what Barash describes as a "positive approach to negative peace . . . [that] distinguish[es] as carefully among the different varieties of peace as we now do about different wars."[29] The five peace scripts in this book are undoubtedly "negative" at times, and each reveals ways that US citizens fall short of an admirable goal because they fail to question their own cultural biases and take stock of the myths of peace. Each chapter cautions us to avoid doing so in the future.

First among the myths we often use to script peace is the belief that *peace is natural*. Versions of this belief appear when people condemn war as a byproduct of a modern, industrialized, technologically advanced society estranged from humanity's original state of nature.[30] We do not need to delve deep into philosophical debates to see how this belief might shape perceptions of current affairs and grant peace rhetoric a coveted moral status. Peace, however, is not necessarily natural, at least not in several significant ways. Some of the oldest relics of past civilizations detail combat, sacrifice, and other rituals of violence in an affirmative way.[31] Even if we exclude the endless wars and battles throughout recorded history, we cannot ignore the structural violence long permitted toward women, children, and other populations deemed "naturally inferior," all of which suggest violence may be more natural than peace. One may reasonably ask, "What do we gain from this pessimistic view of human nature?" In deeming "natural peace" a myth, or at least a simplification, we begin to move past the troublesome binaries of peace/war, natural/artificial, and violence/nonviolence. This correction allows us to grasp better the way an appeal to these distinctions operates in a given time and place, as well as to develop peace advocacy beyond a knee-jerk reaction against war.

Consider how nations across the world chose to remain uninvolved in the Rwandan genocide, whose aftermath led to the First and Second Congo Wars, the latter marking the deadliest conflict since World War II at the time of writing this project.[32] More recently, US politicians and citizens express hesitancy and ambivalence toward the Russian invasion of Ukraine. To *not* engage, the thinking goes, maintains one country's natural peace or, even worse, simply allows the "natural course of events" to transpire in a far-off, uncivilized land. This myth offers citizens the pleasure of feeling like they are pro-peace while allowing a situation antithetical to peace to continue. When the dominant culture of a nation defines what is "natural" and "peaceful," as seen repeatedly in this book, the myths of peace tend to perpetuate racial, gendered, and class-based inequalities.

The second myth of peace builds off the first by claiming that peace is not only natural but *passive*. In this view, peace is a default position that lacks depth compared to other political beliefs. This assumption also animates isolationist appeals that claim the moral high ground by urging nations to do nothing. We see this in contemporary responses to injustice abroad, such as the mistreatment of Uyghurs in China, but also in responses to domestic issues, such as homelessness.[33] Doing nothing, the thinking goes, is an intrinsically peaceful stance, while intervening in another's problem will disrupt our comfortable state of being. This myth presents peace as a property or object that one might possess and protect rather than an activity or gift you extend to others. We hear versions of this belief when people criticize activists, arguing that they create conflict and sow discord.[34] Of course, peace is no default or passive position; it is as contentious, lively, and prone to debate as any public policy. When we treat peace policy as passive, we deprive it of a meaningful engagement with politics and culture, excluding it from the public sphere where it gets its energy and makes its impact.

The third myth of peace draws from the first two to assert that *war and peace are diametrically opposed*. In the abstract, we can list many differences between the two, but they are harder to see in practice. A quick survey of wartime discourse will disabuse most of the idea that the terms "peace" and "war" are used with consistency across time and place. People confronting conflict tend to be pragmatic, responding to the real-world problems before them instead of consulting a handbook or philosophical treatise on peace. As a result, we see peace discourse take on diverse issues, beliefs, values, and emotions characteristic of a given time and place. As a rhetorical critic, my focus is on this realm of public affairs: the dynamic, disputatious world of politics where citizens battle over definitions of violence, harm, and coercion every day. The appeals to peace in the public sphere are ever-shifting, nomadic, and protean; they may easily traverse and betray ideological boundaries.[35] This does not mean that there is no meaningful difference between war and peace. Indeed, we must carefully analyze how citizens rhetorically mobilize that dichotomy—sometimes masking a "negative" peace as a "positive" one.

The fourth myth tells us that *peace is not an organized position* and lacks coordinated, collective action except for perhaps a few sterling examples. One need only glance at peace theorist Gene Sharp's compilation of nonviolent strategies to see how creative and dynamic peace protest can be.[36] In its most extreme form, this myth denies that anti-war activists are activists at all. For those who contest war and fear the label "dissident," this is surely an attractive idea. This myth reassures peace advocates and their opponents that they are merely reacting to some form of unacceptable violence like any reasonable person ought to rather than pushing against the grain. This assumption may even explain why there are relatively few studies of peace organizations in US history. If peace is a short-lived, knee-jerk response from isolated individuals, then how could we ever analyze its formal qualities? Peace activism, as this book shows, is activism in the purest sense—a collaborative, structured, and organized type of social action with rhetorical patterns. In fact, discrete peace organizations with official names, resources, and adherents tend to be among the few remaining voices of dissent once a war is afoot. To presume that peace is just an emotional reaction lacking order is to ignore major groups of resistance during moments of significant national and global change. Peace activists must not only organize to offer a compelling vision of peace against these myths but, if they are to succeed, also must script their dissent in the drama of their time to intrigue the populace. Peace scripts express this dual struggle in both "positive" and "negative" ways.

The fifth myth tells us *there is only one peace*. Definitions of peace are as diverse as conflict itself, and even the most single-minded peace movement cannot avoid influence from the issues, controversies, and values of their time. A rhetorical analysis of peace gives us a way to trace these scripts of peace and catalog the various types of "negative" peace that circulate throughout American history. My effort to debunk this myth motivates every page of this book as I shift from civil war to imperialist conflict to wars for democracy. Each type of armed conflict calls forth its own set of ideas, arguments, and policies that shape the debate over that war's legitimacy. As definitions of warfare shift, expand, and break down, so too do definitions of peace. Moving past the belief in a single, monolithic "peace" makes it possible for a more intricate study of how people oppose warfare—whether as advocates of "peace," "anti-war" dissidents, or staunch "isolationists"—and, in doing so, see how each offers a new script for future generations.

This brings us to the final myth that tells us *peace is a utopian or idealistic position*. The "flower child" trope during the 1960s and 1970s is a prime example of how this myth shapes perceptions of peace in the United States. "Yes, certainly these kids mean well," the thinking goes, "but they don't have the slightest clue how the real world works nor the guts to make the tough decisions required to keep a nation safe. Such naivety belongs safely tucked away at music festivals or college campuses." The condescension dripping from this myth reinforces its blatant attempt to gate-keep civic discourse by banishing some styles of peace talk in order to protect ostensibly "serious political deliberation." The opposite couldn't be truer. Peace activists prove time and again to be doggedly pragmatic, responding to each new crisis with a creative response. For this reason, we cannot study warfare without appreciating the dynamics of peace and anti-war arguments over the years. Each armed struggle hails peace activists and requires them to modify their arguments. Even the most "negative" scripts, ones that use opposition to war as a chance to validate inequality and dehumanization, offer lessons for attaining a "positive" script, even if we always strive imperfectly toward that goal.

I must give special mention to Ellen Gorsevski's rich work on peace rhetoric, which highlights similar myths that cloud our ability and tempt peace-loving people into acts of dehumanization and scapegoating. When analyzing the "rhetorical climate" of peace, she cautions against simplistic thinking to instead focus on new possibilities for peaceful persuasion characterized by what she and others call "rehumanizing" rhetoric. Refusing to perpetuate divisions among people, this type of rhetoric creates common ground by doing the hard work of seeing oneself and others as interconnected.[37] In this spirit, my book explores US history to better understand its "rhetorical climate" and the nature of cultural conflict as it recurs during war—asking why we forsake "positive" and "rehumanizing" rhetoric in favor of "negative" acts of dehumanization? While I focus on "dehumanizing" peace scripts, these offer useful lessons on how to combat the myths that blind us to the roots of violence. To summarize, peace is neither natural, passive, binary, unorganized, nor hopelessly idealistic. These reductive ideas, nevertheless, contribute to the allure of peace that convinces us that nonviolence is an object worthy of pursuit—and of course, it is! But first, we must dispel these myths, asking how they aid in the composition of peace scripts. There is no time when the stakes are higher than during the "emergency context" of war, the special focus of this book.

The "Emergency Script" of War: Undemocratic Dissent during Undemocratic Times

Setting the Parameters of the Peace Script

Interpreting a peace script depends on how we conceptualize warfare, society, and rhetoric.[38] My approach in this regard is founded upon three assumptions: (1) the boundaries among state violence, civil society, and public discourse are fluid and contextually negotiated by members of a nation; (2) the interaction among these three is informative of the shape of US history and national identity; and (3) the mass mobilization of people around a collective identity opposed to war, as expressed in peace scripts, is a key variable for tracking the definitional changes that accompany state violence. Such entanglements of rhetoric, war, and civil society are by no means an uncommon topic in rhetorical studies. Aristotle, for instance, cites "war and peace" as one of the five primary areas of public deliberation, and although he doesn't focus on political dissent, he does highlight the contextual nature of such debates and their impact on a given polity.[39]

Ignoring or downplaying the role of activism during war perpetuates the misleading belief that the battlefront is a far-off, distant place while the home front undergoes only minimal change. Robert Ivie looks closely at this complex dynamic between war and dissent and stresses its role in shaping democratic aspirations.[40] Each peace script, in fact, offers a unique lesson for those invested in "strategies for dissent [and] models of civic behavior that may make it more difficult to dehumanize or enter into war in the first place."[41] When we expand the study of peace rhetoric by looking past the more popular or "epic" moments of history, we see anti-war discourse as a window into studying the democratic culture of a given time and place. Indeed, anti-war movements prove quite capable of integrating wide-ranging, sometimes violent meanings while disguising them as harmless beliefs opposed to war.[42] Peeling back each layer of this symbolic work is the purpose of the peace script approach.

What makes my study of peace distinct? First, I should clarify what this study is *not*. It is not an exhaustive look at peace or anti-war argumentation. Such a study would cover countless activists, orators, and organizations not included in this book. Topics related to peace, such as religiously motivated anti-war movements, would require far greater attention than they receive here. Broader studies of peace, such as those by Gorsevski and Ivie, guide my narrow focus on peace scripts.[43] These works have underscored several ideas that appear throughout my analysis: the act of scapegoating; the rhetoric of de- and re-humanization; the special status of dissent during wartime; and the role of collective identity (or "consubstantiality") in dramatizing public affairs.[44] While I may be the first to use the term "peace script" in this way, many rhetorical analyses of war have implications for peace scripts that inform my approach.[45] To be clear: a peace script emerges whenever a person or group defines "peace," even indirectly. This might range from one-off comments to intricate arguments that tell a person how to act if they want to properly resist warfare. I do *not* consider every dimension of a peace script, which would be impossible in one book. Instead, I focus on how, in rejecting violence of one type, each script offers new justifications for exclusion often based on race, gender, and class. In this way, these five scripts circulated a "negative" peace to their fellow citizens.

Finally, my peace script approach is limited to the frequent public appeals made by social movements during wartime. Clearly, I leave much out of this book. In each chapter, I consider only one organization that uniquely influenced the public discourse against war. By no means were these the only voices critical of war, and certainly not everyone heard their arguments. However, each organization circulated public texts against the war to a comparatively high degree. Because of my focus on the public appeals made by grassroots actors, I primarily rely on archival documents from discrete organizations, such as the Anti-Imperialist League or the Mothers' Movement. There is no doubt that this excludes many voices better known to both historians and the general public. Furthermore, my focus reflects long-standing inequalities: nonwhite and non-male actors are repeatedly pushed to the margins of public life and wartime debate. This lack of representation and diversity is no peripheral concern but the central point of critique that asks, "What are the consequences of peace advocacy dominated by the privileged few?" I also must acknowledge the imperfect nature of the archives, as each organization curated its collections in ways that inevitably leads to distortions and gaps. Regardless, ignoring their public arguments cheats us out of a deeper understanding of the history of peace rhetoric and how citizens have repeatedly use anti-war rhetoric to sanction violence anew.

My hope is that the peace script approach offers a sense of continuity across vastly different moments in national history. During the tumultuous periods of military mobilization, citizens unite to oppose war and, in the process, stylize their dissent with the cultural tools—symbols, identities, and myths—at their disposal. Due to the rampant repression characteristic of the periods discussed, their scripts often express fear, paranoia, and sorrow. Minority groups all too often make up the villains and scapegoats of these dramas of peace.[46] For instance, chapter 1 analyzes the Copperhead script, highlighting how it justified racial inequality by appealing to a resolute manliness indebted to white supremacy, all while taking on the sheen of a harmonious and innocent advocacy of peace. We must not simply discard or ignore these awful arguments but ask why they were persuasive to specific communities and what they can tell us about contemporary obstacles facing the construction of a "positive" peace. The story of the peace script told in this book is not over. It overlaps with an ongoing story of American violence and the myths that give it life by telling citizens that one person's peace demands another person's death.

Combatting the "Emergency Script"

To better understand the negative potential of peace talk, I look at moments when the stakes are the highest: when peace scripts go up against "emergency scripts." Legal scholar Kim Lane Scheppele defines the "emergency script" as the federal response to war that typically involves repressing dissent.[47] These scripts are designed to regulate the home front and keep citizens united in support of the war. These aggressive measures typically entail legislation targeting fundamental rights, ranging from the prohibition of "disloyal expression" in World War I to the suspension of habeas corpus during the Civil War.[48] These "emergency scripts" address extreme, threshold moments—when a nation decides to use lethal force and, typically, how far it will go to prohibit dissent in the name of military success. They rightly garner much scholarly attention, yet we give less focus to the competing scripts written by those who resist war and remind citizens what a nonviolent culture is supposed to sound like.

The grassroots movements that compose these opposition scripts face intense challenges in every direction: from attacks upon free speech to threats of imprisonment to physical violence. Political philosopher Giorgio Agamben labels such tumultuous periods as "states of exception," in which standard laws no longer apply.[49] Mary L. Dudziak expands on this, arguing that "wartime has become normal time in America" and, accordingly, that the erosion of democratic norms may happen well before or after periods we take as "times of war."[50] For instance, in the case of the Spanish-American and Philippine-American War, we do not see the "state of emergency" as clearly as in other conflicts. However, the obstacles facing dissent at this time overlapped with, and in some ways foreshadowed, Woodrow Wilson's severe measures a short time later. An expansive view of "wartime" might connect the repression of far-Left activists at the turn of the century with the new policing practices in the colonial Philippines. Here, the government perfected new policing techniques—what one scholar calls the "rise of the surveillance state"—of which activists at home faced the brunt.[51] Jeremy Engels and William Saas similarly challenge the traditional boundaries of wartime by highlighting a newfound cultural "acquiescence" to perpetual war that presents new obstacles for peace advocacy.[52]

To better see how a "state of emergency" blurs into a broader sense of wartime, we must examine the grassroots movements that form during what are characterized as "perilous times" when the nation collectively fixates on war.[53] These anti-war movements are crucial to the health of civic life because their adherents speak out at great personal risk to test how much democratic dissent will be allowed. As this book shows, protest during wartime, targeted and stigmatized as it may be, often reflects a narrow pool of citizens whose socioeconomic privilege affords them such risk. Their arguments against war, recorded in their peace scripts, thereby reflect their limited perspective. Far from rejecting all forms of violence, these scripts tend to repackage exclusionary ideas of race, gender, and class into powerful new narratives about national identity and citizenship. They are, undoubtedly, "negative" scripts, but ones that help us chart the course for a lasting, "positive" peace as these scripts live on well past the "time of war."

What's at stake in this battle of scripts is nothing less than the quality of democracy. Ivie puts it succinctly: "Democracy's formidable challenge may be most clearly indicated on the occasion of war."[54] War threatens the foundation of democracy because its hallmarks—cooperation, deliberation, persuasion—are met with calls "to coerce, combat, and destroy" the enemy.[55] When a nation abandons persuasive efforts in favor of combat, it must still preserve a democratic culture invested in free speech, open deliberation, and nonviolence for whenever the state of emergency ends. Nevertheless, we see a vicious clampdown on free speech and public dialogue in most of these chapters. To truly understand why this happens, and why military conflict is a fixture of society, we must interrogate the shortcomings of war's critics. Throughout these "negative" scripts, a "narrow definition of the common good" rises in prominence that distorts perceptions of who is the cause of discord and who, accordingly, must be removed from society to return to peaceful living. Those who protest war in this way mimic their belligerent opponents in "practices of extreme Othering."[56] Analyzing the contradictory nature of such peace dissent is integral to explaining why the United States, despite such high democratic aspirations, seemingly cannot help but go to war.

Scholarship beyond peace studies support these observations. Prominent social movement scholar Sidney Tarrow labels dissent toward war a key variable in the formation of nation-states that shapes culture, laws, and political ideologies over time.[57] Common distinctions, such as enemy and ally, take on heightened meaning in the chaos of the war's "state of emergency" as nations scramble to send their citizens to fight. Dissent during wartime thus demands a special place in the pantheon of public address, despite its relative lack of study from communication scholars. As Ivie states, "vigorous dissent and debate are especially critical in times of national crisis," yet this is also when the government and society so often stifle dissent.[58] The result is a hardening of war culture as its rhetoric and myths seep into peace advocacy.

Whenever debate and deliberation over military policy are stymied or legally prohibited, deep-seated assumptions and misconceptions about war and peace permeate public discourse. During these states of emergency, scholars must explore what function these myths serve and chart the places they emerge across society. My attention to the topics of race, gender, and class during these moments is an effort to attend to the need to "locat[e] more cultural artifacts of peace-building discourse in the public sphere . . . to refine prototypes of perspective-taking."[59] If we can get a stronger, more diverse sense of how peace is discussed, we can work toward building stronger rationales for opposing the devastation of warfare and the systems of violence it perpetuates. We gain a "firm[er] footing in the underlying culture of values, beliefs, and accepted ways of acting" that impact how citizens view society and conduct peace-building projects.[60] When better to study this than when the stakes are the highest?

Critical-Cultural Approaches to Wartime Dissent

Expanding the Study of War

Although this is a study of peace discourse, it is largely indebted to the study of war rhetoric. Communication scholars, in particular, have introduced innovative approaches to unpack the persuasive layers of war discourse, focusing on the visual to the spatial to the cultural dimensions of conflict and state violence.[61] For instance, the work by Roger Stahl and Barbara Biesecker, each in its way, highlights the role of time in shaping agency and subjectivity during wartime.[62] The peace script similarly offers ways for citizens to experience wartime, sometimes as a fleeting moment to assert their generational destiny by, in often gendered language, "manning up" to save the nation from self-destruction. Recent work by Stephen Heidt considers the rhetorical dynamics of scapegoating, dehumanization, and enemyship by politicians in ways that "resow the seeds of war."[63] My work builds upon Heidt's by looking at how grassroots activists who, while touting peace, set conditions for future conflict. Of course, I am not the first to point out the messy overlap of war and peace discourse. Mark Vail, for example, notes how "much antiwar protest involves reverse recrimination or demonizing rituals," not unlike pro-war demagoguery, and calls for "finding productive models of rehumanization."[64] Robert Ivie also emphasizes the "discursive instability of war's cultural hegemony."[65] In that spirit, this book unpacks how that hegemony may affect conversations over peace. From loosening up the "place" of warfare to reassessing the "time" and "agents" of battle, these critical-historical scholars push me to become more sensitive to nontraditional forms of peace discourse.[66]

Despite numerous studies of anti-war rhetoric, there are few compared to those of pro-war speeches and texts. Fewer still are studies that consider how anti-war organizations reshape definitions of violence through their advocacy.[67] One aspiration of the "peace script" is to bring critical/cultural studies closer into conversation with the study of war and peace. This goal requires searching for marginalized voices throughout the history of peace advocacy, as well as interrogating those that have dominated and overshadowed them. We can thereby better see how anti-war activists might "resist the effacement of difference and the reduction of dissenters to the status of social outcasts and enemies of the state."[68] This book hopes to offer tools for future activists by considering moments when they *failed* to do so—when peace activists emphasized cultural differences to rescript the war debate into one that may "rehumanize" themselves while vilifying others.

While many peace movements reject violence and offer progressive postwar policy, this book shows how easily a "positive" peace can be lost to "negative" appeals if we do not pay close attention. Ivie himself notes the "volatility of positive peace" and its potential to break into "negative" forms of scapegoating and demonization.[69] By holding fast to the Galtung's moral standard of a "positive" peace, we can better evaluate the rhetoric of grassroots activists who may seem eminently "positive" to adherents but nevertheless offer "negative" appeals that legitimize hierarchical visions of society. At one moment, activists may call for a just and equal society for all; the very next, they might establish racial and gendered boundaries for the very same society. By understanding the dynamics of "negative" peace, and all the symbols, myths, and narratives that inform it, we can better see how specific policies, identities, and values create obstacles for peace policies that remain prevalent today.

Finally, I must acknowledge my indebtedness to the tradition of social movement studies. The most obvious evidence of this influence is that the five chapters are all case studies of grassroots organizations with clear protest goals pursued outside official, institutional channels.[70] From Robert S. Cathcart's focus on the confrontational form of dissent to Karma R. Chávez's discussion of coalition-building practices, a social movement rhetoric (or SMR) approach directs me to those who resist a given policy from the margins of society, as well as the larger environment that sparks their resistance.[71] Specifically, I approach social movements as discursive objects and entries into a field of controversy and contestation that hinges on definitional battles even as very material resources and rights are at stake. Kirt Wilson's analysis of the "discursive field" of the Civil Rights Movement and Thomas W. Benson's study of peace posters are both exemplary in this regard.[72] Recent work by Amy Pason, Christina R. Foust, and Kate Zittlow Rogness also highlights the discursive dynamics of dissent, emphasizing the interconnectivity among social movements, counterpublics, and society at large.[73] This book shares this attention to protest texts and their relation to a broader field of ideas, opportunities, and political structures, such as the "emergency context," that shape struggles for power. Far too often, these contexts also determine which voices get heard and which are marginalized.

Scripting Race, Gender, and Class

If we read peace as a dynamic, contextually constructed appeal open to contradiction, we start seeing seemingly unrelated concepts resurface in debates over war. Chief among those is race, which animates responses toward war to a shocking degree and tends to characterize its "negative" dimension in US history. Repeatedly, the threat of military conflict becomes a call to safeguard whiteness. To conceptualize this work, I draw from scholars such as Eric King Watts, Ersula Ore, Lisa Flores, Kirt Wilson, and Lisa Corrigan, to name only a few, who have clarified the connections among race, rhetoric, and violence.[74] For instance, Flores's work on "racial rhetorical criticism" tells scholars that race is implicated even when we least expect it, often operating in indirect ways that may be tied to other power dynamics.[75] Peace rhetoric, approached with these ideas in mind, must be viewed as a discourse open to possibly—although not inevitably—reproducing racial inequalities by telling us who is "civilized" and who is "violent."[76]

I critique "negative" peace scripts with an eye toward this dynamic, hoping to contribute to a racial turn in the study of war rhetoric. In each case, I ask how anti-war debates tap into discourses on race even when advocates frame peace as a natural, passive, race-blind, and wholly nonviolent position. Natalia Molina uses a similar concept—the "racial script"—to chart the disparate ways that communities are racialized across space and time.[77] A peace script, likewise, grants its readers a set of motives, values, characters, and plot encased in the sheen of harmony. And sometimes it is harmonious! However, in this book we repeatedly see activists depict peace in discordant terms. Some anti-war advocates present their case as a defense against state violence while adorning it with symbols of racial exclusion, using peace scripts as a vehicle to reframe white supremacy as harmless advocacy for nonviolence.[78] While my project is historical in nature, understanding how race and ethnicity shape our inherited definitions of "peace" can shed light on why more recent conflicts, such as the war on terror, the immigrant detainment crisis, or the oppression of the Uyghur community, evoke such divisive responses.

In movements dominated by white men, which comprise four out of my five case studies, the opposition to war can gain traction by framing the conflict as an assault on white masculinity. Race, once again, intersects with gender. Casey Kelly's work observes an affinity between white masculinity and concepts common to war, such as "death, victimhood, and fatalism," which are also taken up by those advocating peace.[79] Consider the Spanish-American War and the decades-long Philippine-US conflict that ensued. A "critical war approach" points to the interlocking debates over race, eugenics, and economic inequality that turned the imperialist war into a referendum on national culture. Some pro-war advocates dehumanized Filipinos, as other scholars have noted, but some *advocating for peace* also used the conflict to reestablish whiteness atop the US hierarchy. Like traditional scripts, we must read these social movement texts as narratives filled with characters, motivations, values, and dramas that valorize certain races and ethnic communities at the cost of others. The dominance of peace activism by white-majority organizations only underscores the utility of whiteness as a "strategic rhetoric," in Thomas K. Nakayama and Robert L. Krizek's words, that redirects pacifist feelings toward violent ends.[80] In short, a protest history of US war—essentially the story of our peace scripts—is partly a history of the nation's racialized identity and its violent manifestations.

Gender plays no less a role in peace rhetoric, directly and indirectly. Many scholars have noted the gendered way US society discusses the soldier and military sacrifice.[81] Those who oppose war do not necessarily reject this gendered language but offer their own take. Claire Sisco King mines this relationship, noting the "role violence plays in constructing white masculinity and the consequent fetishizing of bruised, bloodied male bodies."[82] Thus, one might say that if narratives of white masculinity fetishize war, they may also fetishize peace and its martyrs. In analyzing the public texts of anti-war movements during wartime, we can better appreciate how activists accomplished such work, what cultural norms they sanctioned in the process, and what the legacies of these words may be. To be clear, I am not arguing that any one individual or organization consented to all the racial or gendered dimensions of these scripts. Yet, appeals to gendered and racialized violence recur across the movements under consideration and are inseparable from each movement's "negative" potential.

Finally, my focus on how gender, race, and class operate through peace appeals draws upon the uptake of intersectionality in rhetorical studies. Since Kimberlé Crenshaw's foundational work, scholars have used intersectionality as a lens to see public discourse without isolating only one variable of power and instead seeing how multiple vectors of privilege "interlock" or "intersect."[83] Cindy L. Griffin and Karma R. Chávez's work on intersectionality urges scholars of rhetoric, specifically, to challenge old assumptions about who speaks on behalf of marginalized groups.[84] This challenge bears directly on my project: Why is it that during "states of emergency," white, middle-to-upper-class men seem to speak for all peace advocates? The peace script approach uses insight from intersectionality to answer this question, demanding that we take stock of each element of oppression, whether gender, race, or class-based, even when they seem irrelevant at first glance. In fact, some movements in this book, such as the Henry Ford Peace Expedition, thrived off the assumption that the group was free from partisan issues and the trappings of gender, race, and class. Nevertheless, Ford's movement existed, in large part, because of its leader's tremendous socioeconomic privilege. To little surprise, the consequences of his script tended to harm the marginalized communities whose voices, particularly those of women, he claimed to represent.

Consider Copperhead rhetoric: a troubling web of race, gender, and collective memory that reveals the prevalence of whiteness for a major segment of Civil War peace advocacy, replete with fragments, antecedents, and "sediments" for contemporary scripts. The "diffused, normalized sets of assumptions" found in their peace rhetoric still contributes to the reproduction of race-based inequalities.[85] By interrogating these assumptions and their articulations alongside appeals to peace, we can formulate new routes of subversion to ingrained inequalities and work toward a lasting, "positive" peace. Following recent calls for scholars to challenge the depth and complexity of whiteness in rhetorical studies, this book offers the peace script to help demonstrate how white supremacy finds shelter in unexpected places. Readers will surely see parallels to current events, which I draw out at the conclusion of each chapter.

A Note on the Selection of Case Studies

Upon first inspection, identifying major wars seems easy to do. However, after a closer look, the standard indicators (battles, declarations, treaties) muddy the timeline. From frontier conflicts pitting settlers against indigenous populations to the Barbary Wars expanding an early nation's naval powers across international waters, one thing becomes clear: it is nearly impossible to find a time absent of violent conflict on the North American continent, at least since initial settler encounters.[86] Labeling a conflict as "war" or "battle" is both a political and rhetorical act: political, because it imposes upon actors a set of rules meant to confer winners, losers, aggressors, victims, heroes, and villains, rhetorical because these labels influence how conflicts are perceived and, in turn, how communities remember or forget certain periods.[87] Consider how often citizens discuss wars as generation-defining events that bestow a deeply felt sense of meaning and purpose, acting as a sociological anchor to valorize behavior and entire cohorts of people.[88] While some wars persist as landmarks in national memory—the Revolutionary War, most obviously—others barely exist as a footnote, such as the Korean War.[89] Still, despite precarious definitions of war, scholars must assert some boundaries for their study.

My project analyzes the US Civil War, Spanish-American/Philippine-American War, World War I, World War II, and the Vietnam War. Each impacted national identity by forcing citizens to reconsider the role of government, the extent of civil liberties, and the appropriate style of war and peace advocacy. There were anti-war movements before the US Civil War, and one deserves special mention here. Amy Greenberg convincingly argues that the US-Mexican War (1846–1848) provoked the first national anti-war movement.[90] Resistance to this conflict was more widespread and diverse in its sources and appeals than negative reactions to conflict in any previous US war in the young country's history. As a rhetorical antecedent to the Civil War this conflict is also key. In fact, appeals to the "Mexican-American War" make up part of the anti-war rhetoric engaged in by Lincoln's opponents. I choose to start with the Civil War because its cultural, political, and legal impact and the massive resistance these changes sparked across the North and South were widespread and unprecedented, ultimately heralding a new era in US history. Whether one describes this point as the start of "modernity" or not, the Civil War and the period after witnessed an extraordinary rise in federal power at a time when the very legitimacy of a democratic republic was under dispute.[91] Circling around this transformation were voices critical of the government's ability to wage war with impunity. Similarly, the Spanish-American/Philippine-American War, World War I, World War II, and the Vietnam War all sparked a significant degree of domestic protest. Each is a moment when the government's exertion of power stretched across society, and, in turn, citizens contested and reframed the acceptable limits to national authority, coercion, and military control.

While the five social movements I consider possess significant differences, their similarities are vital to this book. First, each partook in a larger process of contesting one form of national violence by reframing another, supposedly more legitimate, type of violence. While limited to the available archives, the public texts of these movements indicate the kinds of appeals citizens may have heard on behalf of peace. Secondly, to varying degrees, each movement engaged with an "emergency script" and, occasionally, matched the government's undemocratic response to dissent with undemocratic peace rhetoric. As these movements countered state power, they leveraged a vision of citizenship they saw as under attack and needing to be protected at all costs. Finally, each movement, directly or indirectly, offered a boundary to national identity that implied some marginalized group or some culture labeled "Other" that was usually based on racial, gendered, and class-based markers. By using the language of peace, each movement scripted a new version of who America is supposed to be—what makes the country an exception to the rest of the world as a nonviolent, harmonious, and civil place.

Finally, I want to address the matter of platforming heinous rhetoric. Even when critiquing abhorrent views, we still risk republicizing them. There is no easy solution to this very real concern. In a sense, the problem gets to the heart of rhetorical historiography, forcing us to ask how to retell and challenge narratives of the past without merely advertising the dominant discourse that drowned out other voices. At the same time, how do we fully discuss past injustices without bringing even the most subterranean prejudices out to light? I'll be relieved if my project has landed somewhere in a responsible middle position: one that considers the popular discourse of a specific time while attempting to connect my critique to larger ideological currents that resonate today. Is this the perfect answer to a complex methodological and moral problem? Far from it, but my hope is that people engaging this book will not read the repugnant voices of the past and feel relief or self-satisfaction that they live in a distant time safe from such ideas. Instead, my ideal reader would feel a mix of shock, anger, and perhaps guilt in realizing how prevalent these arguments remain today and how easily prejudice, hierarchy, and scapegoating can permeate society, infecting otherwise noble belief systems, even those as seemingly unproblematic as "peace" rhetoric.

Chapter Previews

My project begins at the Civil War to consider how Northern anti-war activists rescripted antebellum culture to define their peace. The Copperhead movement mostly grew out of Midwestern regions with indirect ties to the South. Historian Jennifer L. Weber identifies three phases of this movement from 1861 to 1865 and notes several enduring rhetorical qualities, such as an insistence upon a narrow interpretation of the US Constitution.[92] Politicians such as Clement Vallandigham, Daniel Voorhees, and George Pendleton led the movement of Peace Democrats while engaging issues related to economics (e.g., paper currency), law (e.g., habeas corpus), race (e.g., slavery), and politics (e.g., republicanism).

In chapter 1, I examine how the movement, through its public speeches, pamphlets, and editorials, penned a peace script for the Civil War with appeals to a generational memory predicated on a gendered interpretation of activism. By mobilizing appeals to true "men," such as Andrew Jackson, the Copperheads crafted an influential retelling of peaceful US society that countered abolitionism. In the process, they justified a new sense of acceptable violence that foreshadowed postbellum rhetoric, particularly the Lost Cause narrative. The Copperhead peace script, in short, reframed cultural logics of race, gender, and memory to support notions of white supremacy.

Decades later, the Anti-Imperialist League grew out of a collective frustration over the protracted Spanish-American conflict, particularly the US military's belligerence in the Philippines beginning in 1898. Touting an impressive lineup of public intellectuals, including Jane Addams, Mark Twain, and

William James, the Anti-Imperialist League actively contested US warfare overseas for decades. Their focus on the Philippine-American conflict lasted until around 1902, when the US declared the war was over. Nevertheless, the organization continued to influence peace activism throughout the Progressive Era leading to World War I.[93]

In their peace script, the Anti-Imperialist League (AIL) asserted a cosmopolitan view of national violence that fixated on the racialized nature of citizenship. Far from the more overt racialization of the Copperheads, the Anti-Imperialist League employed more indirect cultural rhetoric to sanction a new type of exclusion. Additionally, the Anti-Imperialist League made frequent use of the memory of previous conflicts, particularly the US Civil War, to narrate a history opposed to current expansionist projects, articulating in the process a new ideal of US society based on racial hierarchy, economic isolation, and moral superiority. Of course, divergences from this rhetoric existed, but chapter 2 looks at the less-considered dimensions of the AIL protest that circulated in its literature. This peace script foreshadows problems with future debates over warfare, global citizenship and colonial subjects.

Indeed, public opposition to World War I was strong in the years leading up to US involvement, at which time the government suppressed anti-war dissent to an unprecedented degree.[94] Many women, nevertheless, continued to fight for the end of the war while pursuing their rights as citizens.[95] No single peace movement in the States, however, claimed as much international attention as Henry Ford's Peace Expedition, a late-1915 social movement event. Ford, the eccentric automotive tycoon, leveraged his privilege and wealth to recruit a ragtag team of anti-war protesters to sail aboard his "Peace Ship" from New Jersey to Europe, where they were to hold a series of public events aimed at ending the war. Largely a publicity event—in a way, the most purely "cultural" movement of all under consideration—Henry Ford's Peace Expedition was an extravagant example of what is now called "astroturfing," or the creation of a social movement by a wealthy donor.

Through reading the Henry Ford Peace Expedition story in newspapers published across the globe, in chapter 3 I describe how the event publicized a peace script built upon a cultural spectacle indebted to Ford's socioeconomic position; few citizens could rival Ford's deep pockets and create a peace movement from thin air. In doing so, Ford reduced the perception of anti-war activism from a diverse group with nuanced policy proposals to a "spectacle movement" driven by a singular personality lacking a concrete strategy or plan. Ford's peace script, as a result, leeched vital rhetorical resources from other activists, revealing the harm of spectacle rhetoric. The Peace Expedition professed a universality that was, in fact, more a reflection of US citizens' fixation on industrialism, celebrity, and serialized dramatic entertainment. Ford's script insisted upon a timeless, ahistorical quality but, in reality, embodied a specific disposition toward progress and ingenuity that left critical questions about nationalism, citizenship, and cultural difference unanswered. This absurd script of peace foreshadows serious issues at the root of nationalism, self-determination, and violence that would inform the terms of peace following the Great War.[96]

World War II marked a rarity: a generally popular war. Organizations such as America First protested intervention, but the nation was mostly on board following Pearl Harbor—not least because of the unprecedented use of state-sponsored pressure and propaganda.[97] Nevertheless, as many as six million women—roughly 13 percent of the voting population in 1948—claimed adherence to one of the more extreme anti-war movements in history: the Mothers' Movement, the subject of chapter 4.[98]

Mostly comprising Midwestern, white Christian women, the Mothers' Movement offered a vision of peace predicated on what its adherents took to be the "traditional" definitions of femininity and Christianity, while in fact representing a very narrow definition of both. While the Mothers' Movement found religion a powerful resource for constructing peace, its members twisted it into a virulently anti-Semitic, racist, and nativist version of isolationist rhetoric. They bolstered this peace script through appeals to national memory, casting events and characters foundational to US identity in extreme opposition to the war. The reframing of violence offered by this organization reveals frightening antecedents to the fringes of the subsequent New Right movement, as seen in the John Birch Society and movements well into the twenty-first century.

Finally, at the end of this century of war lies the Vietnam War, a generation-defining event. The Vietnam Veterans against the War (VVAW), one of the largest and longest lasting anti-war movements from that period, conducted several of the era's better-known protest events. Chapter 5 examines what happens when the experience of warfare was so radical—in some cases so *traumatic*—that it fundamentally altered the returning veteran's ability to be a citizen as previously understood.

By listening to the voices of VVAW activists from oral histories, pamphlets, and the *Winter Soldier* documentary, I describe how their peace script subverts the citizen-soldier ideal. In doing so, they challenge viewers to bear witness to the contradictions of individualism and collectivism that define the military system and patriotic duty.[99] VVAW activists who partook in the violence they indict drastically reframed the cultural logics of war and peace rhetoric by demanding self-critique. Their script, not simply replacing one type of violence for another, hinged on the recognition of one's role in a violent system, a task essential to building a "positive" peace.

Productive Failures of "Negative" Peace

This book's central aim is to illuminate an understudied legacy of racial, gendered, and class-based violence written through the language of anti-war activism. Each peace script studied herein tells us which models of masculinity, whiteness, and/or ethnic citizenship were presented as the proper alternative to war by a vocal segment of the population. Each movement thereby acts as a guide to uncovering how war and peace may be intertwined with the rhetoric of exclusion. In the end, the peace scripts surveyed in this book, each more or less "negative," each composed during periods of war and repression, offer new justifications for social hierarchies. Just as each war adds new legal and political measures often unprecedented for the nation, so too does each war catalyze new debates over what counts as peaceful civilization that echo throughout future generations. That we continue to hear intolerant assumptions about race, gender, and class animate national conversations only speaks to the need to better understand how the language of peace might contribute to discrimination, as well as offer an alternative path forward.

These peace scripts are characterized by failure of two kinds. First, each chapter tells of a failure of goals: none of the movements brought an immediate end to the war. Second, each marks a rhetorical failure: no movement defined a perfect, "positive" peace. While the reader could easily imagine less exclusionary definitions of peace, we must ask if a *perfect* peace is even possible and, if so, what is required to obtain at it? Here again, Johan Galtung's body of work is instructive. We can use Galtung's tripart definition of violence to describe the movements covered in this book as prone to justifying "cultural" violence regarding race, gender, and class. They do so, however, by scripting them into ostensibly high-minded critiques of "institutional" and "direct" violence.[100] This suggests how members of each group likely didn't feel their peace script to be reactionary, myopic, and unsustainable for a lasting peace. To them it sounded like a thoroughly "positive" or even "perpetual peace."[101]

Nevertheless, under Galtung's terms, the movements in this book fail: each, to varying degrees, composed a "negative" script of peace that disregarded fellow citizens. However, this judgment is useful only to a point without attending to the texture of their arguments and appreciating how they can help us arrive at a better future. What we see is how each movement offers appeals to a "positive" peace at least on occasion—some more than others, such as the Anti-Imperialist League and the VVAW. For some members of the Copperheads, for example, their vision was nothing more than a call for a postwar order founded upon the US Constitution. To those within the upper tiers of society, privileged enough to escape the worst of the plantation slavery, this may have sounded admirable. Needless to say, the Copperheads used this language to push for a racially segregated, thoroughly "negative" vision. An essential condition for formulating a "positive" peace is a close consideration of the history of peace scripts. Once we take a serious look, we begin to see how the language of "positive" peace can collapse into the "negative." This doesn't mean we abandon efforts for peace. Only that we must try harder.

So stand the peace movements in this book: sketches of peace that give lifeblood to forms of violence.[102] Fundamentally, all of these peace scripts are about defining "civilization" less through a formal argumentative structure and more through a narrative, hence, the "script" approach. It is not "war" or "peace" alone, but culture, collective memory, and national identity through which these peace scripts compose their stories. They tell their adherents what is worth preserving, what is sacred, and, if threatened, what must be defended at all costs. Adherents are the actors who perform this act of protection, tirelessly rehearsing it in hopes of upholding its worldview.

These public texts, however strange they may seem to modern readers, help explain our current state of peace or lack thereof. Attending to these peace scripts, written at highly charged moments, can tell us why, for instance, the sector of peace activism was stigmatized or deserted for a period of time; why certain groups were friends of peace while others shied away; which resources, rhetorical or otherwise, peace organizations could avail themselves of. These scripts, furthermore, allow scholars to trace the cultural contestation over a host of terms that revolve around the idea of peace: "civility," "self-restraint," "nonviolence," "harmony," and "social justice," to name only a few. When we look at anti-war rhetoric long enough we begin see how easily it can exploit and amplify deeply reactionary feelings across society. Put simply, it offers the ever-satisfying power of the "negative," a resounding and defiant, "No!" to those pushing for military conflict. The language between pro- and anti-war activists, ironically, blurs, as both sides seem to cry, "You are either with us or against us!" Suddenly, the stage is set: the peaceful versus the bellicose. The consequences of this drama last for decades, even centuries. While the prospects for US peace may seem bleak, and its terms still heavily debated, the nation's past scripts remain available to us to read, to discuss, and to critique so as to better craft new scripts of dissent, vulnerable as they may be to the allure of violence.

1

Rehearsing a Masculine Peace in the Copperhead Movement

On Wednesday, October 19, 1859, Clement Vallandigham, Ohio Congress member and future leader of the Northern anti-war movement, paid a visit to John Brown, the radical abolitionist now in custody for his raid on Harpers Ferry several days earlier.[1] Lamenting the "paroxysms of rage ... [and] vulgar but impotent vituperation" that such a "casual conversation" sparked across various presses, Vallandigham sought to set the record straight.[2] The public reasonably struggled to imagine any such "casual conversation" between the two men: Vallandigham, a staunch states' rights advocate opposed to federal limits on slavery, constantly hearkened to a narrow interpretation of the Constitution as the bedrock of American civilization; Brown, a militant anti-slavery activist who grew weary of the "laws of man," sought to violently assert emancipation. Rarely would two worldviews seem more likely to collide.

This meeting, far from hostile, illustrates the complicated nature of violence. For Vallandigham, there was much to admire in his enemy. Brown's "muscular" body and "cast iron face and frame" displayed someone he found "bold," of "singular intelligence," and "as brave and resolute a man as ever headed an insurrection."[3] What could lead a man of such "coolness, daring, persistency," and "firmness of will and purpose unconquerable" to commit "murder" and "treason"?[4] Vallandigham, never the absolute pacifist, did not oppose cunning, audacious acts of violence—indeed, he seemed to admire this in Brown. Vallandigham felt his error was in the misuse of his manly nature. Brown's character, so "sincere, earnest, persistent," was led astray and perverted by the abolitionist cause, an overzealous movement that distorted the proper foundations of civilization.[5] In gazing at the enemy, Vallandigham was aggrieved not by his violence but by his submission to the wrong type of violence, by his performance of the wrong peace script.

Vallandigham's campaign against the Civil War, known as the "Copperhead" movement, offered its own version of peace.[6] In the process, these activists reframed the boundaries of violence with a special focus on race and gender. To allow the war to continue was not merely to encroach upon civil liberties, to enact unnecessary economic legislation, or to unconstitutionally interfere with the institution of slavery—although it was all of this and more in the eyes of many. As the Copperheads scripted the conflict, the Civil War was but a symptom of a much larger disease: a cultural scourge upon American manhood that weakened the pillars of Anglo-Saxon civilization millennia in the making. Allowing the federal government to abolish slavery was thus equivalent to civilizational suicide. In the Copperhead script, abolitionists were the unmanly villains hell-bent on exacting a violence far greater than slavery. Vallandigham's heroic persona was the nation's best chance to defend the white supremacist culture under attack. For many of these activists, a lasting, "positive" peace required nothing less.[7] Make no mistake—this peace script was thoroughly "negative" because it perpetuated inequality and resowed seeds of conflict that would characterize the Reconstruction era. Adopting a "positive" approach to such failed scripts helps anti-war activists of today better anticipate how cultural assumptions about race, gender, and class might distort peace appeals.[8]

First, I situate the Copperhead movement within a broader US debate over cultural violence and, as the war went on, an increasingly repressive climate for democratic dissent. In this "emergency context," Vallandigham's movement circulated public appeals for peace throughout the North. These appeals offered the readers an insidious script that I analyze through the speeches of three prominent Copperheads (Clement Vallandigham, George Pendleton, and Daniel Voorhees) and the anti-war Democrats' response to Union League publications, the Society for the Diffusion of Political Knowledge (SDPK) newsletter. Copperhead rhetoric rescripted the war through three main appeals: to a notion of "manly resolve" in the face of the effete Abolition movement; to a generational memory that placed citizens at an epoch of Anglo-Saxon history and demanded immediate action; and to white supremacy, not always as an incidental part of a larger legal argument but as the bedrock of national civilization. If citizens forgot any of these three themes of the Copperhead identity, then the Abolition movement would succeed in undermining US civilization, forsaking the only foundation by which political life obtains any peace at all. Ultimately, Copperheads could use these cultural narratives about masculinity and race to compose a new defense of white supremacy. Their peace script also exploits several myths of peace—that it is natural, inherently good, and free from partisanship—to falsely suggest that the antebellum status quo was a "positive" peace. We may wish to dismiss this work as a failed attempt at peace, but it can teach us about the racialized rhetoric we must still confront to achieve a lasting, "positive" peace in the United

States. What is most surprising is not that these citizens proffered a reactionary and sometimes violent framework of society. Instead, what is noteworthy is that they seemed to share the same aspirations and even the language of "positive" peace: appealing to harmony, civility, and nonviolence, while in fact distorting these ideas in the service of a deeply undemocratic and "negative" vision of the world.

PEACE AND PROTEST IN VIOLENT TIMES

LINCOLN'S STATE OF EMERGENCY

Abraham Lincoln was not the first US president to impose strict regulations upon civil liberties. The Alien and Sedition Acts of 1798, for instance, illustrate how long-standing the tension between granting freedom and repressing dissent has been throughout national history.[9] Nevertheless, historians, political philosophers, and scholars of rhetoric have noted a unique "emergency context" during the Civil War.[10] Even if Lincoln himself was not always thrilled by either his wartime measures or their implementation, such as in Vallandigham's banishment from the Union, there is little doubt these actions fostered a hostile environment for those critical of war.[11] On eight occasions, he suspended habeas corpus, which, to be clear, is granted under the Constitution "in Cases of Rebellion or Invasion the public Safety may require it."[12] Estimates vary, but somewhere between thirteen to thirty-eight thousand citizens were arrested by military authorities, with some specifically detained for political expression.[13] These severe measures assisted in the pursuit of a quick war but had serious consequences for the quality of peace discourse.[14] In this undemocratic climate, the Copperheads, a group led by politically prominent men, dominated the public perception of wartime opposition, telling Northern citizens who anti-war advocates were, what they believed, and who they blamed for the chaos. In addition to making protest a severe risk for the average citizen, these draconian measures allowed the Copperheads to focus on more popular issues, such as protecting civil liberties, rather than their more divisive topics, such as slavery.[15]

To be clear, the Lincoln administration did not create the Copperheads' racial and gendered peace. These men drew upon a tradition of dehumanizing political opponents and, particularly, enslaved people.[16] Additionally, the Copperheads were not the only anti-war advocates at the time, and their influence may have been only marginal in terms of affecting presidential policy.[17] However, no anti-war group organized more formally than the Copperheads, who circulated many public arguments through speeches, editorials, and newsletters. Repeatedly, it may have seemed to the average citizen that they alone spoke for all those opposed to the Civil War in the North. Therefore, their peace script is crucial to studying US peace rhetoric because it marks a sustained public effort to persuade the citizenry to oppose war during the largest domestic conflict in the young nation's history. We can see remnants of their undemocratic peace script alive in the Reconstruction era and still to this day. If we hold the history of peace discourse just as important as the social, economic, and political history of a time and place, then understanding the Copperheads' script is necessary to formulate both a full picture of US history and a "positive" peace.[18]

Copperheads for a Golden Age

To understand the cultural context informing the Copperhead peace script, consider the fraternal orders springing up across the United States in the nineteenth century.[19] One such group was the Order of the Sons of Liberty, which rehearsed its version of peace during the Civil War through rituals adorned with Revolutionary War iconography. The Indiana-based group's members, partly inspired by Copperheadism, behaved as they thought any true patriot should in that moment . . . by plotting to overthrow the government.[20] Quoting the Declaration of Independence, these men fashioned themselves as defenders of America's civilizational destiny alongside the likes of Andrew Jackson and the rebels of 1776.[21] The secret society's militancy was a matter of both "patriotism and manhood."[22] Such rhetoric did not, however, strike everyone as civilized or patriotic. The Union Congressional Committee, for instance, published an "exposé" on the "treasonable order of the 'Sons of Liberty'" and labeled them an offshoot of the "Copperhead Conspiracy."[23] The report describes the society, which had proclaimed Clement Vallandigham their "Supreme Commander," as a "despotic" organization and an "enemy" "hostile to the Government of the United States."[24] These "oath-bound traitors," far from the fringe, had some overlap with the Democrats' Chicago Platform, the report concludes, suggesting it all "emanated from the brain of Vallandigham."[25]

And what of that "Supreme Commander"? Vallandigham had years to perfect his own brand of peace, one also rife with cultural narratives about masculinity, race, and civility. To some, his peace was treason tantamount to an act of war; for others, his was a brave voice of patriotic truth. One month before the Confederacy's Fort Sumter attack, Vallandigham gave an infamous speech interpreted by many to support not one nation, not two, but "*four distinct nationalities.*"[26] How could a man, much less a militia, that decried war and professed unity—Vallandigham's speech was called, after all, "How Shall the Union Be *Preserved?*"—be deemed secessionist and treacherous?[27] How were self-fashioned "patriots" also enemies of the state?[28] Analyzing Copperhead rhetoric and its interlocking appeals to race, gender, and memory helps explain how such a polarizing discourse could find a home among some Northern citizens and how radical beliefs did not appear to violate long-cherished definitions of civilized behavior but instead embodied the only path to peace and salvation.[29]

We must not ignore the role of masculinity in eighteenth- and nineteenth-century American rhetoric. Paeans to the manliness of revolutionary fighters are legion.[30] The Declaration of Independence itself laps praise for "manly firmness" against "invasions on the rights of the people."[31] Amy Greenberg describes "martial manhood" as a focus on "strength, aggression, and even violence," which proved popular in the "aggressively expansionist discourse of the Democratic Party."[32] Andrew Jackson's public image, a common appeal for the Copperheads, was of a daring and forceful personality that animated versions of "martial manhood." Susan Zaeske describes how Jackson seemed to have "achieved unquestionable valor, a character trait essential to martial manhood and to any man of honor . . . viewed as possessing a ferocious will."[33] "Restrained manhood," a counter to "martial manhood" popular in Republican and activist wings, drew upon a sense of masculine prudence, of being "morally upright, reliable, and brave."[34] The Copperheads, as Democrats opposed to the Civil War, found themselves between these two models of masculinity, drawing upon their culture to articulate an anti-war vision of a restrained yet vigorous manliness linked with appeals to collective memory and white supremacy.

The Copperheads went to great lengths to patch over the major contradiction in their peace script: how the supposed beacon of freedom to the world could enslave four million people.[35] Many debates preceding the Civil War dealt with slavery indirectly, weighing questions of federalism and free labor, while the essential issue remained: the right to own humans based solely on the color of their skin. Was slavery an unconscionable societal violence, as some activist groups argued; was slavery a necessary, if unsavory, political reality protected by the law, itself the only protector of peace; or was slavery, as others argued, a positive institution that maintained harmony between races?[36] Intense disagreement over slavery contributed to the rise and fall of new political coalitions, such as the nativist and anti-Catholic Know Nothing Party, which marked the continued dissolution of the Whig Party.[37]

The Copperheads scripted their solution through the myths of peace. First, they branded their pro-war enemies as "activists" while their own movement, by comparison, was "restrained" and "natural," a common-sense position not poisoned by partisanship. The Copperheads, so they said, were not disloyal citizens but simply responding to events in a clear-eyed, reasonable way. Indeed, the Northern anti-war movement frequently voiced fear and derision toward the untethered activism they imagined all around them. The Abolition movement perpetuated the worst crimes, in their eyes, but was just one part of a graver problem of partisanship resulting in an ever-expanding executive branch. Whether it was a new spending bill, the conscription act, the suspension of habeas corpus, or the emancipation of enslaved people, any action by congressional Republicans might represent an uncivilized and immoral fanaticism.[38] The growth of new political affiliations, activist groups, freed slaves, and immigrants also likely increased the Copperheads' feeling that their position in the national hierarchy was threatened, amplifying their call to stem the tides of change.

We must ask how the Copperheads penned a new peace script through rejecting the Civil War. While the precise influence of Copperhead activism on politics and society is unclear, we can partly answer this question by analyzing the movement from a rhetorical perspective. Since Frank L. Klement's reappraisal of the Copperheads, a multi-book project that partly rehabilitated their image, scholars have questioned if these activists were, in fact, a real threat to Lincoln and Northern victory.[39] Jennifer Weber argues that the anti-war cause in the North was not a "peripheral issue" but a highly divisive one "whose influence waxed and waned in counterpoint to the Union armies' success and failures."[40] Jonathan W. White suggests scholars focus on "who the Peace Democrats were and what they stood for . . . [with] more weight placed on the Democrats' own terms, rather than on Republican rhetoric and accusations."[41] An investigation into the Copperhead peace script seeks to follow this path. In the speeches of the movement's leaders, we see a script of peace fixated on a resolute masculinity made to withstand the withering effects of anti-slavery activism, of which the current war was the most extreme expression. Their anti-war manliness found strength through appeals to a collective memory inseparable from white supremacy. Despite its shockingly violent implications, a rhetorical analysis of this script can help answer why this "negative" peace seemed persuasive to many Northerners.

Composing the Copperhead Script

Gendered Resolve and Emasculating Dissent

In resisting the changes brought by the Civil War, what cultural elements did the Copperheads avail themselves of to write their version of peace? One of the frequent themes in their peace script is gender, here depicted as a vigorous, resolute manliness opposed to Abolition activism. Not the "martial manhood" of combat and violence, nor the "restrained manhood" popular among Republican activism, Copperhead rhetoric stressed an active manliness centered upon a rhetorical performance: a near-constant insistence on the primacy of "political principles" that transcend specific exigencies. Using Abolitionists as foils, Copperheads fashioned themselves as civilized men unsusceptible to the wiles of political circumstance, doggedly guarding the antebellum status quo.

These appeals to a resolute anti-war masculinity doubled as a critique of activism in US society, blending into discussions over the proper spheres of public and private life. Once again, we see the myth that peace is not an organized position of dissent but a natural failsafe against the irrational and the bellicose. Here, the myth feeds into the Copperheads' broad appeal to civility and self-restraint that, in this case, means standing firm against the perverse femininity of anti-slavery activism. Their peace script offered this "negative" vision of society while presenting it as a "positive" peace for true Americans.

In Civil War era speeches, Vallandigham amplifies this gendered element of the peace script through an attack on the prospects of war. Musing on the crisis in the nation, Vallandigham first points the finger at his own Democratic Party, lambasting the organization as lacking manliness. The party failed, he states, because "it held not, in all things, to sound doctrine, vigorous discipline, and to true and good men."[42] Repeatedly, the lack of "true and good men" is associated with a grave "loss of vigilance and discipline."[43] A hallmark of Vallandigham's peace script was this abiding focus on a masculine ideal characterized by a fortitude and strength to endure the reality of political life. Vallandigham further defines this gender role by contrasts, imploring the audience to act unlike the Abolitionist fanatic, presently overcome by disordered emotions. Instead, he implores the Democrats to "be manly, then, and outspoken, and honest. Act the part of cowards and slave-stealers no longer."[44] The response to unmanly, irrational citizens is a brave and vigorous masculinity that Vallandigham repeatedly performs for the audience in expressly gendered terms: "I speak it boldly—I avow it publicly—it is time to speak thus, for political cowardice is the bane of this, as of all other republics . . . you must take open, manly, one-sided ground upon the Abolition question."[45] The performance of the Copperhead peace script demands manly resolution against Abolition, now framed as a battle between the violent and the peaceable.

In a later address, Vallandigham again underscores the gendered nature of the crisis now expanding from a matter of civility to one of preserving civilization. A resolute manliness, lacking in his opponents, is required to uphold the nation's founding principles as enshrined in the US Constitution: "Maintain [Southern rights] here, within the Union, firmly, fearlessly, boldly, quietly—do it like *men*" and do not succumb to "unmanly terror."[46] In one of Vallandigham's most infamous addresses, he again forefronts the need for a resolute manliness to combat the uncouth sentiments currently dominating politics. In penning a script of manliness suitable for the Copperheads, Vallandigham now goes beyond contrasting Northern Democrats with Republicans. Observing the South's gender dynamics, he commends how "the South, almost as one man . . . are resolved, that, whatever else of calamity may befall us, that horrible scourge of Civil War shall be averted."[47] He then encourages the audience to stay strong by "avoiding the "arous[al of] ambition, or to excite avarice," to reject all "mischief," and stand resolute against the flurry of partisan emotions that may accompany opposition to the Copperhead cause.[48] Vallandigham again praises Southern manliness as "not weak... but powerful, earnest, warlike, enduring, [and] self-supporting."[49] In ignoring the issue of slavery and focusing on gender, these words reveal how selective a peace script may be in integrating cultural symbols, even those associated with extreme violence.

Once the Civil War began, Vallandigham continued to insert this gendered vision of culture into his peace script, linking appeals to harmony and self-restraint to Copperhead masculinity. He framed congressional obstruction, for instance, as an articulation of vigorous manliness. Vallandigham called on the House of Representatives, in a speech reportedly printed and circulated three hundred thousand times across the North, to not pick up arms but to "hold [. . .] up the shield of the Constitution, and standing here in the place, and with the manhood of a Representative of the people."[50] To be immovable, solid, and staunchly behind the Constitution—this is the image of masculinity chosen by Vallandigham that drew rhetorical power from its supposedly anti-war position. The Copperhead script thus denigrates its opponents as lacking in proper masculinity without directly addressing the issue of slavery.[51] What he repeatedly associates with "the individual man, breathing, God-created, exulting in the might and majesty of an immortal and almost omnipotent nature" is "not so much the originating of new principles in politics," and especially not "soul-debasing prostration before political and corporate organization," but "the varied application of the old and established principles."[52] The vigorous manliness of Vallandigham's anti-war rhetoric is tied to standing by eternal principles, seemingly always a position opposed to the Republican agenda that perverts proper manhood.[53]

Other leaders of the Copperhead movement followed suit in depicting advocates of war as weak men overcome with emotions. Writing a peace script this way allowed Copperheads to frame peace as the properly masculine position capable of a "vigorous prosecution of Peace."[54] George Pendleton, a Democratic Congress member and the party's 1864 vice presidential candidate, addressed the House of Representatives in 1861 and depicted the war as an issue of masculinity and self-restraint. In the face of unseemly "agitation and irritation," he urged for inflexibility toward Abolition's unmanly "acts of passion," thereby avoiding any "loss of pride... loss of self-respect... [or] loss of power."[55] Peace, for Pendleton, demands an unyielding commitment to constitutional principles despite one's passions. The "principles of truth and right," Pendleton continues, cannot be corrupted by the "sways and surges in this mad tempest of passion."[56] Only through "faithful observance of the Constitution," he exhorts, may one enact a manly resolve against the Republican usurpation of power.[57]

Daniel Voorhees, a Copperhead politician who oversaw the tumultuous governance of Indiana during the Civil War, also urged manly resolve as the nation's only path toward a lasting peace. Against the "seditious citizen," who succumbs to "overwhelming temptations," one must stand firm by the founding vision of the nation.[58] This firmness, typified by constant identification with the Constitution, offers not merely a solution to the conflict but asserts "the full stature of vigorous manhood"—if only the "constitution shall survive its enemies."[59] One thwarts the challenge to manhood, represented by the maelstrom of partisanship and Abolition, in aligning with the "men who are devoted to the old constitution, who worship reverently after the old forms of religion, who love their country and maintain their own honor—go and ask these men."[60] Voorhees's appeals to a "manly, determined" nature is not an incidental part of Copperheadism but a powerful symbolic resource that scripted their anti-war resistance.[61]

Pro-war arguments frequently invoke a binary view of war, exploiting fears of mortal enemies hell-bent on destruction. The Copperhead script shows how peace advocacy is equally amenable to such "enemyship," as it depicts Abolitionists as a threat to both national security and national culture.[62] Copperheads used this language to transform appeals to manliness into broader critiques of political activism as unmanly, passion-driven mania that violates the sacred spheres of civilization.[63] To be so swayed by the passions of the world, as Abolitionists were wont to do, was both an unmanly political response and a threat to all civilized culture. Pendleton, for instance, called for a public taming of "our passions and our fears" as the war was heating up, demanding all men "assuage angry passions" that obstruct the "feeling of fraternal affection in our people."[64] The entire Abolition movement, for Pendleton, represents a succumbing to "agitation and irritation."[65] Their lack of resolve implies Copperheads possess the proper masculinity, defined by its inflexibility, and allows the movement to again frame the war as a conflict threatening the very pillars of civilization—the "soft and silken cords which encircle the heart."[66] Thus, the only solution is a "calmness of spirit [and] moderation of temper, with determined purpose."[67] Every pro-war element of the conflict reflects a fanatical nature that will lead to "pure, unmixed despotism."[68] Repeatedly, the threat—nothing short of the "perversions of our system"—is described as not merely military, political, or legal but a cultural one: the loss of "social order" and the "disorganization of daily life."[69] By framing the crisis as such, the Copperhead peace script uses its anti-war position to sanction their vision of resolute masculinity.

Vallandigham again reveals the type of gendered work achievable through the language of peace in his interpretation of the Abolition movement. While delivered in the context of the slavery debate, Vallandigham veers off-course to paint his opponents as a fanatical, emotion-driven mob of activists corrupting the sacred spheres of civilization. Once more, manly resolve is needed just as any legal or political resolution. On one occasion, Vallandigham compares the Republican Party's discourse to how "girls of thirteen [talk] of puppy dogs."[70] He again chastises this unmanly exuberance in a discussion over the proper realm of government, describing how activists "invok[e] the government to regenerate man, and set him free from the taint and the evils of sin and suffering; [and in so doing] seeks to control the domestic, social, individual, moral, and spiritual relations of man."[71] The test of manliness, in this case, is to resist the "sort of magnetism . . . [that] all great public movements" bring to the political sphere: "It is one of the peculiar evils of a democracy, that every question of absorbing, though never so transient interest—moral, social, religious, scientific, no matter what—assumes . . . a political shape and hue, and enters into the election contests and legislation of the country."[72] Activism, in short, is improper to the realm of politics and of real men, who must vigilantly guard against such sweeping passion.

Vallandigham uses the exigence of impending war to meld this "negative" script into a broader theory of partisanship. His anti-war movement stands against any temptation to pervert what is properly political, a point made by again framing opponents as "weak men" who are "dazzled and deluded."[73] The issue of slavery is simply not a political matter, and thus the fitting response is to oppose any federal involvement and thereby safeguard the manly realm of politics from the "altar of jealousy and fanaticism."[74] In later speeches, Vallandigham warns of being duped by the "pestilent fanaticism on the subject of slavery," the "thirst for power and place, or preeminence—in word ambition," and the "extreme abolition sentiments" that have perverted every action that the Lincoln administration implements.[75] Repeatedly, Vallandigham bolsters his call to manliness through denigration of the "factious demagogues, conspiring fanatics, and unfaithful public men" who threaten national culture.[76]

Northern citizens could also read about the Abolitionist attack upon manliness in the pages of the Copperhead newsletter, *Papers from the Society for the Diffusion of Political Knowledge*. The pamphlet frequently highlights the "widespread demoralization, pervading the public mind" and the "fanaticism [that] rules the hour" against which men must resolutely protect the antebellum status quo.[77] All actions of the Lincoln administration could take on the unruly, unmanly "reckless[ness]" of Abolition, now the consummate foil to the disciplined manliness invoked by Copperhead protesters.[78] Samuel J. Tilden, at the time a prominent Democrat, wrote a letter decrying the irrational activists occupying the Abolition cause who he believed imperiled civilization.

"Mobs" rule the government, Tilden warns. They are "blind partisans, visionary theorists, impracticable philanthropists, sensation journalists" ruining US culture.[79] To be against the war, as read through this peace script, was to claim one's masculinity. Drawing from a Christian perspective, Edward N. Crosby also calls for the need to be strong against "ignorance or passion" propagated by the Abolition cause.[80] In place of the unmanly and "befogg[ing] intellects controlling the fanatical avenues to public opinion," the Copperheads offer a resolute manliness that rejects all forms of activism, even denying their own activity as such, and frame the war as a submission to emotions destructive to the pillars of civilization—including those that uphold slavery.[81]

Rewriting Generational Memory

The Copperheads bolstered their appeals to masculinity through reimagining a shared past. This new narrative called for true men to defend a timeless tradition, allowing the Copperheads to infuse high drama into their peace script while also aligning it with optimistic narratives of US destiny and divine providence. If Republicans, in calling for an expansive federal government, reimagined the "space" of US patriotism, then the Copperheads countered with an expansion of patriotic time.[82] In appealing not only to the Founding Fathers but also Anglo-Saxon and ancient European roots, they framed the war as an attack on a millennia-long struggle for civilizational progress that reflected their own social position in the United States.[83] In this historical narrative, Republican policies were simply another instance of forgetting one's generational inheritance and, thereby, a subversion of Enlightenment principles of progress and freedom. In retelling episodes of European progress alongside tales of despotism, the Copperheads imbued their memory appeals with a sense of fragility, a feeling that at any moment the nation may recede into an unmanly frenzy—a subversion of all things essential to their "negative" peace.

The way Copperheads integrated generation-defining characters into their peace script deserves special attention. Articles from the *Papers from the Society for the Diffusion of Political Knowledge*, for instance, note "the generation which embraced Washington, Jefferson, Franklin, Madison, and Hamilton" that now guides the way for the current "generation which finds itself . . . in a situation wholly novel."[84] The great men of America's past stand as foils to the present, warning the current generation of their precarious moment in time. For the Copperheads, the Constitution preserves this old wisdom. This document represents not merely an object of national memory but "centuries of human wisdom . . . the principles, rights, liberties, our British forefathers, after five or six centuries of struggle, wrested from the Kings and Despots of England, and affixed to great charters of Human Rights, the Magna Carta of 1215."[85] Stretching far past the US Revolution, the Copperheads script integrated

Anglo-Saxon rulers into the drama of their script, instilling it with a sense of purpose and heroism. Former presidents are made exemplars of how to remember the long Anglo-Saxon struggle, lauded for their brilliance in not creating new principles but rather acting as "condensers" of pre-American "Progress and Civilization," which is to be safeguarded against the current "servile insurrection."[86] The Copperheads carefully situate themselves as the current generation along this lineage of Anglo-Saxon men tasked with preserving a cultural destiny. This rewriting of national memory has a distinctly ethnic hue, now safely shrouded by the language of peace.

Once again, Copperheads activate the myths of peace—which assure them of a natural, intrinsic purity to their peace discourse—and thereby compose a "negative" script that justifies inequality and violence. Vallandigham, for instance, uses the moral language of peace to reinterpret national memory, highlighting the generation-defining drive of US progress that refuses to abolish slavery. On one occasion, he invokes the nation's forefathers to chart the proper political path forward. Unlike the Abolitionist cause, he says, "Our ancestors went to war, indeed, about a preamble and a principle: but these were *political* . . . They were resolved to form a political union, to establish justice and to secure domestic tranquility, the common defense, the general welfare, and the blessings of liberty to themselves and posterity."[87] Posterity must recall that founders like Washington did not become fanaticized by so-called moral issues but remained "purely political."[88] They were man enough, so the script goes, to realize they were not merely creating US principles but eternal ones. This assertion of what counts as "political" helps insulate Copperhead rhetoric from critique by adorning it with the symbols of a much broader generational pursuit of civilizational greatness, the source of lasting peace.

By tying national memory to Anglo-Saxon forebears, the Copperheads reinforced their patriotism while demanding strict adherence to the status quo, which included slavery. Vallandigham tells his followers to remember that founding principles were "fostered still by English princes and nobles, confirmed and cherished by British legislation and judicial decision."[89] He thus admonishes the current generation to defend the Constitution by remembering all the history leading up to it: "By memories of the past, by the history of the tyrannies of Greece and Rome, and the terrors of the French Revolution, I call on all men to demand of the Administration that it obey the Constitution."[90] Jackson, that masculine "tower of strength," understood the "principle and truth" of defending the Constitution, as did Americans' English ancestors, such as the "glorious John Hampden."[91] It is from this long history that the Copperheads' generational appeal is activated for the present audience: "Here, gentlemen, a new epoch begins in our political history. A new order of issues . . . are introduced."[92] The instability of the present moment—and its threat of forgetfulness—is what compels Vallandigham to "trace briefly the origin and history of those grievous departures from the *ancient* landmarks. . . . [that] have impaired . . . the strength and discipline of the Democratic Party."[93] These ancient landmarks are intended to guide the manly resolve of the Copperhead generation and reinforce its "negative" version of peace.

Copperhead rhetoric breaks history into forces of order and peace versus those of change and war to provide their script with a wide range of characters and narratives gleaned from a shared past. Drawing again on religious language, Vallandigham hails "our fathers, in their day and generation," who now offer "one precedent, at least, hallowed by success and *canonized* in world history."[94] Next noting the bravery of "the Irish patriot" who attacked invaders, he stokes a civilizational vision of "one Destiny" under attack by enemies who stand outside the European tradition. In one case, he describes the enemy as "apostles rather of Mahomet, disciples of Peter the Hermit."[95] Later, Vallandigham celebrates how "the hard Anglo-Saxon sense and humane impulses of the American people have rejected the specious disguise of [Abolition's] words without wisdom." Here we see how the Copperhead script creates a manly Anglo-Saxon memory that allows its followers to celebrate their ethnic roots while avoiding the racial crisis that precipitated the Civil War.

Vallandigham again hearkens to a precolonial Anglo-Saxon past to infuse his peace script with a claim to cultural superiority. First noting all national achievements in "science, civilization, wealth, population, commerce, trade, manufactures, literature, education, justice," he attests that the genius founders surely meant to construct a political system with a stronger safeguard to executive power.[96] We then clearly see the connection between the romanticized past and the current anti-statist pursuit of the Copperheads. Vallandigham frames US civilization as one episode in a larger struggle against despotism, recalling the efforts of many non-American actors who struggled for liberty, such as "Littleton and Coke . . . and Plowden," and connecting them to "the Marshalls, and the Storys, the Harpers, the Pinckneys, the Wirts, and the Websters of an age gone by."[97] After Vallandigham's exile from the United States in 1863, he increased calls for anti-war activists to view the fight for peace through a broad temporal scope. On one occasion, he calls on his audience to remember "the spirit of the patriots and freemen of other ages and countries, of the heroes of Greece and Rome, the spirit of Bruce and Tell, of Hampden and Sydney, of Henry, and Washington and Jackson," through which "the men of the present generation" can hope to "survive."[98] Vallandigham then goes further, pointing to the Greeks as "the true study of American statesman."[99] By recalling these "memories of the past, by the history of the tyrannies of Greece and Rome, and the terrors of the French Revolution," the Copperheads seek to compel the current generation to reject unmanly passions of contemporary extremism and instead follow the movement's culturally superior peace script.[100]

The Copperheads frequently use such memories to add excitement to their peace script and amplify the threat of "perversion" to Anglo-Saxon culture that the current generation must resist. As Vallandigham foretells, "Before the close of the last quarter of the first century of the Republic, [military despotism] is about to assume a terrible significancy."[101] To stress the point for the current generation, the present crisis is considered in light of past figures, such as the Duke of Wellington, to caution against receding into tyranny.[102] In James Brooks's epic narration of human progress published in the *Papers from the Society for the Diffusion of Political Knowledge*, he similarly recounts the struggles against absolutism spanning from ancient Rome to the Magna Carta to the US Constitution, noting Anglo-Saxon tyrants in Queen Elizabeth, James I, and Charles I, among others.[103] Vallandigham fears "the golden age of America" will recede into the past as citizens forget the lessons learned from these precolonial struggles.[104] To enact the Copperhead peace script, in short, is to take up the mantle of Anglo-Saxon manliness against the present mob ignorant of the past.

In a commencement address, Vallandigham speaks in stark generational terms, once again importing European culture into his peace script. He reminds his young audience that they "speak the language of the coming generation" and thus must "read history, and learn that the patriot, the hero, the statesman, the orator, whom you reverence or admire in the pages of Plutarch and Livy, or of Hume, Gibbon, and Macaulay was reviled and persecuted . . . [by their] own generation."[105] Whatever persecution the Copperheads may face, it is already sanctified in the memory of these martyrs, whom they must imitate to repel the oncoming tyranny. A failure to remember one's generational inheritance becomes the implied reason Republicans seek new legislation—casting the war in terms of a cultural memory that privileges the performance of a type of white masculinity.[106]

Other Copperheads followed Vallandigham's lead in appealing to an eclectic European past to reframe their peace movement as epochal, one that dares to rise up during "the darkest of all the annals of America."[107] Giving a speech on the suspension of habeas corpus. for instance, Pendleton frames the concept of military necessity as antithetical to the civilization of "free people . . . its history marked by the wreck of popular liberty and free institutions, by the sad tokens of human hopes destroyed and noble aspirations blighted." He then invites the listener to consider their place in history: "As we look back upon this pathway of desolation, and trace it even to our own times and country, we . . . tearfully pray that [US liberty] not be added to the list of victims."[108] Pendleton implores his audience to see the present moment within a broader timeline, "learn[ing] prudence from the heroism of your ancestry."[109] For Pendleton, the issue of the Civil War is a matter of cultural remembrance, and thus, he implores people to consider how the US "stand[s] in the eyes of the civilized world today."[110] The current generation is on the cusp of losing its manhood, of a submission to the "vulgar and low ambition" of "territorial ambition" that makes US civilization look worse than non-Anglo Saxon communities, such as "Russia, and even China." Here again, we see the generational script offered by the Copperheads: they stand at a moment of choice over what kind of culture they want to preserve and, thus, in what way their present behavior should relate to their Anglo-Saxon history.[111]

In the expansive Copperhead memory, anti-war rhetoric incubates violent notions of race and gender, urging adherents to take act like true Anglo-Saxons in combatting Republicans. The practical result of this generational memory, it bears repeating, was often the rejection of emancipation.[112] Voorhees, for instance, asks his listeners to "turn our faces around toward the past" to see the present crisis of national culture. He then frames the debate over the issue of slavery in this language of cultural memory: "We may not ignore [the present crisis]. It is the lineal descendant and legitimate offspring of those days wherein the arts of war and peace first assumed to act for American interests, guided by American valor and wisdom. The importance of the present epoch in the history of the world is, however, simply the importance which attaches to the condition and probable destiny of that universal hero of all earthly dramas—man himself."[113] To identify with the Copperhead peace script is to feel oneself chosen for such destiny—one best for all of mankind, taking place upon a "memorable epoch in history."[114] From Thermopylae to Yorktown, it is now the "American citizen" who must deliberate on the future of government. For Voorhees, it is not merely a memory of the Founding Fathers that citizens must nurture but an understanding of the ancient struggle across Western civilization.[115] Violating the Constitution in any way, as the Abolitionists are figured to do, is depicted as not simply a political error or a lapse in manly conduct but as a cosmic violation of the Anglo-Saxon pursuit of culture and the peace it is meant to guarantee.[116]

WHITE SUPREMACY AND THE ENSLAVEMENT OF CIVILIZATION

The issue of race makes up the final element of the Copperhead's "negative" peace and best reveals the type of violence their script sanctioned. By combining appeals to gender and memory, Copperheads found a new language to justify white supremacy, insulating it within the sheen of a harmless yet manly defense of peace. The tolerance of slavery in US society, even if considered morally repugnant by some, was neither an extraneous issue nor an incidental feature of the Copperheads' insistence on states' rights. The presence of enslaved people—only fearfully considered "Black citizens"—was integral to their script, catalyzing the group to protect a profoundly exclusionary vision of national culture. According to the script, the current generation faced a turning point wherein real men had to choose which heritage to preserve. The Copperhead solution, put simply, demanded the realization that Anglo-Saxon, often Christian, Americans were "the race of liberty."[117] While much of the Copperheads' advocacy of white supremacy was implicitly stated, the moments where leaders directly discussed the role of slaves reveal an essential privilege granted to whiteness.[118]

We can see the scripting of this racial appeal in *Papers from the Society for the Diffusion of Political Knowledge* pamphlets. Samuel Morse, famed inventor of the telegraph and staunch pro-slavery activist, wrote in these pages an impassioned defense of slavery, arguing that the slave system was not the problem but rather a solution to the fundamental inequality of the races. Morse reached this conclusion not through abstract consideration of Constitutional law but through what, to him, was a common-sense look at national civilization, of which "the cornerstone is the inequality of the two races."[119] Morse then asserts we cannot reject "the inequality of the races: by denying that there is this difference, then one race of necessity is superior, and the other inferior, and if the two physically unequal races are compelled to live together in the same community, the superior must govern the inferior . . . The cornerstone cannot be removed."[120] Invoking "the kindly spirit of the Fathers of 1787," Morse stresses again that the inferiority of the Black race is managed by the civilized institution of slavery: "This providential arrangement of conditions in human society has for its end a purpose of infinite and eternal good to both races, a purpose clearly discerned in the light of gospel truth."[121] Here, we see the troubling intersectionality of Copperhead identity expressed plainly in its public texts: an entanglement of race and gender fused into acts of remembering that adorns itself with the vestments of peace while in fact reframing a culture of violence.

The image of an emancipated slave was an effective foil to the Copperhead peace. Readers could thereby rehearse responses to Black citizenship, a prospect they considered with fear and disgust, by framing Black people as agents of disruption and evil. Even Abolition activists, denigrated as fanatics, were redeemable, although dangerously close to the uncivilized nature of Black slaves. Former justice of the Sixth Circuit District, Charles Mason, for instance, reacts strongly to the prospect of emancipation, framing it in stark civilizational terms that the *Papers from the Society for the Diffusion of Political Knowledge* reprinted and circulated. He describes how "under 'Republican' policy, we should, be at once overrun with hordes of this black population, who as a class are indolent and vicious."[122] After detailing the supposed horrors that freed slaves would bring to white society, Mason asks, "Are we anxious to make our State a moral pest-house, to be crowded with these colored subjects of crime."[123] To him, the emancipation of slaves was no peripheral issue; it equated to "national suicide."[124] Treating enslaved Black people as equal citizens was an affront to all Anglo-Saxons had accomplished, "abhorrent to every instinct of humanity."[125] Its violent effect upon society is repeatedly framed in the Copperheads' peace script as graver than any harm slavery might cause. The Copperhead peace script sought to remind citizens of this truth, rife with gendered and mnemonic appeals to a fundamentally violent identity.[126]

Vallandigham's rhetoric relies on a similar insistence upon fundamental cultural differences between Black and white races, implying true racial violence lies in obstructing or forgetting white supremacy.[127] In discussing the role of the federal government, he notes slavery's potential as a civilizing force, reassuring his listeners that "however slavery might be extended, as a mere form of civilization or labor, there could be no extension of it as a mere aggressive political element in the Government."[128] Later, he states he will not "be stopped by that [. . .] cry of mingled fanaticism and hypocrisy, about the sin and barbarism of African slavery. . . . I see more of the barbarism and sin, a thousand times, in the continuance of this war . . . and the enslavement of the white race."[129] Peace rhetoric proves once more fertile ground for growing new justifications to reframe the status quo as nonviolent and civilized. In this case, the myths of peace help obscure or even sentimentalize the brutality of slavery, all while offering a false sense of "positive" peace for those who identify with the Copperhead script.

The Copperhead peace script further links the violence of war to an assault on whiteness through racialized discussions of culture and civilization. Abolition, in "tak[ing] up [the] negro" cause, has "defiled" the "pure altars" of Christianity and thus endangers the infrastructure of national civilization: "the railroads, the banks, the telegraph lines, the express companies."[130] Stressing again the "common descent" of the "Anglo-Saxon stock," Vallandigham underscores the threat of Blackness to peaceful white society, emphasizing the differences of "the negro race, styled now, in unctuous official phrase, by the President, [as] 'Americans of African descent.'"[131] From this perspective, the war violates the white supremacy at the heart of national citizenship, which directly feeds the need for a manly resolve to preserve Anglo-Saxon civilization unless the country succumbs to "enslavement of the white race."[132] In remembering their European ancestors and standing firm as principled, resolute guardians of peace, a citizen enacting this script can feel as if they are preventing an attack on whiteness. Every action of the Lincoln administration, in this Manichean framework of peace, becomes a weak, fanatical perversion of national destiny, a desecration of all that is sacred to the Copperheads, with the ultimate danger being subjugation to "the [false] superiority, of the negro race."[133] Peace, simply put, is possible only through a manly preservation of whiteness, and to script the conflict otherwise is to make oneself a victim of an irrationality unbecoming of real men.

Black enlistment was another topic that animated Copperhead discourse and illustrates its racial views. Pendleton, for example, uses this topic to elaborate on the bonds holding society together and the civilizational instability caused by what he considers constant violations of the Constitution.[134] Later, he laments the threat to US society caused by supposed "negro equality," deciding "it was better that one-tenth of the white people should rule the South, than have this black element introduced into the body politic."[135] Voorhees takes a similar opportunity to underscore the attack on Anglo-Saxon resolve when considering the prospects of emancipation when he implores his audience to remember that "the success of freedom . . . has only been achieved by one distinct race of the human family . . . [who guards against] the licentious violence of the unrestrained populace . . . The Anglo-Saxon race laid its hand on the destinies of the world, and became the champion of liberalized civilization."[136] Copperheads are encouraged to consider "the inequalities of the human race . . . the inequalities which exist between the different races of the earth . . . [to] determine the due supremacy which belongs to our own race."[137] Again we see how the peace script connects its appeals to generational memory and manly resolve to a racialized notion of culture, justifying the violence of white supremacy by fixating on the behavior of the unmanly, "negrophilistic" federal government.[138]

Copperheadism fortified its ugly vision of peace by framing emancipation as a regression of Anglo-Saxon manliness to a state closer to that of the uncivilized slave. In defense of an embattled Democratic colleague, Voorhees takes the chance to valorize Virgil, John Milton, Edmund Burke, and other European figures in his appraisal of European culture, a topic ostensibly unrelated to the matter at hand. He then directly addresses the racial nature of US civilization, praising how the "white man enlarged the boundaries of civilization" when "the Indian vanished into the shades of the forest."[139] The "career of American progress," which stands "without a peer in all of history," is integrally tied to the "natural and inevitable result of the irreconcilable inequalities of the human race."[140] In his words, the Civil War is not only a legal issue but a cultural battle incited by those who dare try the "disgraceful" "experiment of commingling the blood of separate races."[141] Voorhees warns against this project by comparing the current "prosperity" with the "jarring, discordant scenes of the mongrel races of Mexico, Central and South American."[142] The "ravages of fanaticism" presently at work risk preventing, not American progress, but the "Anglo-Saxon race . . . [from] rush[ing] forward again on the bright track of American progress."[143] The supposedly natural and inherent dignity of peace—one of the myths that support "negative" scripts—bolsters the movement's assertion of natural racial hierarchies, given here as a new language of violence to rehearse and imitate under the guise of nonviolence.

Through this language, Copperheads could rescript the violence of the Civil War as not just a legal or political error but as an existential attack upon national culture. Peace and whiteness are inseparable in their model of peaceful culture. Obviously, defenses of freedom and constitutionalism do not need to fixate on race. Furthermore, not every Democrat and Copperhead affirmed, or even likely heard, all the arguments publicized. Nevertheless, a close analysis of their words reveals how Copperhead discourse hinged upon three interlocking appeals that could imbue debates over habeas corpus, free press, conscription, or emancipation with a racial identity. In its extreme form, the Copperhead peace reads as a civilizational fantasy that excludes nonwhite citizens—necessitating radical inequality and the literal bondage of millions of humans as slaves. In looking back through history, their script granted intrinsic peacefulness to whiteness, whereas "the negro race [n]ever attained a higher degree of civilization than is at present exhibited in Congo and Ashantee . . . [and] no wise people will ever in any manner encourage the attempt to elevate such a race to social or political equality."[144] Anything less than a manly assertion of Anglo-Saxon culture was thus antithetical to peace.

Anti-Black Violence: Rescripted and Reconstructed

Although the Copperheads failed to end the war on their terms, it does not mean they didn't succeed in impacting the fringes of US discourse—or even re-emerging at its front and center. On May 18, 1871, Clement Vallandigham, like the prodigal son returning home, attended the Democratic convention in Dayton, Ohio, hoping to guide the party's future. His return from exile marked a return to establishment politics if no real ideological change.[145] The postwar peace, as the history of Reconstruction reveals, might have incorporated new ideas, deployed new appeals, and rehearsed new scripts, but a core belief in white supremacy endured.[146] Consider the platform of 1871. Called "The New Departure," in it the Democratic Party hoped to rehabilitate their image and distance itself from overt associations with Copperheads, who, predictably, became pariahs after the war.[147] Yet Vallandigham's address to the group reveals how Copperheadism, and its "negative" version of civilized, peaceful life, survived in an altered form.

First, Vallandigham laid claim to his audience's memory, demanding once again a bold mnemonic: to now *forget* the Civil War, to place the conflict, along with its moral purpose, out of mind. The Democratic Party could salvage the violent peace of Copperheadism by obscuring the Civil War, "thus burying out of sight all that is of the dead past, namely, the right of secession, slavery, inequality before the law, and political inequality."[148] The period of strife must be declared over, and with it, all questions of inequality. Vallandigham proclaimed, "Reconstruction is complete, and representation within the Union restored to all the States, waiving all questions as to the means by which it was accomplished, [thus] we demand that the vital and long established rule of STRICT CONSTRUCTION [*sic*], as proclaimed by the Democratic fathers . . . be vigorously applied to the Constitution as it is."[149] These are peace terms with clear precedent in the Copperheads' manly credo: a staunch, even ruthless, enforcement of national identity as they understood it. With Reconstruction frozen in the past, the Democratic Party may reaffirm its hearty resolve for the "original theory and character of the Federal Government as designed and taught by the founders."[150] With such selective memory, the party vigorously sought to delete from consciousness the nation's foray into racial politics to bring back a new variation of the antebellum world. Given this focus, it is not surprising that Vallandigham's "new" departure also involved rejecting the "Ku-Klux Bill," designed to address anti-Black terrorism.[151] Radical white supremacist groups, if not directly endorsed, received latitude to act. Meanwhile, the country primarily chose reconciliation over Reconstruction, illustrating how marginal Black life remained in national culture.[152]

Proof that we must interrogate even the most "negative" of peace scripts lies in the simple fact that the Copperhead script never fully went away. Their reactionary peace, characterized by a supposedly manly assertion of a pure Anglo-Saxon culture, would find new life not only in official policies of discrimination but also in the burgeoning sphere of popular culture and its celebration of "melodramatic masculinity" found in far-right extremism.[153] The Ku Klux Klan made use of such gendered social roles, lauding members as real men whose crimes of terror were framed as chivalrous acts aimed at maintaining order.[154] Thus, it is crucial to understand how peace can serve as a sanctuary for white masculine violence—as an engine to reenergize abhorrent elements of racial and gendered discourse through a war-versus-peace binary. The Copperhead terms of peace also help explain the racial violence of US warfare characteristic of the late-nineteenth-century Plains Indian Wars and the Spanish-American/Philippine-American War. Such occasions of "brave" white men killing nonwhite people could bolster the assumption that whatever violence military engagement inflicted, it helped advance a natural hierarchy—and therefore ensure what we might call a "colonizing peace." It is only "common sense," therefore, that it also preserves white America—and so goes the myths of war and peace, marching in lockstep through "negative" peace scripts.[155]

In the twenty-first century, we catch elements of this peace script in the language of extremist groups, such as the Proud Boys.[156] In demonstrations against the removal of Confederate monuments, members of the so-called Alt-Right emerged to "bravely" stand up for the "real American" against a disingenuous "woke mob" that is attacking culture norms, such as masculinity. In the history of US public address, Copperheadism may be dead by name. Still, its "negative" vision that justified violence lives on in multiple forms, offering an unsettling, if predictable, answer to various "race" questions. White supremacy, the anti-Black violence valorized through Copperhead performances of manly remembering, quickly blurs into other, supposedly bias-free, discourses because its racial order registers to so many as "natural"—a positive and objective substrate of national life and civic culture. As the United States lurched awkwardly toward the twentieth century, its most prominent anti-war movement—and one of the nation's most publicized arguments for peace—offered awful guidance. While US warfare would spread across new territories, many debates regarding race would be met with old articulations of a violent peace.

2

Violent Compassion in the Anti-Imperialist League

On November 21, 1899, President William McKinley struggled with the terms of peace despite a decisive US victory in the Spanish-American War the year prior. Two paths lay before him now: to keep the Philippine Islands, a territory obtained after the "humanitarian war" against Spain, or to let the islands determine their own fate, granting them the democracy they desired yet risking a foreign adversary taking control.[1] After much deliberation and prayer, a third option arose—"It came to me," the president would mystically recount.[2] The United States would not take the Philippine Islands but would, instead, baptize the nation in the font of American civilization. McKinley would not be a cruel master of the weak but a benevolent guide to "educate the Filipinos, and uplift and civilize and Christianize them."[3] Thus went the peace script at the turn of the century, conspicuously tied to the language of empire.[4] In matters of colonization, Achille Mbembe rightly observes that "the distinction between war and peace does not avail," and here was no exception, as those keen on war were convinced imperial violence was the proper method for a lasting peace.[5]

But what of those opposed to this violence? Anti-Imperialist League (AIL) members, such as Carl Schurz and William James, mobilized a host of appeals to offer a countervision of peace that, at times, reflected their narrow slice of upper-class culture.[6] To be clear, AIL rhetoric is diverse and, at times, admirable in its ideas, but my analysis of their script considers its "negative" elements to appreciate better the obstacles facing a truly "positive" peace—both during the Spanish-American War and still to this day. A recurring theme across much AIL literature is a faith in American exceptionalism, or the belief that the United States is unique among all other nations whether due to the grit of its hardworking citizens or because of a divine providence bestowed upon its people. Anti-imperialists could invoke this belief in racialized ways, for example to highlight the risk to this exceptionalism when white citizens interact with members of nonwhite nations. American exceptionalism, in this way, operated as a rhetorical means to reframe and justify domestic inequalities. The AIL script also offers a glimpse into the US history of anti-Asian discrimination, seen here in the treatment of Filipinos. To better understand the rhetorical foundations of a "positive" peace, we must pause and ask how the AIL script could integrate abhorrent ideas to voice new defenses of old racial boundaries that placed nonwhite lives ever closer to death.[7] When activists combine the utopian language of American exceptionalism with the myths of peace, we find a peace script familiar in structure but unique in content, one that activates the language of harmony and nonviolence while infusing it, in this case, with a racialized vocabulary characteristic of the turn of the nineteenth century.[8]

This chapter takes a closer look at how the Spanish-American and Philippine-American War inspired a new set of activists to oppose war and, in so doing, generated new defenses of violence. Both expansionists and anti-imperialists used the conflict to debate the essence of national culture, asking what, precisely, made it exceptional.[9] The Anti-Imperialist League, in opposing one form of violence, fortified a type of violent compassion. Although not all AIL texts reflected this tendency and the movement itself was diverse in its claim-making, AIL rhetoric makes a recurring appeal to what could be called "humane exceptionalism." In this vision, US culture is strictly hierarchical along several lines, including racial. Those who identify and rehearse this script distinguish themselves, or so they believe, by exhibiting benevolent self-restraint. Similar claims to superiority were not unheard of at the time, but the AIL built theirs from the language of anti-war rhetoric, bolstering their exclusionary ideas by invoking the moral authority of the myths of peace. Notably, AIL discourse deployed the memory of past conflicts, particularly the Civil War, to rewrite a moral history of US culture that obscured the present moment's crises, particularly those related to racial injustice, now drowned out by cries for humane noninterference. Attention to these rhetorical dynamics illustrates how Jim Crow anxieties about African American enfranchisement influenced US debates over colonialism, as well as views on capitalism and respectability. Ultimately, AIL rhetoric demonstrates how the language of compassion and moral self-restraint, neither of which is incompatible with "positive" definitions of peace, can reproduce "negative" narratives of inequality, for both domestic and foreign consumption. In the twenty-first century, we can hear echoes of such foreign policy talk when countries privilege national interest, however defined, over sustaining international peace.

In this chapter, I provide context for US imperialism at the time, noting how peace organizations at the turn of the century marginalized some of the more radical voices among their own activists. Long-gestating issues of immigration, urbanization, and labor tensions boiled under the pressures of industrialization and sparked what is commonly called the "Progressive Movement." All the while, the Philippine conflict persisted, sparking a wave of protest mostly dominated by the AIL, a richly resourced anti-war organization with valuable ties to the Democratic Party. Because the AIL engaged the Democratic Party's complicated relationship to federal intervention and militarism, this chapter also sheds light on how peace rhetoric contributed to shaping interpretations of "liberalism" at the turn of the century. By renarrating the nation's past, the AIL fused racial and economic appeals into a new rhetoric of "humane" self-restraint that guaranteed US superiority, along with an exclusionary type of citizenship and what was, in their eyes, a moral right to commit violence of a kind.[10] We also see here a problematic appraisal of self-restraint scripted in the language of peace and underwritten by violent notions of race.[11]

War, Race, and Empire at the Turn of the Century

Unlike in the other wars covered in this book, the US government did not enact severe wartime measures upon citizens at the start of the Spanish-American War. Nevertheless, there were significant obstacles facing anti-war protesters that foreshadowed the massive repression characterizing World War I.[12] First, it was difficult to garner sustained public attention toward McKinley's war because its initial phase was so short and decisive. The Spanish-American War, as such, did not accrue mass casualties (on the US side), nor did it require a draft, two factors that tend to amplify anti-war dissent.[13] Nevertheless, a colonial war transpired thousands of miles from mainland America in what we now call the Philippine-American War. Officially, the conflict ended in 1902 but fighting went on for over a decade and sparked vocal if relatively small protest from US citizens.

Secondly, as peace historian C. Roland Marchand expertly shows, peace advocacy was undergoing a major shift of its own, becoming increasingly fashionable, even faddish, among the US middle and upper classes. At the same time, peace rarely commanded the sole focus of activist organizations during this period but was rather tacked on as a secondary or tertiary cause to a broader mission statement. This type of attention fostered a less defined anti-war rhetoric that excluded many voices deemed too "radical."[14] Additionally, the more radical voices faced severe challenges from the government and their fellow citizens, who rejected their critique of US society. Activists such as Emma Goldman, Mollie Steimer, and Eugene Debs, to name only a few, may have felt as if they were in a "state of emergency" typical of warfare given the tremendous pressure—and even imprisonment—they risked. Taking Mary Dudziak's concept of "wartime," we could characterize this as a period rife with nonmilitary "emergency scripts" that facilitated the crackdown on labor and far-Left activists.[15] Furthermore, the radical activism possibly made the moderate antiwar voices even more popular simply by contrast, reflecting the "radical flank effect."[16] Regardless, the result was that a well-funded, conservative-leaning organization like the AIL could take center stage in the public arena of antiwar advocacy and, like other Progressive Era movements, tap into the myths of peace while perpetuating questionable assumptions about US society.

"Genteel" Reform and Imperialism's "Mugwumps"

For a sense of the troubled state of US colonial peace at the time, we can look no further than the deeply anti-Asian pageantry at the Greater America Exposition of 1899 (figure 1). On opening day in Omaha, Nebraska, the president of the event, George L. Miller, spoke with a bravado typical of a bustling empire, boldly declaring that the "characteristics of our new possessions can be more intelligently understood in these grounds than by a trip to the islands themselves."[17] One exhibit included a makeshift Filipino village that, according to a sordid news report, housed fifty "lusty" Filipinos brought to the States by Special Commissioner to the Philippines Henry F. Daily.[18] Another article described how the Filipinos "started to run for their lives" when they saw an oncoming military parade, suggesting lingering obstacles for any "Greater American" peace.[19] The myths of peace—their promise of unity, harmony, and comfort—tore at their seams in Omaha's colonial theater.

The period encompassing the Spanish-American and Philippine-American Wars was fraught with radical change, which citizens met with a variety of responses, ranging from the conservative clamor for a return to the nation's founding vision to revolutionary calls challenging the core of US culture and economic life.[20] Less unified in policy goals, Progressive Era reform groups nevertheless often shared many of the same policy concerns: urbanization, transportation, manufacturing, the market economy, and migration. These phenomena ushered in an unevenly distributed progress and prosperity to Americans and challenged old ideas of US life; in this context, the family, work, gender, and race all took on new significance, and people readily redefined them to meet their own needs. Rhetoricians can see in these new definitions a struggle to reimagine democratic thought and citizenship through appeals across the spectrum of political ideology, from progressivism to the shockingly retrograde.[21] For AIL members, specifically, dreams of national rejuvenation were inflected with more parochial concerns and shared memories stemming from their New England-based "patrician" style of activism. This political model tended to favor limited government and fiscal conservatism while fighting against political corruption through deliberation and gradual change within the system.[22]

Figure 1. Advertisement for the Greater American Exposition in Omaha, Nebraska, 1899. Uncle Sam is pointing to the Philippines and Cuba, with the phrase "The White Man's Burden" below (North Omaha History).

To counter the improper use of US power, the leading anti-colonial organization, aptly named the Anti-Imperialist League, reflected what some scholars call the "genteel" tradition of activism. This strand of social thought generally favored reform over radical change. While not uncommon in the Gilded and Progressive eras, two periods characterized by discrimination against immigrants, this style of dissent gained traction while overshadowing other voices.[23] Radical voices were not only heavily repressed, but in the case of the Homestead Strike, a future member of the AIL, Andrew Carnegie, actively cracked down on them.[24] All the while, as Marchand's history describes, the topic of peace was becoming an increasingly popular issue for upper-class, moderate, and, unsurprisingly, white male-dominated groups.[25] As Robert Ivie argues, when the diversity of peace activism is depleted or obscured, it harms the overall democratic quality of a nation. Such peace scripts help shape the popular perceptions of peace should another "state of emergency" occur. The dehumanizing rhetoric of AIL peace did not bode well for the next challenge to democracy.[26]

To better understand the AIL's socioeconomic dimensions, consider Fiske Warren's life. Warren, the youngest child of a prosperous New England paper mill family, thought of peace in deeply personal terms. Like many from this elite sphere, within which the league would originate in June 1898, Warren's concerns were not material—he felt that idleness and the "lack of nerve force" threatened those blessed with the privileges and luxuries of "modernity."[27] Warren thus filled his time frequenting the commune he founded at Harvard, dressing himself in so-called reform clothing when not practicing nudism, and petitioning for various causes, ranging from vegetarianism to anti-imperialism.[28] Though a notorious "oddball," Warren did what few of his fellow AIL members even thought of: he developed a close relationship with a Filipino activist, Sixto Lopez, while hosting him during his national speaking tour.[29] Indeed, key AIL members, though staunchly against meddling in the Philippines, were wary of such an alliance.[30] Leaders Carl Schurz and George Boutwell reportedly shot down Warren's plan to forge any explicit Filipino-American coalition. It was one thing to campaign against the colonization of a "tropical race," but it was another matter altogether to embrace them or even partake in their culture. Citizens may disagree with the colonization project, but few viewed its victims as equals.[31] This tension is a core element of the AIL peace script, one that says, "Dissent as you may, but maintain a semblance of decorum familiar to our cherished New England customs." Educational treatises, for example, feature in the script as more effective than grandiose acts of resistance.

AIL members could also evade racial matters by focusing on the shifting political alliances and abstract economic theories of the time.[32] For many in

New England politics, the Gilded Age crisis came to a head in the 1884 presidential election when Republicans such as Moorfield Storey, a future AIL leader, defected from the party, citing corruption.[33] He and his fellow defectors were soon labeled "Mugwumps," a word appropriated from Algonquian Indian culture used here to describe independent voters. These New England Mugwumps were men generally rooted in inherited wealth who, rather than call for radical change to the system, preferred steady reform in keeping with traditional notions of decorum and national honor.[34] Their liberalist argument against unscrupulous spending could take on different meanings when, for instance, they considered the Philippine-American War. The AIL combined economic considerations with appeals to the past to bolster their cherished model of laissez-faire individualism, turning it into a paragon of patriotic self-restraint. In the backdrop to much of this economic talk was an unquestioned assumption regarding a natural hierarchy that, far too often, fell along racial lines. Ultimately, the rhetorical union of these moral and economic appeals with racial and cultural assumptions created new justifications for violence, giving expression to the AIL's peace script with contemporary parallels to neoliberal ideology. Such connections were made easier given the decentered nature of the organization. For instance, there were forty vice presidents and no less than one hundred AIL chapters throughout the nation by the end of 1899.[35] Such diffused leadership and messaging made it harder to separate the nobler arguments from the more destructive, the latter of which is my focus.

A fixation on the past, particularly the Civil War's legacy, was another critical tool for the AIL to reframe racial violence and sanction it anew through anti-war rhetoric. Only thirty years earlier, the Peace Democrats, or Copperheads, had mobilized their constituency in opposition to Lincoln's administration and provided justifications for Jim Crow policies that empowered anti-emancipation elements. The AIL reflects several of these priorities, particularly an insistence upon moving past racial questions, a position made all the stronger when combined with new ideas concerning race and ethnicity, such as social Darwinism.[36] For instance, consider AIL member Andrew Carnegie, who could easily patch over racial inequalities through his gospel of wealth ideology.[37] From Secretary of State William Henry Seward's expansive foreign policy to John Hay's "Open Door Policy," the United States was building a justification for empire that offered new horizons for overtly racialized discourse, particularly anti-Asian discrimination. Even opponents to empire, fostering a new language for anti-intervention, could reflect similar attitudes toward ethnic nationalism.[38] AIL members such as David Starr Jordan, the founding president of Stanford University, elaborated on Darwinist theory through their newfound interest in warfare, citing the Philippine Islands as empirical evidence of essential racial and civilizational differences.[39]

From the Spanish-American War to the Philippine-American War

The Spanish-American War stands out today if for no other reason than its brevity. Early on, the United States government framed Spain as an evil colonial master oppressing the abject and helpless Cuban population who bravely sought independence—a narrative that, if kept vague, nicely paralleled America's own revolutionary birth.[40] The war and the conflicts it generated would continue to be contested in this fashion: this was as much about US identity as it was about the foreign populations facing the brunt of the violence. Public opinion in favor of the war grew with each lurid tale of inhumane treatment at the hands of Spain, and by August 1898, the US fleet had defeated the Spanish after a whirlwind four months of nearly uninterrupted American victories. One key question remained: What would the United States do with its new territories? Much of the debate revolved around American exceptionalism. Many expansionists argued that the nation had an opportunity, even an *obligation*, to export its best features, all while gaining global standing alongside our European peers. Other imperialists stressed economic gains, often mixed with a religious zeal to Christianize the inhabitants of the new territories. Undergirding most of this rhetoric was a belief in national superiority marked by an assertion of indomitable strength, as reflected in figure 2.[41]

The idea of a new war was attractive to many US citizens and may help explain why no "positive" peace won out. Historian Caroline Janney suggests that the nation, still divided by the "grays" and "blues" of the Civil War, embraced the chance for a united fight against a foreign enemy.[42] This chapter follows this hypothesis, viewing the protracted Philippine-American War as a proxy for post-Reconstruction memory—or amnesia. Even arguments against imperialism embraced racialized rhetorics and built them into a new and occasionally violent national ideal. While many scholars of rhetoric have observed the dynamics of colonialism in contemporary contexts, there are very few studies of the Philippine occupation, a missed opportunity to consider how earlier debates over imperialism created cultural frameworks that legitimize racial violence today.[43]

To fully understand how peace rhetoric reflected these beliefs, we must closely read the public texts of the AIL because they dominated the critiques of war at the time. Rather than treat the movement as a marginal entity with little relation to major shifts in US culture and politics, I consider how the AIL penned an influential script of peace that could dehumanize Filipinos and other nonwhite populations. While opposed to the violence of imperialism as they understood it, members of the league drew a new boundary for acceptable violence. Appealing to the memory of past warfare, particularly the Civil War, the AIL told the story of a world constituted by a natural hierarchy

Figure 2. Clifford Berryman's *Washington Post* comic of a small Emilio Aguinaldo trying to pry off Uncle Sam's massive boot from the Philippines. Originally published on February 4, 1899 (National Archives).

that required individual self-restraint, itself an expression of moral superiority. Therefore, not intervening was evidence of one's great power, all while justifying the status quo. Ultimately, AIL rhetoric used the myths of peace to reframe exclusionary ideas of race, economics, and morality, resulting in a new script of national culture. Historians correctly point out that there is no homogenous or singular Anti-Imperialist point of view. Still, the AIL's public rhetoric reflects a "conservative bias dissatisfied with the course of American history since the Civil War."[44] This scripting of peace offered a way for citizens to correct, or simply forget, the problems of their day.

At first glance, AIL rhetoric exhibits many signs of a "positive" peace, yet it is imbued with racialized assumptions that dehumanize groups of people. A rhetorical analysis of these "negative" elements is thus required to arrive at an appreciation for what pernicious beliefs stand in the way of a truly "positive" peace. First, I detail the AIL's appeals to a racial hierarchy, focusing on how these arguments combined with celebrations of civilizational difference. Next, I describe how economic history was rewritten by AIL members to prioritize long-held Democratic beliefs regarding government intervention; in their view, interfering with the US economic order, much like its racial order, imperiled national culture far more than any violence meted out against colonial subjects. Finally, I examine how these appeals to economic and racial hierarchy united in a moral discourse that located US strength and superiority within a history of self-restraint. Here, nonintervention takes on near-mythical status, offered as a tonic for modern ills and, most significantly, the only proper script for peace that, nevertheless, obscures the rampant violence of the day.

Anti-Imperialist Peace

Rescripting Race through National Culture

Like earlier peace movements, the Anti-Imperialist League drew upon available resources to challenge warfare and offer its own version of a civilized and harmonious society. What stands out in the AIL peace script is its attention to race, often expressed in two interlocking ways. First, race served as an indicator of essential differences that shaped individual and group development. In this way, the AIL could use race as a justification for legal and economic arguments normalizing current inequalities. Second, this vision of race could amplify ethnonationalist theories of progress and civilization.[45] Together, the AIL could use this racial rhetoric—about individuals, groups, and entire civilizations—to defend the ideal of a national culture made up of fixed racial differences that demands noninterference in matters both domestic and foreign. In this peace script, past conflict, such as the Civil War, underscored the logic of noninterference, as AIL members reminded readers how that terrible struggle involved the federal government's meddling in racial matters. In its most extreme form, AIL advocacy sounded like a version of ethnic nationalism, suggesting, for instance, that Anglo-Saxons had already paid the price for playing "racial politics." The path toward national healing, this "negative" peace told its adherents, required that citizens discard divisive racial concerns in favor of a genteel acceptance of national culture. Such is the supposedly "humane" path toward lasting peace.

Elements of "positive" and "negative" peace coincided in AIL rhetoric as ambiguities in methods and goals lingered in key documents. Such vagueness is evident in the official AIL platform. First, we see an immediate reference to the national history of war and race, noted with a tinge of disappointment if not irritation. The passage hearkens to the US promise to grant liberty to all men: "We regret that it has become necessary in the land of Washington and Lincoln to reaffirm that all men, of whatever race or color, are entitled to life, liberty, and the pursuit of happiness."[46] What, precisely, the granting of liberty looks like is left unstated in this key document, yet the question of racial liberty animates much AIL rhetoric. Given the decentralized nature of the organization, where different branches could publicize clashing views on race, a clearer statement on what enfranchising racial minorities entails would have helped better guide the AIL peace script. As we will see, the AIL's vision of "granting" liberty to "whatever race or color" appears less like an active pursuit of social justice and more like rigid noninterference intended to maintain national culture and racial homogeneity.

The AIL repeatedly couches anti-Asian sentiments in the myths of peace to make its script seem "natural" and "harmonious." For instance, a racialized peace informs the work of prominent AIL member Charles Francis Adams Jr. A Civil War veteran who found success in the ruthlessly competitive railroad industry, Adams grounds one of his anti-imperial addresses in a racialized narrative of US history. First, he stresses the significance of national memory, placing himself within a generational lineage: "I put my foot in the tracks of our forefathers, where I can neither wander nor stumble."[47] In this sacred space of patriotic memory, Adams begins an excursus on civilizational differences, discussing Ottoman, European, and Spanish histories before landing on a hallmark of AIL reasoning: "If there is one historical law better and more irreversibly established than another, it is that, in the case of nations even more than in the case of individuals, their sins will find them out,—the day of reckoning may not be escaped."[48] Adams's rhetoric slots the United States into a system, even a cosmology, made up of nations with a unique destiny. While the individual citizen plays a crucial role in the AIL script, the league oscillates, in Adams's speech and elsewhere, between the individual and the nation, often implicating race and ethnicity in the process. For instance, within his discussion of civilizational fate, Adams reaffirms America's racial and ethnic identity, describing how "America has been peopled, and its development, up to the present time, worked out through two great stocks of the European family."[49]

Adams's scripting of peace naturalizes racial exclusion—in effect if not in intent—by highlighting Anglo-Saxon superiority. Again addressing racial history, Adams acknowledges "how the country at large has carried itself in turn towards Indian, African, and Asiatic is a matter of history. And yet it is equally the matter of history that this carriage, term it what you will,—unchristian, brutal, exterminating,—has been the salvation of the race. It has saved the Anglo-Saxon stock from being a nation of half-breeds."[50] For Adams, this racial makeup of the States has brought about, albeit violently at times, a type of benevolence toward "inferior races," one "clearly voiced by Lincoln." By invoking Lincoln, Adams imports the respect and admiration attributed to that president into his vision of peace—ironically—characterized by the supposed racial purity of Anglo-Saxon stock. Adams's peace, deeply exclusionary and unequal, is thus presented as a reaffirmation of the natural order intended to help the "half-breed, the Mexican, the mulato" assimilate because "the Anglo-Saxon is . . . essentially virile and enduring . . . [and made strong] due to the fact that the less developed races perished before him. Nature is undeniably brutal in its methods."[51] The struggle, brutal as it may be, must be accepted. And so goes the role offered in Adams's peace script to its adherents: to preserve the Anglo-Saxon race through cautious engagement with other peoples.

In this racialized peace, Anglo-Saxon culture strengthens through interaction, but not assimilation, with "inferior" races—a lesson Adams brings to bear directly upon the Philippine conflict. He repeatedly naturalizes the violence of this racial hierarchy, justifying this blatantly "negative" order by presenting it as an evolutionary process whereby the stronger races, at best, might keep weaker races safe. He grants the individual right to life for one deemed to be of a weaker race, but only when placed below Anglo-Saxons, whose culture is the means to guide others toward participation in national culture, not entirely unlike McKinley's missionary vision. Adams draws the limit for this process at the current conflict, concluding that "the Philippines . . . do not admit of assimilation." They are simply too different in custom, climate, and manner. The "miracle" of US civilization is that Anglo-Saxon stock endured and raised up those it nearly exterminated, yet for Adams, Filipinos and "races less developed . . . especially tropical" lack this possibility, being instead locked into their own civilizational trajectory. National pride and cultural development, in such AIL texts, depend upon racial inequality and essential differences acknowledged only through the lens of Anglo-Saxon superiority.[52]

Other AIL texts echo Adams's racialized rhetoric and expand these "negative" elements into a broader call for noninterference, which may have seemed "positive" to some readers. For instance, Edward C. Pierce, in a piece called "The 'Single Tribe' Fiction," urges against the inclusion of the Philippines into the United States due to glaring racial differences. First, and somewhat ironically, Pierce notes Filipino cultural advancements, only to segue into claims about their incompatibility with US culture.[53] He rejects comparing Filipinos to "wild American Indians" because they are more civilized and, therefore, well set on their own national trajectory. Citing zoologist Dean C. Worcester, Pierce declares, "the civilized Filipinos are as homogeneous as the Swedes and Norwegians," each of these categories representing a self-contained, if unequal, national unit. Thus, we ought to allow Filipinos to continue on their natural trajectory—the proper path toward global peace.[54] If major differences exist, it is evidence of the evolutionary struggle toward civilization engaged in by each race: "They are a mongrel race, formed by the survival of the hardest-lived traits in a varied and cosmopolitan (Oriental) ancestry."[55] Again, we see the myths of peace at work in the AIL's insistence upon a *natural* order necessary for peace, repeatedly depicted as essential racial differences. These differences are evidence of a larger civilizational process involving discrete nations. This peace script's domestic and international implications are notable, as AIL members used this framework to argue that America should resist disrupting the natural order, at home or abroad, and thus preserve Anglo-Saxon superiority. In short, the AIL peace, expressed in these publications, frames radical noninterference as a means toward racial purity—and tremendous inequality.[56] Of course, not every AIL document supported this view, but it pervaded the organization's rhetoric to a surprising degree.

George S. Boutwell, an AIL founder and president, echoes this line of racial reasoning and combines it with appeals to national memory.[57] To win African American citizens to the anti-imperialist cause, Boutwell awkwardly frames the issue of peace as a referendum on Lincoln's fight: "If the negro race have not learned to love liberty for the sake of liberty, and to hate despotism because it is despotism . . . then their freedom during five and thirty years has been a failure."[58] He then directly addresses African Americans: "I say to the negro population of the North: Men of your color, eight to ten million of them in the Philippine Islands, are denied the right of self-government," asking them to make the same sacrifice that Anglo-Saxon Americans made for them.[59] A toxic combination of ignorance and racial condescension, Boutwell's rhetoric nevertheless reflects several AIL trends.

First, this passage reaffirms the belief that a lasting peace must acknowledge discrete racial cohorts who each have a role in upholding civilization. Secondly, Boutwell speaks to an anxiety over federal interference and African American enfranchisement. The failures of Reconstruction and the rampant discrimination toward African Americans and other minorities are thus minimized, veiled by Boutwell's insistence on a strict hierarchy of racial difference. For him, the matter comes down to acknowledging the civilizational process whereby supposedly weaker races must "show . . . that [they] are ready to make some sacrifices" or else accept the status quo.[60] Black citizens, treated here as racialized subjects subordinated to America's civilizational process, have simply not sacrificed enough for peace. In rejecting imperialism, however, Black citizens can exercise self-determination and individual will in advocating for governmental noninterference. As we will continue to see, the Philippines serve in AIL rhetoric as a referendum on race, assimilation, and the sacrifices a white-centric peace requires.

Boutwell continues to connect the annexation of the Philippines to the contested memory of the Civil War and aspirations for racial harmony. In one instance, he bemoans a US flag flying over the Sulu Islands, where "the protection of the American flag [stands] over slavery" once again.[61] In another address, Boutwell stresses the legal and cultural implications of the Thirteenth, Fourteenth, and Fifteenth Amendments (often referred to as the "Civil War amendments"). Notably, he does not apply these to a progressive program that extends freedom and liberties but instead mentions them to incite a fear of cultural diminishment.[62] After asking the audience to consider the meaning of Lincoln's life and sacrifices, Boutwell reminds his listeners that if America were to annex any territory, whether Puerto Rico, Cuba, Guam, or the Philippines, the inhabitants would legally become citizens with equal rights. While praising Lincoln's emancipation efforts, he stokes new racial fears, asking, "Is there one man who will advocate what we call universal suffrage for the semi-barbarians whom we have taken into fellowship?"[63] Boutwell's rhetoric reveals, once again, how malleable the rhetoric of peace may be. Here, opposition to warfare is a chance to demand "harmony," but only if one maintains a vision of national culture predicated on rigid racial differences.

References to previous wars comprise some of the AIL's more impassioned pleas against war. Their peace script, however, betrays a profoundly ambivalent, at times even contradictory, use of these appeals. For instance, rather than amplify the message of racial equality inherent to the outcome of the Civil War, AIL members reframe that conflict as a case study on the delicate racial makeup of national cultures that should be interfered with only with great trepidation. In this way, the league's peace script invites readers to view the Filipinos as an "uncivilized," "mongolian race" whose inclusion into the United States may degrade the country.[64] The Civil War, Boutwell states, should remind us that "every acquisition of territory comes with this question: Are the people inhabiting this territory to be received as citizens and as our equals, or are they to be treated as vassals or as persons not yet fully emancipated?"[65] Far from extending freedoms to others, the memory of the Civil War delivers a racial lesson that curbs the desire to enfranchise other races. If pursued, the inclusion of Filipinos risks the "enslavement" of national culture and a loss of Anglo-Saxon civilization—often treated as if they are the same thing.

Similar framings of peace characterize Carl Schurz's work. In one address, he portrays a racialized vision of the United States as the natural order of things. In his words, every nation comprises discrete racial actors who guide its civilizational course. The issue is not admitting difference but failing to recognize its natural, even harmonious, role across the globe, which does not tend toward equality. The moral citizen, thus, must be resolute and disinclined to meddle with a culture's trajectory. Schurz, himself an immigrant, tells his audience of such racial differences: "Their population consists in Cuba and Porto Rico of Spanish Creoles and of people of negro blood, with some native Spaniards and a slight sprinkling of North Americans, English, Germans and French; in the Philippines of a large mass of more or less barbarous Asiatics."[66] When this diversity is framed as natural, any meddling risks spoiling the already fragile demographic makeup of each nation-state and its evolutionary fate. The racial stakes are high to Schurz, who asks the audience to "show me a single tropical country into which a stream of Anglo-Saxon, or more broadly speaking, of Germanic immigration" has survived.[67] The AIL turns climate itself into an advocate for their version of peace, as if each season, or the absence of one in some far-off place, attests to the natural order of ethnic nationalism.

AIL members occasionally suggest that the real violence of war, in the case of the Philippines, is in the resulting racial integration, an event depicted as catastrophic to harmonious living. If ignored, essential differences—"in language, in traditions, habits and customs, in political, social and even moral notions"—will lead to "the moral ruin of the Anglo-Saxon republic."[68] Far from contradicting the North's mission in the Civil War, Schurz implies that citizens align with Lincoln's spirit when they guard the nation against racial heterogeneity. He states, "We have still to atone for our long toleration of slavery. The ills we thus have we must bear as best we can. But would it not be sinful folly to add to them tenfold the incorporation in our bodypolitic of millions of persons belonging partly to races far less good-natured, tractable and orderly than the negro is?"[69] Echoing the words of Clement Vallandigham and his Copperhead movement, Schurz's peace script upholds racial differences to maintain US culture. Strict noninterference can absolve citizens of the sins of the Civil War, as opposed to the continued enfranchisement of racial minorities or any federal guarantee of equal treatment. Otherwise, Schurz warns, we will witness "the transformation of 'the United States of America' into 'the

United States of America and Asia."[70] Thus, we see the dystopia that threatens the AIL's peace in some of its public texts: a disfigured racial amalgamation of inferior Asian subjects.

Samuel Gompers, the prominent labor leader, similarly depicts peace through racialized rhetoric and stokes anti-Asian sentiment. Gompers asks, "Can we hope to close the floodgates of immigration from the hordes of Chinese and semi-savage races coming from what will then be part of our own country?" He argues that preserving the racial character of America is part of a larger mission to maintain "humane conditions" at home and to honor the "men who help to make this homogenous nation great."[71] Peace, in short, is only possible through racial purity. Moorfield Storey, a founding member of the National Association for the Advancement of Colored People (NAACP), also expresses demographic anxieties when urging against imperialism. In a statement given before Congress, referencing Lincoln's own dealing with so-called inferior races, Storey warns of future embarrassment spurred by the racial integration of Filipinos, connecting noninterventionist policy with ethnic nationalism—a rhetorical move already familiar in the AIL peace script.[72] He continues to advise that "the great trouble is that we do not recognize the fact that the Americans and the Filipinos are different. We say they are inferior and imagine that we can take a Filipino and make him an American. We do not recognize the essential difference, and we do not treat them sympathetically."[73] To be truly peaceful and humane means understanding racial differences and treating each accordingly. For the AIL, this practice is part of a script maintaining national culture.

Here, we see again how anti-war protest offers new justifications for racial and ethnic discrimination that, to its adherents, might falsely appear like a "positive" peace. Storey, to his credit, is more nuanced than Gompers when he discusses "difference"—we will find no prolonged racist diatribe here. Nevertheless, he and other AIL members surround their often vague racial "observations" with an insistence upon America's unique culture and civilizational superiority, which could easily justify noninterference toward other races. At best, perhaps, this script casts racial and ethnic groups as leaders of their own nations set on particular civilizational trajectories.[74] William Jennings Bryan, a controversial (and somewhat fickle) AIL ally, viewed Filipinos as members of an entirely alien people, arguing they were "so different from us in race and history that amalgamation is impossible."[75] Here, expansion is no mundane policy debate but a question over the fate of "Anglo-Saxon civilization." Framing the issue as one of ethnic nationalism allows adherents to demand a white-centered peace or none at all. Through this rhetoric, members such as Bryan could use racial difference to prioritize white individualism ("Anglo-Saxon civilization has taught the *individual* to protect his own rights") as well as the collective unit of ethnic cultures ("American *civilization* will teach him to respect the rights of others").[76] The war debate again allows dissenters to reaffirm the homogenous qualities of US culture, with grave racial implications.[77]

David Starr Jordan, the first president of Stanford University, made his own overture to ethnic nationalism while injecting social Darwinism into the AIL peace script. Jordan warns that the "Anglo-Saxon or any other civilized race degenerates in the tropics mentally, morally, physically," and thus, the United States cannot hope to survive there.[78] Citing other nations, such as China, Korea, Siam, and Turkey, Jordan underscores the "social decay" intrinsic to engaging with Filipinos, drily stating that "their population cannot be exterminated on the one hand, nor made economically potent on the other, except through slavery."[79] This deeply disturbing assessment could be viewed as a byproduct of a deeper faith—no less disturbing—in a global order naturally composed of different ethnic and racial groups. The AIL script, in these passages, slots each group into a Darwinian struggle, represented here as a brutal game. In this worldview, involvement with other races or cultures brings "decay." As another AIL member reminds his Chicago audience, the nation has finally moved on from racial corruption—the Civil War "destroy[ed] the last vestige of this hateful policy of racial bigotry." To now engage with Filipinos "is not the upward way of civilization but the backward descent to barbarism."[80] The AIL peace script equivocates on the meaning of barbarism. Is it a result of excessive military force? A result of social or political repression? Or is it the natural product of racial diversity? This ambiguity, made possible partly because AIL rhetoric was so diverse and proliferated across dozens of local chapters and thousands of pages of publications, created a rhetorical opportunity for activists and readers: to gather all these negative consequences into a single discourse of peace that privileged the homogeneity of US culture. By echoing the myths of peace, the AIL script could frame this homogeneity as "natural," "nonpolitical," and "harmonious." As the next section describes, these tenuous appeals to race could also permeate discussions over the national economy. Again, we see how malleable peace rhetoric can be in generating new justifications of violence.

The Economy of American Greatness

For some AIL members, the economy was a way to judge national culture that could now be expressed in the language of peace. During this period of rampant wealth disparity, it is significant that an organization that overlapped with the Progressive movement took a strong noninterventionist position that combined economic policies with anti-Asian sentiment. In the AIL view, obstacles to empire-building in the Philippines could reaffirm a laissez-faire attitude toward prosperity. Just like racial inequalities—both near and far—economic inequalities ought to be handled in a hands-off way. Each ethnicity will naturally reveal its level of production and value if only citizens are patient enough to allow it. Ongoing disputes over tariffs, inflation, and currency were quite abstract, but the AIL script offered a way to ground these discussions by tying them to racial visions of national superiority. Understanding how the AIL fused these elements into their peace script sensitizes us to how citizens can use seemingly race-neutral topics, such as the economy, to justify racial and ethnic violence and weave these into arguments for peace.

One reason for this malleability is that the meaning of peace depends on how one defines war. Charles Francis Adams Jr. offers a troubling prescription for peace by making war a matter of race and economics. Hearkening to the nation's revolutionary fight against unfair taxation, for instance, he reminds the audience that economic prudence is essential to America's project. He then segues into the matter at hand with an eye toward race: "Here again, as between the policy of the 'Open Door' and the Closed-Colonial-Market policy, the superior race is amenable to its own conscience only. It will doubtless on all suitable and convenient occasions bear in mind that it is a 'Trustee for Civilization.'"[81] Alluding to the controversial issue of post–Civil War pensions, Adams mentions a $200 million pension payment whose burden falls upon the "unfortunate tax-payer" if the war continues.[82] For Adams, opposition to the Philippine War aligns with the long-held rejection of a strong central government. He expresses this argument in racial terms that seem all too familiar: the "superior race" within the United States must persist in its civilizational mission by rejecting "the 'Pauper Labor' of Europe and of the inferior races . . . [and instead follow] the principle of unrestricted industry and free labor." Laissez-faire economics combines with laissez-faire cultural development, demanding that each race be left alone to achieve whatever peace nature allots it.

AIL members repeatedly define the free market through racial units that correlate to distinct national cultures, a perspective that sanctions anti-Asian rhetoric through the language of peace. Consider Adams's comments: "China, unlike Poland, is inhabited by an 'inferior race,'" and the US system of commerce is threatened by the "introduc[ion] into our industrial system [of] ten millions of Asiatics."[83] Here, we clearly see the ideal economy suggested by AIL members: an ethnonational market free of government interference except to enforce—out of compassion—the border between fundamentally different nations and peoples. Anything else will undermine the cultural hierarchy and, thus, any real chance of peace. By rejecting federal involvement *abroad*, the AIL scripted a new defense for a *domestic* economy similarly shorn of federal regulations. While its implications abroad are important, I must stress how amenable this racialized vision of peace was to the brutal Jim Crow practices of the day.[84]

Few members channeled economics into their vision of peace more directly than Edward Atkinson, an economist and founding member of the AIL. In his 1896 address titled "The Cost of an Anglo-American War," Atkinson foreshadows many arguments that framed economics and ethnicity as central to war calculations. After rejecting the pro-imperialist maxim that "trade follows flag," Atkinson admonishes the audience that the flag only attracts attention through its "symboliz[ing of] energy, personal liberty, intelligence, and a just government."[85] These qualities align, in Atkinson's eyes, with particular ethnicities, and so he repeatedly stresses that "it follows that the self-interest as well as the moral and political welfare of the people of the United States are bound up in a close commercial union with the other English-speaking peoples."[86] Retelling the history of Anglo-Saxon conflict, including yet another discussion of the Civil War, Atkinson reaffirms a racialized economic vision, pleading for policymakers not to interfere with commerce or else risk flooding the US market with the wasteful activity of weaker races.[87]

Speeches by George Boutwell similarly frame economic interaction with the Philippines as a corruption of national culture.[88] The "cheap labor of Asia," he warns, will invade the American market, spreading as "a menace to every manufacturing town and city in the country." In his view, this invasion will occur because of the obligation to recognize such people as equal subjects.[89] Again appealing to Civil War memory, he cautions that if we feel things are unfair now—"if some mills were transferred from the North to the South in pursuit of cheap labor"—things will only worsen along racial and economic lines. He asks, "May not whole towns, and with stronger reasons, be transferred from America to Asia?"[90] For Boutwell, interaction with Filipinos means Americans will "be degraded to the condition of the people of the East."[91] Anti-Asian sentiment seeps further into a revisionist history that amplifies ethnic nationalism.

Boutwell might concede Filipinos *could* achieve equality with Anglo-Saxons someday through great effort. However, the current economic reality is proof of a basic racialized hierarchy that imbues the proper path toward peace. For Boutwell, acquiring the Philippines will create a "free ingress to the Mongolian race" and diminish Anglo-Saxon free markets. Simply put, the United States will see its civilizational progress stall if leaders allow inferior races to interact with its economy.[92] For Boutwell, the matter doubles as a referendum on the Civil War's legacy, again obscuring Jim Crow repression and stoking anti-Asian rhetoric: "With every acquisition of territory comes this question: Are the people inhabiting this territory to be received as citizens and as our equals, or are they to be treated as vassals or as persons not yet fully emancipated from slavery?"[93] In a twisted remembrance of Reconstruction debates, he warns that once Filipinos are on US territory, they will forever be citizens of the United States. Just as "carpet-baggery" ensued in the vacuum of slavery, he reminds his audience, the US population will be exploited—in his words, "enslaved"–by "the most degraded laboring populations of the tropical Pacific Islands."[94]

Other AIL members stress the economic perils of imperialism in cultural terms, thereby masking Jim Crow inequalities with their script of peace. Carl Schurz, for instance, warns that occupying the Philippines will bring about a period of economic pain "when every American farmer and workingman, when going to his toil, will, like his European brother, have 'to carry a fully armed soldier on his back.'"[95] Incorporating Filipinos will not bring prosperity but more likely a cultural backslide because the weaker races are unlikely to contribute to the US economy. Depictions of colonialism's economic burden illustrate how arguments against imperialism could support a white-washed interpretation of the Gilded Age and America's racial legacy. For example, Schurz contrasts the future crisis with the supposedly pristine industrial history of America: "We simply produced, in our factories as well as on our farms, more things that other nations wanted" and thus prospered unlike inferior countries.[96] Rather than acknowledge the race-based inequalities ravaging the economy, or the more complicated legacy of US treatment of indigenous people, Schurz warns of a frightening tomorrow that depends upon a false nostalgia for a peaceful past.

Economic discussions continued to animate appeals to a peace predicated on racial inequality. Former president Grover Cleveland, himself an AIL member, alludes to a supposedly simpler America—"the days of 'Uncle Tom's Cabin' are passed"—and claims that citizens must now make productive economic members out of "the nearly nine millions of negroes who have intermixed with our citizenship . . . [where] there is still a grievous amount of ignorance, a sad amount of viciousness and a tremendous amount of laziness and thriftlessness."[97] Repeatedly, the AIL script for peace calls for a "material prosperity" to enhance the nation, yet in their view this prosperity is achievable only through nongovernmental means, *not* through enfranchising more nonwhite citizens.[98] The nation had already assimilated some racial minorities, the argument goes, so let's not create further obstacles by inviting more inferior people. Labor and race, once again, meld together to shape a violent anti-imperialist peace script.

Demographic anxieties serve as another means to tie racial inequality into a "natural" economic order. Consider William Jennings Bryan's anti-imperialist compendium, *Republic or Empire? The Philippine Question*. In these pages, politicians and thinkers across the spectrum cite the economic toll of war and colonialism while repeatedly stoking racial fears.[99] Of particular concern for US peace is the prospect of an "influx of Malays."[100] This economic assault on labor would render the States "The Poor Man's Load."[101] Such racialized appeals were powerful ways to criticize federal intervention while reaffirming Anglo-Saxon's place atop the hierarchy. Senator and former Confederate major John W. Daniel uses this rhetoric to fuel fears of civilizational collapse. He warns that "we are breaking down our history, repudiating and belittling our principles, and seeking to subvert the whole theory and settled tenure of American progress and of American rule, just to get and embody in our Commonwealth some scattered, barbarous, or savage islands."[102] Echoing Southern arguments heard during the Civil War, citizens must preserve national homogeneity in the face of irrational federal intervention. The myth of peace as a natural, utopian order dovetails again with appeals to a racial and ethnic hierarchy.[103]

Another recurring economic argument against imperialism stresses the danger of tropical climates: for US markets, laborers, and Anglo-Saxon culture. Repeatedly, AIL members ask how the physical attributes of US citizens—typically meaning "Anglo-Saxon" men—could be compatible with the tropics. Adams, for instance, suggests the notion of equality is bunk when "applied to human beings of different race in one nationality; manifestly [more so], in the case of races less developed, and in other, especially *tropical*, countries."[104] Boutwell also laments the effects of "the most degraded laboring populations of the *tropical* Pacific Islands" interacting with American laborers.[105] Carl Schurz asks his audience to "show me a single instance of a *tropical* country in which people" developed a stable nation hospitable to Anglo-Saxons.[106] Indeed, "all efforts to get men of Germanic blood to become the bulk, or even a large part, of the laboring force of any *tropical* country, have utterly failed. It is not only the low rate of wages prevailing there that repels them, but the *climatic conditions* which cannot be changed."[107] Andrew Carnegie concludes that "subject races and *tropical* conditions, cannot be realized by Europeans."[108] Through this language, AIL members perpetuated anti-Asian views that reinforced a worldview of discrete nations made of ethnically homogenous actors with different chances for economic prosperity. Those comfortable in the tropical climes are best left there away from Anglo-Saxon culture.

David Starr Jordan, proponent of eugenics that he was, went furthest in stressing racial discrepancies and their economic implications. US civilization—the keystone of peace—simply cannot survive the tropics. He details how, in his view, the climate degrades white culture: "The Anglo-Saxon or any other civilized race degenerates in the tropics, mentally, morally, physically," resulting in the "decay" of economic and social institutions.[109] If US culture depends on free Anglo-Saxon labor, as Starr describes, then economic nonintervention takes on a cultural dimension. In this framework, it is compassionate to leave Filipinos alone, letting them arrive at their natural state of development. Simultaneously, to leave white Americans alone is not merely an impersonal economic policy but a cultural imperative to prevent the "*enslavement* of American labor."[110] Class inequalities among white citizens, not to mention those between white and nonwhite citizens, are thus explained by an economic argument fixated on racial "fitness" for specific environments. In such passages, the AIL script ties the entire history of the States—even the memory of Lincoln, "The Great Emancipator"—to the economic vitality of Anglo-Saxons, now made the bedrock of peace.

Negative Peace as Violent Compassion

The Anti-Imperialist League, despite the previously detailed language, had progressive members whose ideas could help build a "positive" peace. How do we square the nobler ideas with the ignoble, often retrograde, peace script composed in some of AIL's public texts? We must remember that few of these ideas, repugnant as they seem now, were considered out of bounds at the time. Furthermore, the league's activities suggest it was a place for active debate and disagreement, so it is unfair to assume each member consented to every argument.[111] However, as an influential voice for peace advocacy—in terms of membership, resources, and public attention—we must analyze this organization's peace script, publicized during the Spanish-American and Philippine-American War, with an eye for its potential to stoke ethnonationalist sentiments. Consider Mark Twain, an eclectic and mostly progressive figure for his time. Even he left open the question of what guaranteed America's exceptionalism. While concluding that the subjugation of Filipinos was incompatible with national greatness, he rarely disputed that the nation was, in some way, exceptional among all nations. Instead, the details of America's greatness, I argue, were offered by the surrounding AIL rhetoric. Echoing the racial and economic appeals to noninterference, the league frequently contended that US virtue, even superiority, lies in self-restraint.

These arguments served three functions that together reinforced the already-described ethnonational vision. First, these appeals reassured readers that the United States was, in fact, superior among nations, including the Philippines. Second, these calls for "humane" restraint toward those lower on the moral hierarchy did not reject violence in principle, only in this instance. In the end, the decision to hold back the full arsenal of US power only served to further remind people of that very power. Pulling one's punch was still an acknowledgment of one's ability to throw one full force. Finally, the AIL's moral argument against warfare reinforced the Gilded Age status quo. To enact and rehearse the AIL's peace script in this way demanded an affirmation of basic structural inequalities in the country. Altogether, these three functions animated a rhetorical vision of brutal compassion, or what one might call "humane exceptionalism." Here, America validates its economic and racial superiority by expressing self-restraint toward inferior foreigners. This self-restraint, nevertheless, legitimizes the potential of future violence. Ultimately, extreme noninterference and self-restraint enforced the current racial and economic hierarchy inseparable from the ugly legacies of white supremacy and capitalist exploitation. This undercurrent of violent rhetoric that fuels "negative" peace scripts is part of our national history of peace and the broad cultural context that must be acknowledged in pursuing "positive" peace proposals.

We can see shades of "humane exceptionalism" in the AIL's official platform. The anti-colonial text implicitly reinforces a geopolitical vision of strong and weak nations. Decrying current policies that violate the spirit of Washington and Lincoln, the AIL then claims they are opposed to the "doctrine of international law which permits the subjugation of the weak by the strong."[112] Not only does it not deny the superiority of the United States, the AIL platform reaffirms it as fact. The organization then establishes a hierarchy of grievances: "Much as we abhor the war of 'criminal aggression' in the Philippines, greatly as we regret that the blood of the Filipinos is on American hands, we more deeply resent the betrayal of American institutions at home."[113] The AIL peace script thus invokes a classic isolationist argument: whatever the suffering of others, we must prioritize our own problems. Echoing David Starr Jordan's argument against warfare—that combat sends the strongest men to die while the weaker men are left to populate the nation—the AIL platform suggests the worst part of war is not the harm done unto others but the threat it poses to national superiority: to the "great people [who] for a century" pursued freedom and liberty and now throw it away and tarnish the memory of Lincoln.[114]

Adams calls for a brutal compassion that illustrates how anti-war rhetoric can legitimize past violence in the name of a falsely "positive" peace. First, he states that if racial violence seems inevitable, it may still be useful: "the knife and the shotgun have been far more potent and active instruments in ... dealings with the inferior races than the code of liberty or the output of the Bible Society."[115] Even in anti-imperialist writings, Adams affirms the utility of US power. Here, however, he urges restraint, asking the United States to not take on Filipino subjects, stressing the need to "put implicit confidence in the sound instincts and Christian spirit of the dominant, that is, the stronger race."[116] Colonizing the Philippines is not about treating all humans as equals in the eyes of God or relative to the US Constitution. Instead, Adams frames the debate as a chance to affirm the natural system of nations made up of unequal races. Ultimately, the AIL's peace script frames the issue as a moral imperative for the superior race to reject fighting inferior races or risk losing hard-fought cultural progress.[117]

The AIL peace script repeatedly framed colonization as a process of cultural degradation, which complemented appeals to American exceptionalism as the natural path to peace. Readers likely felt themselves the benevolent, yet strong, star of the show. League member George F. Edmunds, a Vermont senator, underscores the exceptional trajectory of US progress in his anti-war tract, reminding citizens of "the golden future [that] will draw nearer and nearer, however much the present may be clouded."[118] Clearly, the "golden future" is not a perfectly peaceful process, at least not as generally understood. By adhering to "humane exceptionalism," however, the United States remains selective of the types of violence allowed to be sure they align with a proper, even compassionate, extension of a mighty national culture: "A[n acceptable] war that was begun for humanity, as we alleged, has been continued for [an unacceptable war of] conquest."[119] Lincoln's memory is invoked in this framework, which again does not reject violence or argue that all humans are equal but underscores the special role of national violence, past and present. It calls upon its adherents to respect such memories—ensuring that "the dead shall not have died in vain"—by not misusing national power.[120] Boutwell continues by stating that ending the imperialist war "relieves us from the suspicion that we are to cooperate with England in an attempt to subjugate the *weaker* states of the world to the domination of the Anglo-Saxon race."[121] His ideal of nonintervention is thereby a way of "vindicat[ing] the character and example and teachings of Washington and of Jefferson . . . Lincoln and Grant" by not fixing the inequality and domestic turmoils of another nation.[122] Instead, the supremacy of an Anglo-Saxon nation is reasserted by what it chooses not do. In this case, the ideal of nonintervention meant *not* subjugating the weaker races abroad, yet such calls for restraint echoed calls for nonintervention in domestic issues, as well.

Carl Schurz also wrote extensively about how the imperial war deviated from US exceptionalism, and as such was an absolute misuse of the nation's otherwise legitimate strength and force.[123] Schurz, who echoes the genteel style of his peers, depicts self-restraint toward the weak as "the character of a gentleman." Again, the appeal to humane and compassionate treatment justifies a system of inequality, as he reminds us that "there is one duty [of] *strong* men and *strong* nations . . . It is that the strong should scrupulously abstain from abusing their strength when dealing with the *weak*."[124] It bears repeating how the AIL script, as seen here, does *not* reject state violence so much as offer new cultural justifications for it. Schurz's rejection of violence reassures the reader of intrinsic American power, stating that "our manifest *superiority* is so great that there would be little glory in our triumph."[125] Indeed, the nation is clearly "strong enough to '*whip*' anybody whenever we like."[126] The AIL offers its audience the ultimate wish fulfillment: to have the moral high ground inherent to "peace" without disavowing one's might and right to use force.[127]

Schurz's rhetoric demands closer investigation because, in at least one instance, his writings served as argumentative guidelines for all AIL members.[128] In this text, titled "The Issue of Imperialism," he underscores US supremacy over other nations and cultures, telling his readers that "no pusillanimous" spirit or loss of "patriotic pride" will befall the nation if we cease "arbitrary rule over subject populations."[129] In fact, US superiority would only be bolstered by showing restraint toward the weaker Philippine Islands—indeed, he states that "the world knows how strong we are." Echoing appeals to economic and racial nonintervention, Schurz reminds fellow members that national supremacy will not be diminished but enhanced through restraint.[130] To carry forth the exceptionalism begun by Washington and Lincoln, he states, requires a staunch display of self-restraint that grants America the status of "the greatest of all existing worldpowers [sic] by its moral prestige."[131] One ensures economic and national supremacy, according to the AIL, by refusing to hurt the weak, inferior races—but only in this instance. Again, the AIL takes a generic call for humane treatment and combines it with a hierarchical system to reaffirm US violence and exceptionalism with little thought given to the rampant violence impacting nonwhite people domestically and abroad.[132]

One noteworthy AIL project was the publication of soldier letters to offer citizens the chance to read firsthand testimony regarding the Philippine War's brutality.[133] Rather than explicitly denounce the racism and atrocious accounts of violence presented in these letters, the league printed the letters with almost no commentary. Thus, the collection could reinforce a pervading sense of incompatibility between Filipino and US culture. Racial animosity toward Filipinos is matter-of-factly documented in some letters, as if such feelings are the inevitable consequence of an ill-conceived war.[134] "Humane exceptionalism," as the guiding concept for the AIL peace script, offers a place for such animosities to fester. Rather than rebuke racial intolerance, the league presents it as evidence of essentially different nations and peoples. For example, in considering the greatness of the United States and other nations, Storey reminds the audience that "self-government" is the sign of civilization and, no matter how far behind the Filipinos may be, the States must not diminish in moral standing by possessing a weaker people against their will.[135]

Carnegie contributes to this line of thinking by praising the exceptional humanity embodied by the restraint of Americans and "the English-speaking race."[136] Put simply, US culture is irreconcilable with Filipino culture, and the recognition of this fact will maintain national greatness and peace. Carnegie asks, "Has the influence of the *superior* race upon the *inferior* ever proved beneficial to either? I know of no case in which it has been."[137] He proceeds to envision the unnatural and immoral consequences of this ill-begotten route toward peace: "If, in our humanitarian efforts . . . we should bring a hundred

[Filipinos] to New York, give them fine residences on Fifth Avenue, a fortune condition upon their remaining, and try to 'civilize' them . . . they would all run away if not watched, and risk their lives in an attempt to get back to their own civilization."[138] US superiority, and the peace it offers, demands self-restraint, not as a gesture of equality but as an enactment of ethnic greatness. Carnegie continues, "No *superior race* ever gave [civilized governance] to an *inferior* without settling and merging in that race," an option that is unbecoming and degrading to national culture.[139] Former president Grover Cleveland also situated his anti-war stance in an acknowledgment of US superiority, reminding readers that "American citizenship means more than any other citizenship.[140] To preserve American greatness means not to *reject* violence but to reject the cultural violence incurred by taking on Filipino subjects.

In sum, appeals to self-restraint combined into a toxic rhetoric of "humane exceptionalism," a motif within the AIL peace script that tied together disparate attitudes over race, economics, and nationalism. Together, they bolster a vision of Anglo-Saxon supremacy and support of noninterference. With the inferiority of nonwhite people predicated on self-restraint, the AIL legitimizes a boundary to acceptable violence that celebrates the status quo as the proper and natural way. Those lowest in the hierarchy—typically nonwhite and non-male citizens—have only themselves to blame for their suffering. To ask for intervention is not only an individual display of weakness but a violation of peace-loving Anglo-Saxon culture.

Conclusion

The AIL peace script, an odd mixture of "positive" and "negative" appeals, foreshadowed an oncoming wave of ethnonationalism in the twentieth century. This message of racial inequality also has contemporary parallels. In early 2020, the coronavirus (SARS-CoV-2) pandemic disrupted the global order, bringing everyday life to a halt.[141] After weeks of ambiguous and dismissive remarks regarding the pandemic, President Donald J. Trump followed a familiar script when declaring a state of emergency: deny responsibility, target an enemy (he picked China), and act tough.[142] Though citizens will not fully grasp the consequences of such rhetoric for decades, the history of war and peace offers warnings and predictions. The global emergency sparked new laws and political debates while people all over the world tried to make sense of the chaos. And what of the peace script during an emergency of this kind? Early on, we could see how racism and classism were exploited by some opposed to government intervention in handling the coronavirus. White supremacists, according to a *Time* report, saw the pandemic as a new opportunity to achieve their utopia.[143] Radical capitalists deemed the sacrifice of some as intrinsic to the freedom of the market. That some may die was just a rule of nature—that mythical wellspring of peace—which we must resolutely accept, if not celebrate.[144] Even more resonant of AIL discourse was the rise of citizens across the spectrum who saw the path back to peace paved around, or fenced in from, ethnic Others, particularly Chinese and Asian Americans.[145] The scapegoating and dehumanizing of Asian Americans was likely perceived as a "positive" peace by some advocates despite being grossly "negative" by Galtung's standards.[146]

For the early twentieth century, the Anti-Imperialist League offered a curious assortment of persuasive resources for peace advocacy. Consider renowned activist Jane Addams, who stood before an audience of anti-imperialists in Chicago roughly one year after the Spanish-American War.[147] At the start of her speech, titled "Democracy or Militarism," she invokes her own vision of American exceptionalism: "None of us who has been reared and nurtured in America can be wholly without the democratic instinct. It is not a question with any of us having it or not having it; it is merely a question of trusting it."[148] US citizens, she believes, possess an inherent democratic quality if only they dare to acknowledge, or even interrogate, it. To be a citizen means to partake in this active democratic culture, to feel its impulse as essential to our existence. For other AIL members, this concept likely took on a diverse array of progressive and retrograde meanings.

Addams, however, concretely defined her terms. Rather than reaffirm an exclusionary vision of American greatness, as many of her colleagues did, she countered "humane exceptionalism," stating, "We may make a mistake in politics as well as in morals by forgetting that *new conditions are ever demanding the evolution of a new morality*, along old lines but in larger measure. Unless the present situation extends our nationalism into *internationalism*, unless it has thrust forward our patriotism into humanitarianism we cannot meet it."[149] The nation exercises its greatness not through rigid adherence to the past or embracing a ruthless laissez-faire ideology but by daring to evolve, even if doing so violates old definitions and practices. For Addams, democratic culture is pragmatic and thus able to transcend the limitations of nationalism and patriotism if occasion requires. The shared experience of humanity—the dignity of every person due to the basic fact of their existence—is fundamental to her script of peace, which demands "the unfolding of life processes which are making for a *common development*" beyond social and territorial boundaries.[150] Sadly, Addams's cosmopolitan view of world peace would remain marginal in AIL rhetoric, out of step with its scripting of foreign people and national values. Perhaps her script demanded too much improvisation from anxious citizens.[151]

This chapter has argued that the AIL peace script mobilized appeals to race, memory, and economics to reaffirm exclusionary narratives of US life.

The mere thought of Filipino citizens inspired some members to forward an ethnonationalist ideal of civic life that demanded resolute nonintervention. The league, simultaneously, found new ways to praise America's homogeneity—now the source of its superiority. They declared, in various ways, that the nation achieves peace through an enlightened self-restraint that all too often saw nonwhite foreigners as inferior, not even worth the fight. Although there were some exceptions, this peace script could encourage adherents to embrace Anglo-Saxon supremacy and its right to violence. This "humane exceptionalism" offered a way to celebrate one's power by refusing to pulverize "weak" and "inferior" Filipinos. For those identifying with the script, such brutal compassion was constitutive of lasting peace. Like Copperhead rhetoric, elements of the AIL peace script illustrate the reactionary potential of anti-war opposition.[152]

3

Scripting a Spectacle in Henry Ford's Peace Expedition

On September 4, 1933, Henry Ford's "Peace Ship" sold for scraps. Eighteen years after its ill-fated trip to Europe seeking to end the Great War, the ocean liner, once a symbol of innovation not unlike Ford's Model T, was now "junk."[1] The average citizen struggling to obtain a living wage or employment of any kind during the Great Depression probably did not mourn the passing of this anti-war relic. Across the Atlantic Ocean, events unfolded similarly as nations searched for some sense of stability, even if it meant scrapping their own symbols of peace. Although the Western world experienced unprecedented violence during World War I that left millions dead and millions more grieving, Henry Ford's Peace Ship, rusted and useless, testified to the lack of a compelling postwar peace. By 1933 many countries in Europe operated somewhere between the lethal chaos of war and an ideal harmony of peace, pitting types of violence against one another in escalating dramas. All sides, nevertheless, tended to script their actions in the language of peace.

This chapter considers how Ford's ambitious, widely publicized movement fits into this broader landscape of peace. Ford gave to the world a peace script as flashy as it was tenuous—a perfect product for quick, punchy headlines. Scholars, however, have largely ignored Ford's voyage, likely because of its most prominent feature: the use of spectacle as an argument. Rather than highlight a specific policy, organization, or philosophy, Ford simply threw his wealth at any activist who would accept his invitation to sail to Europe in the winter of 1915 and "get the boys out of the trenches by Christmas"—details be damned.[2] Traditionally, scholars treat spectacles as superficial events or objects lacking complex meaning, but I consider how the spectacle scripted peace in a way that thoroughly reflected Ford's world, specifically his socioeconomic privilege, and its serious repercussions for peace advocacy. Understanding this process is integral to formulating a sustainable, "positive" peace for today.

First, I discuss how rhetorical studies can best interpret the protest dynamics of a spectacle. As seen in Ford's movement, spectacles propel grand visions posing as universal into the spotlight. Like all social phenomena, spectacles originate in specific racial, gendered, and class-based systems of power. Next, I give an overview of the war debate at the time, focusing on how Ford fits into the broader legacy of dissent, industrial culture, and war sentiment, as well as how he largely avoided the throttling of civil liberties that followed his protest journey. Finally, I analyze how Ford's expedition played out in the press. His peace script was written almost entirely through printed news and thus reflects several of that medium's biases. Believing in the centrality of advertising, Ford built his movement in the weeks leading up to the voyage as a personality-driven, visually rich PR campaign that dodged concrete plans or policies.

The emphasis, if there was one, was on the astounding fact that the expedition was happening at all. Rather than elaborate upon facts, the event's very *facticity*—its bare existence—became the focal point of the movement, magnified through Ford's persona and dramatized through narrative elements of tragedy and comedy. Once the spectacle was underway, the coverage alternated between a ridiculous, ironic frame and an idealistic, sympathetic one, both spotlighting Ford over any specific policy. To interpret the peace script as citizens likely read it at the time, I also consider the coverage surrounding the articles on Ford's expedition. These mostly fall into two types: intense, frightening accounts of the war's carnage or lurid stories of treasonous plots, which either made Ford's movement seem dangerous or rendered it simply laughable.[3] In the end, this spectacular peace script inundated the reading public and responded to the demand for entertainment, although not without any negative consequences. Ford's movement damaged the moral credibility of pacifism by stifling other activist voices. The few anti-war activists who survived Ford's fiasco would soon face intimidation and repression by the federal government. Unlike the movements described in previous chapters, Ford's peace movement was not explicitly racial, gendered, or classist. However, it shares several similarities with the Copperhead and AIL movements. First, Ford's is a "negative" peace script because it fails to outline any sustainable or equitable postwar world, opting instead to simply reject war. Second, although its cultural claims are not as obvious, Ford's voyage depended on his extreme cultural privilege. We see this most clearly when considering whose voice it favored (often his own) and whose it ignored, namely, those of the diverse pool of anti-war activists at the time.

Depleting the Social Movement Field: A Rich Man's Spectacle of Peace

The spectacle shares with the peace script a reliance on culture. While peace activism frequently draws from the cultural well to imagine a more harmonious world, the spectacle amplifies cultural symbols to the highest degree. Both deal with collective memories, shared narratives, and powerful emotions to influence how the public perceives certain issues and identities. Like peace rhetoric, spectacles tend to get short shrift from scholars, possibly due to an assumed shallowness: they are seen as fleeting, one-dimensional events.[4] Early analyses of spectacles spoke of them as blunt instruments employed to bludgeon hapless audiences.[5] More recently, scholars have moved past this model, asking how images and mediated performances, while still intense, extravagant, and politically reductive, create a dynamic field of meaning for audiences that does not escape the trappings of race, gender, and class.

The spectator, simply put, should not be treated as a mere cog in a linear process of meaning-making but instead taken as an active participant in creating the spectacle and its resulting discourse.[6] The persuasive work that goes into spectacles is not a flat, unidirectional event that defies deep interpretation. Instead, we must interrogate the spectacle as a reflection of dominant visual and rhetorical themes across cultural communities. Spectacles abound with content that crystallizes into often-bizarre objects of public infatuation that, upon closer study, tend to be highly selective and representative of a segment of society. Indeed, a spectacle could not transpire and sustain itself if there was not already an abundance of cultural symbols to command the attention of onlookers as something recognizable. Dismissing the depth and the specificity of spectacles risks relegating key texts, such as Ford's peace script, to the margins of history.[7] By recognizing the actual complexity of spectacles, we can understand how Ford's movement relates to the other chapters of this book: all tap into cultural rhetoric to compose their script. Here, such appeals are not explicit. Nevertheless, in the baldly "negative" nature of Ford's appeals—to end the war and little else—he not only silences the already-marginalized voices around him, particularly women activists such as Inez Boissevain, Jane Addams, and Rosika Schwimmer, but perpetuates existing inequalities by totally ignoring them. In essence, Ford makes such matters irrelevant to peace.

Through a close reading of the spectacle's life course in the press, this chapter asks how Ford's movement used various symbols, narrative arcs, and myths of peace to script its anti-war advocacy. Ford purposefully conducted his movement through newspaper coverage, and it accordingly took on qualities of print culture, such as a reliance on big, dramatic personalities and a dependence on the news cycle. While this chapter considers the symbolic depth of spectacles, I nevertheless agree with critics about a spectacle's outcome: it tends to damage the issues it focuses on, especially when it draw on social movement causes. However, spectacles are not the sole cause of such degeneration. We must not hold Ford exclusively responsible for the loss of resources, both material and symbolic, inflicted upon the anti-war activist sector.

Spectacles are effects or byproducts of popular thought and emotion. They bestow a rhetorical style that is sensationalistic but not strange or unfamiliar; they are made possible through an array of ideas and feelings that have *already* permeated the public sphere. If spectacles are momentary explosions of meaning, then culture and memory are the powder keg.

We must pause here and ask, Whose spectacle was this? Of course, in a white male-dominated society, a spectacle will likely reflect many values and assumptions associated with that culture. Sometimes, this bias may be indirect, working in a way Matthew Jackson and Krista Ratcliffe describe as the "racial enthymeme."[8] Henry Ford's Peace Ship operates this way because it maintains a total disregard for the racial implications of war, not to mention the ongoing struggle for Black equality within the United States. Similarly, Ford glosses over issues of gender and class in his radically naive presentation of peace. This does not mean these topics are absent in the spectacle. Rather, we see yet again how whiteness, for instance, can be "strategic" rhetoric, reinforcing an unequal status quo by dismissing race while subtly giving credence to white-centric symbols and systems of power.[9] Ford's script casts its actors in this way, to display their investment in the establishment by completely ignoring all other matters of politics, privilege, and inequality.

A Progressive Spectacle?

Henry Ford's protest occurred on the cusp of the most extreme wartime measures against civil liberties in the nation's history up to that time.[10] He got a taste of this new atmosphere when reports circulated that he could be prosecuted under the Logan Act because he was a private citizen interfering with foreign policy.[11] When President Woodrow Wilson decided to enter the war, he implemented severe laws, such as the Espionage Act of 1917, stating that "disloyalty . . . [must be] dealt with a firm hand of repression" and that a disloyal citizen "had [already] sacrificed their civil liberties."[12] It must be stressed that other movements against the war had emerged with far more admirable peace scripts than Ford's before Wilson enacted these laws, but none had his global reach. Furthermore, the Peace Ship pulled these movements, such as the Woman's Peace Party, under its umbrella—to the detriment of many. Jane Addams, for instance, was heavily criticized at this time, and her alleged association with Ford only fed the critiques once the States formally entered the conflict.[13] In this repressive context, there was a general lack of robust antiwar dissent, and for many, the lingering memory of the peace movement may have been associated exclusively with Ford's ridiculous trip overseas.

Scholars of Progressive Era rhetoric have long noted the contradictions characterizing the period.[14] New grassroots organizations sprang up to inspire domestic reforms taking aim at rampant inequality, discrimination, and lack of political enfranchisement, to name only a few. These projects brought new tensions, such as between the habit of celebrating individualism while calling for governmental or community-based solutions. War discourse was no exception to such incongruities.[15] Alongside debates over militarism and empire—and of particular significance to World War I peace rhetoric—was an ongoing fascination with industrialism, embodied by men like John D. Rockefeller, J. P. Morgan, and Andrew Carnegie. From "robber barons" to "captains of industry," these figures attracted admiration and repulsion, making for quick reference points for the promises and pitfalls of unrestrained capital.[16] Henry Ford, born in the Midwest to a family of modest income, was a common star in this rhetorical work. Renowned for his fortune made from the Model T, Ford was widely known as the man who made automobiles affordable while revolutionizing workplace conditions.[17]

Ford's reputation as a car magnate was also a visually mediated phenomenon, foreshadowing a key part of his peace script. Inseparable from the consumer culture he targeted in his advertising, Ford became a fixture across the United States with his instantly recognizable name embossed on the roughly fifteen million Model Ts sold from 1908 to 1927 (figure 3).[18] The growth of mass consumption added another dimension to the visual culture of the Progressive Era and, as Pearl James describes, helped form a new national consciousness that blurred the lines between private consumption and public advertising.[19] Henry Ford's identity existed within this symbolic process, which offered new possibilities for politicians, business people, and activists to reach across traditional boundaries of civic life. Unfortunately, as we shall see, it also created new ways to distort information, sensationalize news, and unite readership in derision and mockery.

Ford's spectacle also gained notoriety because he tapped into trends that overlapped with anti-war organizing. Over the previous two decades, peace advocacy had undergone major shifts, such as the Anti-Imperialist League's expansion beyond the narrow New England tradition of genteel reform.[20] Drawing elites from business, science, and culture, the Anti-Imperialist League united a broad swath of ideologies and resources under the banner of "peace."[21] The organization, nevertheless, foreshadowed the coming trend as described by the historian of peace C. Roland Marchand: increased participation in peace organizations for moderate, nonconfrontational activism. This expansion of peace activism satisfied affluent members with a safe expression of reform and political engagement with the United States government and beyond without demanding risky commitments.[22]

The "idols of the age," businessmen such as Carnegie and Ford, occupied influential roles in these peace organizations. The clubs typically focused on process-oriented projects, such as establishing international arbitration

Figure 3. Advertisement for Ford Model T with Henry Ford's face below the caption "Buy a Ford—and Spend the Difference" (Henry Ford Organization).

through "peace congresses."[23] The projects were often plagued with unclear goals; it was not uncommon by 1914 to find in the ranks of these groups members from other movements, such as women's suffrage, urban reform, Protestant missionaries, or experts in the realm of science, labor, law, or business. This big cast of characters likely gave members a sense of diverse collaboration and a global perspective that proved, in many cases, quite tenuous or even counterproductive.[24] Notably, during this period of social movement growth, nearly every peace-affiliated organization retreated from a strong antiwar stance—or else lost resources—and tended to focus on other issues, such as suffrage.[25]

We thus begin to see how "peace" was primed for a spectacle: it was popular, inspiring, and vague. While Ford is not representative of the entire the activist pool, he dominated the public perception of peace advocacy during a critical period of US build-up to World War I intervention. Historian Michael Kazin describes peace advocacy at the start of World War I as a vibrant network full of suffragists, socialists, lawyers, politicians, and more. He notes it as "the largest, most diverse, and most sophisticated peace coalition to that point in US history."[26] While acknowledging the movement splintered across various "fashionable" groups, Kazin remains sympathetic to grassroots activists and stresses the repressive tactics of the government that pulverized threats to US military goals.[27] I try to find some middle ground: between the valiant-but-overwhelmed activist narrative and its popular-yet-dilettante activist counterpart. One way to better understand why peace activism could be so large yet ineffectual is by considering the peace script of Ford's spectacle. The cause for peace was popular enough to grab the people's curiosity. It was not, however, so well-established that either Ford's distortions or the government's repression would cause public ire. This liminal space of activism—popular yet without punch—resembles obstacles for contemporary global protest, where struggles persist long after a cause has achieved massive popularity.[28]

Although Ford's movement failed, his pro-war competition had no easy task.[29] A deep-seated hesitancy to sacrifice civilian lives in a war across the Atlantic clashed with a rise in anti-German sentiment stoked by US and British propaganda. President Woodrow Wilson tried to appease both militarists and noninterventionists by framing the issue as one of "preparedness." Yet, stories of saboteurs, traitors, and German U-boat attacks increased calls to intervene. By April 2, 1917, Wilson voiced the majority opinion, declaring war on behalf of the Allied cause.[30] When Ford's voyage began near the end of 1915, Wilson was at a critical point in this debate over US "neutrality." Although the president offered vague words of support to Ford's cause, Wilson undercut the peace mission during his own December 7, 1915, address. Speaking just as the *Oscar II* set sail upon the Atlantic Ocean, the president stated that "preparation for defense seems to me to be absolutely imperative now."[31] The address naturally rankled the passengers of the Peace Ship and gave the group of journalists aboard new drama to report. As the nation continued to deliberate on the war issue, Ford's "motley crew" expressed their version of peace most ostentatiously, appeasing the public's interest in pulpy entertainment while rendering peace frivolous and silly.

Ultimately, Ford's script laid bare the myths of peace and damaged the public reputation of pacifism by advertising its most ridiculous version to the world. While other work considers the intragroup dynamics of the movement he led, we must also account for its rhetorical work—its public efforts to persuade through the media that dramatized it.[32] The global reach of Ford's Peace

Ship coverage was so impressive, even if often ridiculous, that it may have been one of the most publicized peace organizations in US history up to that time. Scholars must, therefore, examine the style of the peace argument as written in the headlines. Across the three dimensions of the coverage I consider—the buildup, the voyage, and its surrounding media—Ford portrayed "peace" as a character-driven crusade torn between the comic and the tragic frame. Both proved productive for scripting a global spectacle but left little symbolic resources for activists outside of Ford's carnival of peace.

Scripting a Spectacle of Peace

Casting the Star of Peace

The initial coverage of the Peace Expedition framed it as a character-driven movement indebted to its leader's privileged position in society. Ford's platform allowed him to insist that his vision—although Rosika Schwimmer helped shape it—was the only peace to consider. He thereby drowned out the diverse voices of peace all around him. To best describe the way the movement was constructed, I limit this section to the coverage that circulated prior to the *Oscar II*'s departure from Hoboken, New Jersey. These articles frequently depict Ford as a fearless, if idealistic, titan of industry whose master plan lacked practicality and coherency. Nevertheless, Ford's public image hit a vein within mainstream America. In these pages, we can see a fascination with wealthy personalities that combines with visual evocations of technology, protest, and war. On a smaller scale, Ford's ethos aligned with the long-held fixation on "process" common to peace activism, evidenced by his choice to visit The Hague to assemble a committee. The coverage of Ford, however, stresses nothing beyond the process, just the sheer fact that Ford's voyage might happen at all. The resulting peace script alluded to these rhetorical contexts without forcing the reader to consider a substantive argument for peace. In the end, we see a flattening of peace rhetoric at the very moment of its popularization. This flattening did not impact everyone equally. Ford's rhetoric pushed women, in particular, into a double bind: they were granted publicity through his movement but in a way that further silenced them.

In one of the first reports of Ford's plan from August 24, 1915, the *Wall Street Journal* introduces the fight for peace by focusing on big personalities. The article declares, "Henry Ford says that he will use his wealth in a campaign for universal peace and denounces advocates of military preparedness." The brief article juxtaposes Ford with another spectacular personality of the Progressive Era, noting that Ford "predicts that Thomas Edison will never use his brain to make anything that will destroy life or property."[33] As a preface to Ford's project, peace advocacy strikes the reader as a competition engaged in by celebrities and titans of industry like Edison and Ford, who marshal their genius to combat forces of evil. The template is thus set: big, flashy names in the headlines, followed by sensational claims (or just gossip) that grab the reader's attention without concrete policy or plan.

Over the next forty days, numerous articles followed suit, repeatedly depicting the cause for peace as a brash plan devoid of specifics, one that had emerged from the mind of a daring industrialist who aims to succeed by sheer force of will. For instance, Ford grabbed headlines during this period by brazenly commenting to the media that perhaps "the best thing that could happen would be for the nations of Europe to go bankrupt."[34] In another article, he ostentatiously claims, "If I had my way I would tie a tin can to this joint Anglo-French commission and chase it back to Europe."[35] Such articles present no clear plan or policy. Instead, Ford's peace script taps into a cultural fascination with industrialists and their will to succeed through sheer bravado. Other bold personalities, notably Theodore Roosevelt, amplify the drama and suggest peace politics is driven by power and charisma. In an October article, for instance, the former president deems Ford unfit to be a US citizen.[36] Priming the public for a showdown between strong men, the movement gained more attention as it left out concrete planning. We can see in it the crystallization of long-gestating political and cultural elements from peace activism: supposed icons or geniuses taking big, if ineffectual, shots at reforming the world in their image while other voices are marginalized.

Mere weeks before the Peace Ship was to set sail, coverage continued to focus on Ford's personality, reducing the peace script to a character-driven spectacle. Articles from November 1915, for instance, minimized—or simply ignored—specific actors and peace plans. The *Gazette Times* quotes Ford's bald pronouncement: "I am willing to give all the money I've got and to go anywhere if my doing so will aid this movement." Notably, there is a brief mention of Rosika Schwimmer, a key architect of the movement, who was granted only a bit part in Ford's script.[37] From this date onward, major US and international newspapers carried almost daily coverage of Ford's peace plans, yet most depicted the peace movement as just a Ford-centric pursuit. Sometimes the language had curious parallels to the visual spectacle of war itself, adding to the peace script's spectacular qualities. On November 25, for instance, the *Philadelphia Inquirer* framed Ford's peace project as an entry into combat, running the headline, "Ford Will Send Ship to War."[38] This is one of many times that the movement borrowed the language and imagery of war to frame its anti-war stance in a visceral way. While it is tempting to dismiss such language as part of a spectacle's drive to entertain, it also suggests proximity between peace and war rhetoric at the time—a deep-seated fascination with violence and sacrifice in the name of broad, yet vague ideals.

The *Inquirer* article underscores the project's lack of planning, further framing the peace as an extension of Ford's personality and little else. He is quoted saying, "Just who will be aboard the vessel, where they will go, and whether the delegation will have official standing, is something that has not been decided." The only takeaway is Ford's audacious guarantee, a tagline that would become infamous: "The boys will be out of the trenches by Christmas."[39] Stressing the popularity of his movement, Ford vaguely states that "it was announced that *all peace societies* and *all individuals interested in the peace movement* would be interested in some way in the mission of the ship." The only details given for this dubiously universal pursuit for peace is that the group will help set up a conference for neutral nations to draft a peace plan.[40] Ford ends by again foregrounding his personality—the great motif of his script—in lieu of facts or plans. A reporter asks if the Wilson administration supports Ford, to which he coyly replies, "We will tell you that later."[41] Like Max Weber's "charismatic personality," who eschews reason for impulse and asks their followers to simply have faith, Ford promises success with no elaboration, underscoring the ethos-driven essence of his peace rhetoric.[42]

During this period, news coverage let Ford speak for women and, thereby, tied their advocacy to his negative peace. One headline in the *New York Times* simply read, "Ford Aids Peace Move by Women," but gave no substantial coverage.[43] Repeatedly, women are made present but voiceless and ultimately irrelevant in the reports of Ford's spectacle. Consider a November 1915 *New York Times* article on Ford's "Crusade" that reports, "the idea of the peace ship originated in the brain of Mme. Rosika Schwimmer of Hungary, delegate from Austria-Hungary to the Women's Peace Conference at The Hague." The article, which stresses a general lack of planning or support for the movement, also associates Jane Addams with Ford's romantic pursuit. When the article finally cites Schwimmer's words near the end, it is already framed in the context of Ford's persona and bravado. The article includes a letter to the *Times* that casts suspicion upon "the two women who got Henry Ford to charter the Peace Ship." Schwimmer's romantic partner is also mentioned ("a German officer in the trenches") before the article notes she "spent some months in Germany after attending the Women's Peace Congress at The Hague and is known as a pro-German." The women—and by proxy, women's peace advocacy—are called into question: "Why not show up the truth?"[44] In the spectacle of Ford's movement, women play only a minimal or even dubious role.

Ford's peace script, circulating as global news, continued to play into character-driven coverage even when it had the semblance of a concrete plan. Commissioning the *Oscar II*, probably the most concrete part of the plan, was itself reported with an emphasis on Ford and his lack of planning. For example, the *New York Times* front-page headline read, "Ford Hires Liner in Peace Crusade... Details Still a Bit Hazy." Rather than credit Schwimmer or others for their contributions, Ford describes the plan's origin as a random inspiration. He claims it came to him "overnight" and that with his blueprint, he will "crush militarism... even if... the vessel might be torpedoed. I do not consider danger. I don't think I have [ever] been afraid." Once again, we see how Ford's brash personality defines peace advocacy. He amplifies the spectacular quality of this peace with the language of war, discussing the "weapon" he will use: "the greatest weapon of modern times—the wireless [i.e., radio waves]." With this weapon of communication, he will shoot messages of peace directly into the trenches.[45] When questioned if neutral or belligerent nations will support him, Ford retorts, "That question is not up for consideration. We are going to get behind the work done by The Hague peace conference... It is my earnest hope to create a machinery where those who desire can turn to inquire what can be done to establish peace."[46] Refusing elaborate answers, Ford appeals only to blind faith in his process, not uncommon to peace activism of the era. Yet, now this faith is tied as never before to the persona of the charismatic tycoon.

Personalities continued to rule the day in Ford's scripting of peace. Names big and small frequented the articles—from famed politician William Jennings Bryan to department store magnate John Wanamaker to well-known activists such as Jane Addams and Helen Keller.[47] Additionally, news articles from this period referenced many US governors as potential guests aboard the ship, likely increasing the regional coverage of Ford's movement.[48] The frequent citation of these names, sometimes simply printed as lists, ensured that personalities would remain at the heart of the movement's coverage. One headline simply reads, "The Expedition of Notables," illustrating the focus on who may or may not make the journey instead of attention to the *what* or *how* of the anti-war event.[49] A front-page article in the *New York Times* similarly emphasizes the size of the movement rather than any concrete policy and is accompanied by a long list of potential passengers. The headline itself underscores the popularity of the project: "Ford Now Planning an Overflow Ship."[50] The focus on Ford and his revolving cast of characters kept the movement in the news cycle, especially as everyone referenced publicly responded, often declining the invitation.[51] One article included a harsh critique of Ford's lack of planning from activist and professor Anna Garland of the Woman's Peace Party—an organization Ford claimed to represent.[52] Nevertheless, even this gave his movement greater attention, as his detractors added their names to the litany of people drawn into the spectacle event, amplifying the sense that peace planning was a drama of personalities.

As the date of departure approached, Ford again drew upon the rhetoric of war, blurring the line between the spectacle of war and the spectacle of peace. He repeatedly pointed to the "carnage" overseas, lamenting the "wicked waste of life" that forces young men to be "like cattle to the slaughter house."[53] To counter the horrors of war, he scripted his peace as a countermobilization of troops, at one point claiming to be recruiting "young men with 'sand' to go along and hurl *bombs* loaded with 'faith.'"[54] Controversially, Ford discussed plans to weaponize communication technology and get radio signals into the trenches with messages designed to induce soldiers to drop their guns.[55] His wild threat to "bomb" the trenches and stoke a military strike was the focus of several articles during this period, all while other reports trickled in that the government might prosecute Ford for meddling in foreign affairs.[56] All of this could shift the spectacle of war for the US reading public from a distant battlefield to the Peace Ship, distorting the lines between the peaceful and the bellicose. Both sides now had belligerent leaders standing with their own troops.

When defending his mission, Ford doubled down on what he knew best: himself. Speaking about his ability to accomplish anything, he declared, "Europe is exhausted and is really only too ready to find a legitimate excuse to cease killing. The Peace Ship, *coming from the power they all respect*, will give them that excuse, and there is no doubt it will bring peace."[57] Again, we see the scripting of peace as a cultural spectacle with a tabloid-worthy personality under the spotlight. Far from meaningless rhetoric, the Ford spectacle reflects the ongoing interests of the reading public at the time, giving them drama if little else. One spectator rightly observed that Ford's personality may be honorable and "sincer[e], but his methods are strangely spectacular. He has been a great deal in the public eye."[58] Indeed, in what appears to be his first official public address regarding his movement, Ford barely says anything beyond his slogan—"Out of the trenches before Christmas, never go back." He does offer vague accounts of himself acting as a sort of CEO for peace who conducts meetings and ties together loose ends.[59] It comes as little shock, then, that international coverage at this time mostly reported on Ford and his brash personality, as even the *Irish Times*, for instance, ran the headline "The Ford Fireworks."[60]

In his final address before the grand voyage, Ford mobilized all aspects of his persona to cement his spectacular peace script. First, he lambasted critics of the movement, which he now referred to as a "business proposition." Few peace advocates would be so bold as to reject the word "peace," but so Ford proceeded, replacing it with his new word of choice: "construction." Perpetually vague, Ford persisted with innuendo and bluster: "There are plans afoot, big plans." In his words, the fight for peace was to be nothing short of the pinnacle of cultural achievement: "the greatest utterance of all humanity ever heard on earth."[61] In taking on the role of the oracle—"all those things are going to be made known," he mystically promises—Ford ends the initial phase of the movement. Peace is thus scripted as a character-centric campaign infatuated with its own existence, freely using symbols of war to publicize its spectacle. This set the stage for the ensuing coverage of the Peace Ship as a spectacular event flailing between tragedy and comedy. These familiar plots follow certain narrative arcs that, in this case, ended in a failure that damaged the rhetorical resources of peace activism through the very process of its popularization.

For a fuller picture of Ford's peace, consider all the voices that the movement silenced and marginalized. In claiming to speak for all anti-war advocates and then offering only his "negative" peace, Ford made race, class, and gender-based reform irrelevant to his script. The irony is that these are the very same elements that made it possible for Ford to command so much attention. Consider Professor Anna Garland, the officer of the Woman's Peace Party, whose refusal of Ford's invitation was buried on page 6 of a lengthy story about his ambitious plans. Garland's concern lies in Ford's lack of preparation for the task ahead: "I cannot conscientiously accept your invitation unless positively assured beforehand that at least ten men well known and deservedly trusted as peace advocates of experience and good judgment form the leadership of the expedition. . . . [I] cannot too strongly express regret that such preliminary steps were not taken before public, and, as regards some items, inaccurate statements were made."[62] In the dramaturgy of Ford's script, Garland's words receive little attention because he already claimed to speak for women and, as we will see, set them up as one scapegoat for his spectacular failure.

Spectacular Characters in Action: From Tragedy to Comedy

The Ford Peace Expedition placed its livelihood in the hands of the media but gave them little to work with. Journalists made up about one-third of the passengers and they churned out new reports, sustaining a robust cycle of coverage that rarely escaped comedic or tragic frames of peace.[63] Although bolstering the intrigue of the movement, the coverage gave the journey a fated quality—it was either destined for comeuppance due to Ford's hubris or, for the more sympathetic, ruthlessly struck down in its noble pursuit. In either narrative, peace advocacy compared unfavorably to the news of the Great War, itself a tragedy of the highest order that needed serious solutions. The Ford movement could make resistance to war appear more harmful or morally repugnant than the war's harsh reality. To other readers, peace advocacy scripted this way made light of the ultimate human sacrifice. The coverage of the voyage, it must be underscored, focused mostly on white men of middle- and upper-class backgrounds; such was the way Ford arranged it. Although superficial in its messaging, this spectacle of peace operated through the symbols and attention such men were already granted in society and culture. That their words and actions came to represent a falsely "positive" peace is a tragic reminder of how spectacles can easily find cachet in US society by ignoring inequalities and making complex issues insubstantial to the matter at hand.

Figure 4. "First Photographs Made Aboard Ford Peace Ship," *Philadelphia Inquirer*, December 28, 1915.

The christening of the voyage was an episode ripped from Shakespearean comedy. The opening day followed the script as laid out in the previous weeks, taking its character-driven, visually provocative elements and rendering them ridiculous. For instance, one notable member who accepted Ford's invitation, Dr. Charles F. Aked, encountered Ford's "bouncer" upon trying to board the *Oscar II* and, after a reported altercation, resentfully stated that "the peace voyage is a matter of little moment to me."[64] *New York Times* front-page coverage continued to highlight the frivolity of these affairs. Consider the following reported events: a gift of squirrels bestowed upon the expedition; an impromptu wedding ceremony; an admiring fan/activist leaping into the Atlantic Ocean to swim after the departing vessel.[65] Far from incidental features of the movement, these comic tidbits make up its narrative drive because few other details stood in their way. Ford himself flatly announced on the day of departure, "I know little of the details of the working plan of the peace conference."[66]

The movement continued to express itself as a ridiculous event, rife with petty quarrels, tedious distractions, and ironic behavior. These elements worked together to frame the fight for peace as a comedic spectacle that traded nuance for popularity and, upon closer inspection, spoke to the movement's gendered elements. For example, reports noted that when the emcee of the christening event was asked to acknowledge Jane Addams, he was overheard asking, "Jane who?" followed by "Who's Mme. Schwimmer?"[67] Readers were likely to laugh or shake their heads in mild amusement at these accounts of large personalities ignorant of key members, sadly both women now completely ignored. This general sense of disarray, however, amplified the movement's spectacular qualities, granting narrative fulfillment to comic voices that now claimed to represent the entire sector of peace activism.

To cap off the inaugural event, Governor Louis B. Hanna of North Dakota took matters from the silly to the embarrassing. He was observed "lipp[ing] something that seemed to be 'I am for preparedness,'" just as Ford told the media that he intended to stop all policies of military preparation.[68] Far from serious political campaigning, the Ford movement undercut, or "short circuited," any such expectation, offering in its place frivolous and ridiculous anecdotes.[69] One spectator summed it up: "As it was in the beginning of the Ford peace plan, so it was at the pier today. Nobody knew where to go, nobody was in charge of anything; nobody knew anything except that here was a ship that Henry Ford was taking to Europe to stop the war, to get the boys out of the trenches by Christmas and lots of other things." This description, accurate as it was, contradicted any sense of a dignified peace mission, with its continued focus on Ford's personality. And what else would a diligent reader learn of peace from the coverage? Among the sundry items a reader might find were more personality-based absurdities, such as William Jennings Bryan's firm rejection (a one word statement, "No") when asked if he kissed the expedition's newlywed bride.[70]

In dramatic work, either tragedy or comedy will traditionally dominate a plot. In a political spectacle, however, fragments of both can easily coexist and sustain readerly attention across a spectrum of identities and emotions. For example, opening day coverage of Ford's movement incorporated tragic and comic elements that made it fodder for the press while cementing its image as an outrageous mission led by an eccentric personality. Ford was quoted dramatically stating, "I am sincere in this. I shall sail on the steamship. This is the most serious thing in my life. Last night in this hotel I drew up my final will and testament. I executed papers . . . to my son."[71] While some may read the movement as a prolonged episode of buffoonery and incompetence, others may read such passages as tragic moments: a peace script that tells of a well-intentioned protagonist who, whether through hubris, naivety, or idealism, risked his livelihood and suffered tremendously.

Other elements, perhaps silly to some, could express great pathos. The *New York Times* notes that activists sang the hit song "I Did Not Raise My Boy to Be a Soldier," which drew on maternal feelings.[72] The article also includes a statement from renowned scientist Luther Burbank, who dubbed Ford a martyr, calling the movement the "clearest demonstration of the Christ principle in the history of this planet."[73] While Ford himself hedged expectations at the final moment, flatly declaring that he "will keep alive the thought that peace is possible," the coverage often evoked the image of a noble crusader up against indomitable evil, suggesting an inevitable sacrifice for the greater good, like Christ's own death.[74] Other reporters described Mrs. Ford weeping like a widow of war as well as receiving vicious threats from opponents such as Theodore Roosevelt.[75] This coverage of Ford's embarkment evoked a tragic frame, making the cause of peace seem both destined to fail and devoid of complexity—like a well-worn tale of which one already knows the ending.

The ensuing coverage of Ford's voyage fortified a peace script written through the dynamics of drama and spectacle. Some of the most humorous, albeit puzzling, comments came from the esteemed passenger Charles Aked, whose professed ignorance bordered on the unbelievable. He told the press, "For myself, my mind is a blank. For: First I don't know Ford very well. Second I don't know what we hope to accomplish, and Third I don't know how we are going to do it."[76] His statement deflates any hope for a principled or serious peace plan while fueling the narrative of silly characters fretting about a disorganized peace mission. Later, Aked echoed his previous comment when interviewed during the *Oscar II*'s detainment in Kirkwall, Scotland: "Where am I going? Why am I here? I do not know?"[77] Aked's obliviousness in the face of the serious task at hand did little to counter developing stories of squabbles onboard Ford's ship, eventually giving way to endless mockery with headlines such as "Even Have War on Ford's Peace Ship."[78]

The casual reader was unlikely to venture beyond this scripting of peace. The tragicomic style already aligned perfectly with the character-driven construction of the movement. Nothing in the spectacle required a reader to go beyond the escapades of brash characters and their general lack of organization. Instead, several elements filled in any gaps of understanding: a fascination with charismatic businessmen, the spectacle of industrial technology, and the tradition of superficial reform that had developed over the last couple of decades. As a spectacle of peace, the movement was now locked into a cultural narrative of absurdity and irony, which tracked with the overall thrust of the Ford peace script. Indeed, parodies began to pour forth: one editorialist for the *Wall Street Journal* penned the poem "Pepper and Salt" to mock the voyage, viciously rhyming that "No *Lusitania*, this, if sunk / Its passengers on deck or bunk / If, sink thro' the waves, fire-kissed / They never, never will be missed . . . Sail on' proud ship of peace / The crop of fools will never cease."[79] The *Spectator* ran a satiric tale of the "Ship of Fools," while the *North-China Herald* dubbed them "fourth-rate faddists" and "joy riders."[80] Other editorials described the movement as "nuts," "a wild goose chase," or a "farce" of "freaks and faddists."[81] Other international coverage was only slightly more positive. The *Times of India* called Ford a "quaint crusader."[82] Capitalizing on the flood of derision, one US newspaper advertised a "new timely burlesque" about the Ford Peace Ship, noting the "cranks, squirrel mascots and dips, nets and peace delegates" sure to make the audience laugh.[83] Such coverage emphasized the ridiculous quality of the Ford movement, amplifying the cultural spectacle of peace it had become.

If readers could suppress their laughter, they likely would be struck by a new wave of tragic rhetoric that again framed Ford as a martyr for peace. Aked, defending the cause to a reporter, stated that "ridicule never hurt a principle." The movement, in the face of widespread mockery, persisted with its idealistic "appeal to all that is most enduring in earth and heaven."[84] Rather than elaborate on policy, Aked's editorial in the *Inquirer* stresses only the dedication of the activists—the simple persistence of the movement rather than any facts associated with it—in the face of all obstacles: "What if success comes? [. . .] What if we turn out not to be blithering idiots after all? What if this startling, *spectacular advertisement of peace* succeeds in loosing the pent-up good will of war-stricken Europe?"[85] Stronger defenses could have been made, but few could have been more accurate. Surely, the "spectacular advertisement of peace" was vulnerable to ridicule, yet Aked's words could also strike a sad tone for those sympathetic to the plight of well-intentioned but hapless do-gooders.

Such was the fate of the "freaks of the peaceship" (as Aked put it) and all who identified with its script: to be destined either for mockery or a miraculous, if ill-defined, moral victory.[86] Once the ship reached its destination of Christiania, Denmark, hilarity ensued that amplified the spectacle of peace. Reports of the "queer freight of the wonderful ark" leaned heavily on irony, as writers noted the "squabbles mark[ing the] peace ark's voyage."[87] A *New York Times* article satirized the movement by highlighting its preoccupation with process over substance. It describes "meetings and lectures without end . . . characterized by an extraordinary absence of any realization of the size of the task undertaken." Ford plays a comic role, likened to "the inventor of a successful fire-extinguisher setting out to extinguish Vesuvius" in a passage that recalls the comic narratives of an arrogant protagonist destined for comeuppance.[88]

To top it all off, Ford abruptly abandoned the peace mission upon arrival. After all his bragging and guarantees of success, the leader effectively ended the movement the instant it was to begin. The *New York Times* ran a front-page headline that surely evoked snickers or eyerolls from readers: "Ford Abdicates; Sails for Home." The article offers a ridiculous account of his secretary, E. G. Liehood, "dumbfounded at the news" and Mrs. Ford denying that anything suspicious or sinister is afoot despite the bizarre announcement.[89] All this bestowed an ever-greater sense of disorder and farce to peace advocacy. As the movement winded down, reports of outrageous behavior ramped up. With little plan of action and virtually no official reception, the crew continued to act out its farcical peace script with tales of passengers "playing craps during church service," the running of a "mock trial, in which the Rev. Dr. Jones was charged with concealing himself in his whiskers," and photographs printed of peace leaders playing "leap frog" (figure 4).[90] Taken together, all the squabbling and disorganization cemented the peace movement as characterized by frivolity and absurdity, as a spectacle that made peace a cultural text of mockery.[91]

We must not forget the gendered consequences of the Peace Ship. Inez Boissevain, a prominent suffragist, stated the matter succinctly during an early exit from the venture: "We have appeared to the public what we are in fact, a confused mass of amiably intentioned persons of vague thinking and no collective planning."[92] By now, little could disabuse readers of the accuracy of Boissevain's withering critique. The consequences for the embarrassment would severely impact women because they experienced two silencings: when Ford first claimed to speak for them and again when they were laughed at or made the scapegoat in the aftermath of the voyage. Schwimmer, for instance, was reported to have "refuse[d] to indicate the plans of the neutral countries of which she is supposed to have knowledge."[93] Another article reports her "unsympathetic behavior" as the "reason for the failure of the mission."[94] The average reader, believing Ford represents all peace activists, would find little sympathy for the women's movement when its members were so marginalized and represented in such a minimal way. Jane Addams, similarly, faced backlash despite her threadbare association with Ford, as the *Chicago Daily Tribune* stated that she is "in denial" over an "alleged quote from Ford crediting her with the whole idea and him just the money."[95] Other prominent men, such as William Jennings Bryan, could offload responsibility onto women, rendering women's activism irrelevant or worse. The *Gazette Times* reports that Bryan said the failed "pilgrimage . . . emanated from the Women's International Peace Party and that [Ford] simply financed it."[96] In this way, women played the role of the scapegoat for the irrational and negative elements of Ford's script, revealing again how his peace spectacle harmed those it claimed to represent.

Scandinavian newspapers similarly dealt with the peace movement, asking if the "Ford Expedition's Fiasco [Is] Complete?" only days after its arrival.[97] Fulfilling that which seemed predestined, the Ford movement went as the *San Francisco Chronicle*'s front page stated: "Flash! Bang! Peace Party Is Forgotten."[98] The spectacle of peace concluded its comedic arc with Ford washing his hands of the whole thing, "admit[ting] an error" and now "disabused of [the] idea that the war was cause[d] by militarists or munition men."[99] Adding an almost unbearable degree of irony to his representation of grassroots activists, Ford told the *New York Times* in a front-page story that he "now blames the people . . . The people most to blame are the ones who are getting slaughtered."[100] From a man of the people to a misanthrope, Ford traveled the spectrum of the war debate while making a mockery of peace activism. His script could thus travel far and wide upon seemingly contradictory paths as only a wealthy white man of the time could afford, and the script meant less and less the more ground it covered.

If not self-parody, readers likely judged these final days as a tragic culmination of peace advocacy. For instance, reports occasionally depicted Ford as a man foiled by the subterfuge and ulterior motives of those around him. Rosika Schwimmer, unfortunately, played the role of villain in more reports, predictably framed in the previously described gendered terms.[101] The *San Francisco Chronicle* encapsulated the tragic take on Ford's peace script. Comparing him to Christ, the article expressed "sorrow" about the derisive coverage Ford received: "Laugh as you will at the spectacle of a man chartering an unarmed ship and sailing across the ocean with the avowed purpose of calling a halt to the most gigantic conflict in the annal [*sic*] of human bloodshed, and there remains the simple truth that [Ford] is animated by that divine impulse which moves in everything that works for the brotherhood of the races."[102] Ford's innocent nature makes him a martyr who, as with the comic buffoon, is destined to fail. Either narrative the peace script evoked was one of guaranteed failure—a spectacle built to burn bright and extinguish quickly.

Ford was thus the great man tragically thwarted by those around him. The *Gazette Times* noted Ford's "tired and overworked nerves" frayed by the "strain of staying with [the] party."[103] Other Scandinavian newspapers stressed his purity. *The Verdens Gang* called Ford "helpless as a child," while the conservative *Morgenbladet* noted his "infinite tenderness and fertility in ideas," although failing, even here, to specify what those ideas were. The *Tidens Tegn*, a self-described "moderate Liberal paper," depicted Ford in similar terms, describing a man "not of this earth. He lacks not culture, but education, and has no realization of European conditions. His is a fatal plan."[104] The tragic spectacle of peace, realized in the fragile idealism of Ford's character, thus reached its natural conclusion: the sacrificial lamb slaughtered for the cause of peace. The automotive tycoon certainly suffered for his actions and, not dissimilar to the victims of war, was depicted as a man overwhelmed by the terrible events around him. Henry Ford, "the Dove of Peace," who "Br[oke] its Wing," thereby ended his spectacle of peace.[105]

Flanking the Peace Script

Just as the socioeconomic context helped sustain Ford's spectacle, the surrounding coverage impacted his message, highlighting or obscuring certain elements of the peace debate. Although it can be hard to see at first glance, this coverage could amplify the movement's dramatic flair. In considering the reports and headlines beside the articles previously discussed, I seek to reconstruct the experience of someone following Ford's voyage in the press. I ask: What else would they read? What prominent headlines would likely catch their eye and potentially shape their interpretation of peace advocacy? Most articles fall into three categories: (1) coverage of traitorous behavior; (2) coverage of gruesome warfare; and (3) coverage of suspicious pacifist sentiments. These headlines made peace activism appear as either a disgraceful and trifling pursuit or another tragedy among the Great War's many horrors. At worst, the surrounding coverage depicted peace advocacy as a haven for disloyal or un-American agents. Obviously, none of these frameworks bode well for the prospects of peace, yet all could feed the spectacular qualities already discussed.

Opening day coverage best illustrates these trends. For instance, the *Gazette Times* covered the voyage's ridiculous commencement, with its tales of an impromptu marriage and squirrels, with the following headlines beside it: "Kaiser's Pacific Agents Indicted," "Teuton U-Boat Fires on Flag of Uncle Sam," and, cryptically, "Plotters."[106] Roughly six months after the sinking of the *Lusitania*, readers on this day probably noticed the headline telling of another U-boat attack. Furthermore, discussions of disloyal citizens and saboteurs gave little aid to the credibility of Ford's ragtag crew. In comparison, the frivolity of Ford's movement might strike a reader as disrespectful to the war's life-and-death events. Ford's character, and thus his peace script, was temperamentally unfit to accomplish the task at hand. Worse still, the Peace Expedition might itself be a sanctuary for enemies and traitors, a topic of no small concern for a nation at the brink of war. The next day's edition followed suit, publishing a blistering critique of Ford by former president Theodore Roosevelt, who deemed the inaugural event a "ridiculous and mischievous junket" in an article with the following headline right beside it: "Germans May Arrest Ford's Peace Party."[107] If a reader skimmed this page, what were they likely to make of the "determin[ation of Ford] to cross German territory" in violation of US "regulations"?[108] The peace spectacle, read within the rhetorical context of the front page, likely seemed dangerous or at least ill-equipped to deal with the realities of war.

Shocking coverage continued to border Ford's "negative" peace, reinforcing a sense of either tragedy or buffoonery for his spectacle. For example, besides the front-page article titled "Ford Puts Off Date for Ending War," underscoring the leader's "vague[ness]," the *New York Times* ran the following headlines: "Uncover German Plot to Embroil U.S. with Mexico," "Submarine Sinks One American Vessel, Perhaps a Second; Another Shelled; Austria Sinks Entire Munitions Fleet," "Germans Mass to Attack Allies," and "Congress Cheers as Wilson Urges Curb on Plotters: Wild Applause Greets the President's Denunciation of Disloyal Citizens."[109] Peace advocacy, as represented by the Ford movement, was juvenile and impractical compared to these accounts of dangerous belligerents within and without the United States.

If a reader did not choose to see the Peace Expedition as a childish attempt to solve an intractable problem, they may have read it as a risky, even deadly, enterprise. Ironically, the dramatic elements of comedy and tragedy that gave the Ford script such an expansive media life were the same as those that diminished the cause of peace. The cultural feelings and expectations that fuel the demand for such sensationalism can prove too pulpy to sustain a movement, especially when the surrounding coverage is so pointed.[110] Imagine a reader scanning the article "Peace Programme for Ford Party Announced," which offered no actual program, and then immediately sees the neighboring headline: "Can See No Hope of Peace in Address of German Chancellor."[111] Someone might reasonably liken Ford's own lack of peace planning to that of Germany, a comparison that would be quite devastating by the end of 1915.

The endless flow of coverage regarding traitors and enemy attacks offered little aid to Ford's movement. The *San Francisco Chronicle*, for instance, reported on a "Woman Held as Witness in US Bomb Plot Probe" beside front-page coverage of Ford's peace ship. On the next page, reports discussed a suspicious organization accused of misconduct, inconveniently named the National Peace Council. Worse still, reports quoted the group's praise of Ford as "the great American philanthropist."[112] Such associations could damage Ford's credibility while nevertheless bolstering the sensationalism of his peace script. Similarly, the *Gazette Times* ran "Ford's Party Not Popular" beside "Man Suspected of Steel Plant Fire Arrested."[113] While these reports do not make direct connections, this type of coverage, repeated for weeks, was bound to leave the impression of Ford being either another unruly element in the chaotic war or worse, one of a contingent of dangerous saboteurs.[114]

The topic of wartime contraband arose beside reports of Ford's peace ship, again placing the theme of disloyalty next to the nation's leading peace script. The *New York Times*, the *Gazette Times*, and the *Chicago Daily Tribune* all ran stories about the peace ship's detention by British authorities and the discovery of contraband aboard.[115] Beside another *New York Times* article on the affair ran a separate report on a "plot" to attack Du Pont. The *Gazette Times* also noted this plot beside their front-page coverage of Ford's detainment. The next day, the *Gazette* ran another tantalizing headline—"Plot to Destroy Welland Canal: Hamburg-American Sleuth under Arrest as one Conspirator"—beside coverage of the Peace Ship and the announcement that William Jennings Bryan's "peace propaganda" may undergo a congressional "probe."[116] Some readers would understandably gain a negative impression of Ford's movement through such sinister associations and tales of traitorous agents with ties to peace.[117]

The *Philadelphia Inquirer*'s coverage of the war beside Ford's spectacle made peace look like a dangerous farce. Consider the headlines around just one Ford-related article: "Canal Conspiracy Mere Incident in Nation-Wide Plot"; "French Take Purser Off American Ship"; "Plot to Blow Up Plants and Bridges at Niagara Foiled"; and "Socialists Vote to Pursue War."[118] In this frightening world of intrigue, the Ford movement's ridiculous qualities seem inappropriate at best. If this was the only information readers obtained about anti-war activism, then the pursuit of peace looked awful. Spectacular, no doubt—but peace was made of the stuff of tabloids and yellow journalism. In the process Ford's movement, as depicted in the press, diminished the persuasive power of peace advocacy, attaching the cause to tawdry and sinister stories. In comparison, President Wilson's indecision at the time, criticized though it was, seemed prudent.

If not farce or treason, then tragedy characterized the Ford movement, as stories of peace blurred with the many causalities of the vicious war. The *New York Times*, for instance, ran the front-page headline "Ford Finds Peace Elusive" next to the following: "British Evacuate Part of Gallipoli but Will Hold Seddel-Bahr Base; 6 Big Ships, 100,000 Men Lost There."[119] Such loss—100,000 men dead in a single campaign—was an inconceivable tragedy, a landscape of death in which Ford's own tragic pursuit languished. On

Christmas Day, the *Philadelphia Inquirer* ran front-page articles on the war and Ford's ship, making the latter appear as one tragedy among many. The article reported that Ford was abandoning his peace movement—disheartening news for the Yuletide, which ironically, coincided with the date Ford had previously guaranteed success. Beside the gloomy news ran the following headlines: "Fighting in West with Artillery Is Reported Violent" and "Half Starved Allies Taken Prisoner."[120] The *New York Times* ran similar front-page coverage, depicting Ford's spectacle of peace as another victim to unstoppable forces.[121] Whether it be "7,200 Men Needed for Marine Corps," a brave American "killed in war," or a mob attacking a European leader with axes, the Ford Peace Expedition suffered by residing next to such stories. In this rhetorical context, peace was lost among the countless horrors of war.[122]

As a spectacle, Ford's peace script could traverse from the United States to China to India, availing itself of sensational narratives and personalities. Of course, a wealthy white American man could command attention with far fewer obstacles than a group of women, poor Labor activists, or racial minorities fighting for basic rights. Although popular, the media's characterization of Ford's expedition drained peace activism of vital resources and left those about to face Wilson's repression of civil liberties in the lurch.[123] In his outrageous disregard for social issues, Ford reflected the trends of peace advocacy as held by the privileged class. Nevertheless, his peace was a far-reaching script that conjured both extreme derision and deep pity, sometimes in the very same article. As rehearsed through Ford's script, peace felt inconsequential, naive, or traitorous. His was a "negative" peace destined for failure.

Conclusion: Global Peace, Reconsidered

The silencing of women, immigrants, and other marginalized people by a wealthy and overconfident man may not surprise twenty-first-century readers. Today, social movement scholars have labeled such an event, when a rich person creates the impression of grassroots activism, as "astroturfing." In today's corporate world, such lines frequently blur as the lobbyist and the advocacy group morph into one animal, as seen in the labyrinth of groups related to the Koch Brothers and their "activism."[124] Of course, political leaders also make use of this tactic, from organizing "spontaneous" mobs out in the street to the rising trend of online "astroturfing" aimed at pushing certain narratives.[125] In all cases they attempt to hijack public discourse by appearing to represent a broad swathe of its members. It should not shock us that these discourses actually reflect a narrow slice of culture and ideology because their very existence is often indebted to unimaginable wealth and social privilege. Thus, we see in Ford's peace script an important precursor to the political machinations of today.

The immediate fallout from Ford's media spectacle did not bode well for the future of peace advocacy, either. Rather than simply blame him for the diminishment of World War I peace activism, this chapter argues that Ford's peace script, like those before it, was the result of long-gestating cultural trends indebted to socioeconomic privileges, such as whiteness, masculinity, and wealth. These combined with other elements to grant Ford's vision of peace a unique place in the context of global war. From the idolization of business tycoons to the preference for process over policy to the love of sensationalist news, Ford galvanized the rhetorical trends of the Progressive Era and offered his own charismatic personality as the star of his peace. This script offered little concrete actions, values, or ideologies but satisfied the love of a good story.

Ford's debacle foreshadowed a broader struggle to create a sustainable postwar order. While Wilson successfully brought the United States into war, his career was also defined by his attempt to convince the world what that war's peace should look like. Experiencing his own surge in global popularity, the president nevertheless found little consensus regarding his vision. Historian Erez Manela describes the global implications of these postwar deliberations as a tragic "Wilsonian moment." The president's idealism excited people across Europe, the Middle East, and Southeast and Eastern Asia, giving the impression of an international peace debate far surpassing the reach of Ford's own. Unlike Ford, Wilson's words included specifics: the promise of national self-determination, something long denied to many groups across the world.[126] In a matter of months, Wilson embarked on his own ambitious voyage in the United States to drum up support for the League of Nations. Rhetorical critic J. Michael Hogan details this odyssey for peace, noting how Wilson's speechmaking gradually gave way to more sensationalist and demagogic tendencies, exemplifying a type of peace script that would rise in the interwar years.[127] Ford's movement, which petitioned for peace through the absurdity of political spectacle, now seems like the canary in the coal mine, foretelling of a grueling postwar future.

What of the activists who stayed the course after Ford quit? Unfortunately, many were worse off after his spectacle of peace. To see evidence of peace's weakened position, look no further than the massive repression of dissidents upon America's entry into World War I. Consider also the number of leading peace organizations that shifted away from opposing warfare toward safeguarding civil liberties.[128] Eugene Debs, a prominent anti-war voice, was imprisoned and Wilson—the supposed pursuer of peace—denied his pardon.[129] Jane Addams privately feared that her association with Ford would ruin her career.[130] This chapter suggests several reasons she may have unfairly lost some credibility, if not the incentive, to speak out for global peace. Efforts to capitalize on the lingering confusion and resentment toward war resulted in many interpretations and distortions of World War I during the following decades.[131] The nation's repertoire for peace offered little for anti-war groups as the memory of Ford's spectacular failure faded from memory. The coming generation would see the gut-wrenching result of a world unpersuaded by peace, as a terrible trend emerged: citizens composing persuasive visions of peace through violent and undemocratic scripts.

4

Maternal Peace and Memory in the Mothers' Movement

On August 1, 1947, following a five-year legal battle, Elizabeth Dilling declared "victory."[1] The Chicago activist, notorious for opposing US intervention in World War II, saw the successful outcome of her sedition case as one triumph in an ongoing existential battle. She described the federal government's refusal to appeal the ruling as a win "for every American opposed to Marxian, one-party totalitarianism."[2] Dilling did not direct her anger at some faceless bureaucratic machine or banal policy dispute. Her crusade was against something far more sinister, an insidious disease spread by a cunning enemy who had infiltrated all facets of US life. The average citizen may not have viewed her grassroots organization, the Mothers' Movement, as anything more than a harmless, albeit colorful, offshoot of Charles Lindbergh's more popular "America First" isolationist movement. Dilling, however, depicted her work in historical, even cosmic, terms. She was not simply defending herself against allegations of sedition but protecting an entire way of life. She, and the women who read her newsletter, dared to take a "stand for constitutional, Christian Americanism" against a "malicious prosecution" that ran a "farcical 'trial'" to smear their cause.[3] Her anti-war script, to those who identified with it, was the only path for a lasting, "positive" peace, and it demanded bold action to safeguard a sacred way of life against evildoers hell-bent on destruction. Her peace, nevertheless, was thoroughly "negative."

This chapter investigates how two leaders of the Mothers' Movement, Dilling and Lyrl Clark Van Hyning, forged such a script during World War II. Like the other movements in this book, the Mothers' Movement is a product of its time, indebted to the socioeconomic inequalities that allowed them to keep protesting when the costs were too high for many other citizens. The federal government expanded roughly tenfold during this time, reaching deeper than ever into the lives of civilians in the name of war. The Mothers' Movement offered a language of resistance that drew heavily from contemporary white, middle-class femininity.[4] Taking cues from fellow isolationists, movement leaders combined appeals to gender, class, and race into a virulent anti-Semitism that was integral to their desired peace. Like many conspiracy theorists, the Mothers' Movement could script any newsworthy item into the high drama of their worldview. At each turn of the war, they saw instances of evil Jewish actors exploiting a foreign conflict to desecrate the Christian foundations of US civilization. While religion has been conspicuously absent from this book's survey of anti-war movements thus far, many peace activists throughout US history have appealed to Christian principles and biblical interpretation. Perhaps few have done so with the acrimony and dehumanizing effects of the Mothers' Movement. To be clear, the Mothers' Movement asserted a narrow interpretation of Christianity that obscured the diversity of the faith, particularly its more progressive denominations. In the logic of the movement, such people were not real Christians.

The Mothers' Movement marks another instance of how opposition to war can weaponize the myths of peace—of its supposedly natural, apolitical, and nonviolent qualities—to justify cultural exclusion. The movement's rhetoric is a catalog of specious reasoning that makes full use of a conspiratorial style: rife with obscure references, tenuous connections, and endless lists bereft of substantive referents. Of course, this didn't appear to be the case to adherents. Dilling and company offered the reader a moral sheen of peace that masked their frightening vision and bolstered their worldview with appeals to harmony, nonaggression, and virtue. Different topics could draw a reader in: the critique of big government, a lament over the loss of traditional gender roles, or a rebuke of secular attacks on Christian faith. All these, however, became warped and twisted into a fearful narrative of persecution that, ironically, required the persecution of others. If readers felt threatened, we must ask who they made the aggressor. Like clockwork, the movement returned to Judaism as both a religion and a race hardwired to dominate and deceive. This anti-Semitic fixation fueled the movement's reimagining of US history, often expressed in paranoid retellings of national events. The Mothers' Movement peace script, nervy and tense, foreshadows a strand of post–World War II ideology, itself proffered as "peace." If we take the rhetorical history of peace as necessary to formulations of lasting peace, then we must consider how the Mothers' Movement scripted these elements together into a wicked, deeply undemocratic vision of the United States.

First, I briefly note key cultural shifts after World War I, a period full of demagogic rhetoric. As the crisis in Europe escalated into World War II, isolationist groups in the States also reframed a host of grievances regarding gender, race, and class. As this book has argued thus far, these cultural elements do not exist apart from anti-war advocacy. Furthermore, when war ushers in a climate hostile to democratic dissent, we see undemocratic articulations of these concerns rise in prominence and prove remarkably capable of using the language of peace. Dilling and Van Hyning were prominent among such activists, and, notably, their movement was among the few publicly opposing the war after the Japanese attack on Pearl Harbor, when most Americans supported intervention. I interpret how the Mothers' Movement peace script justified violence at this time through three main appeals, all displaying a conspiratorial style. Specifically, I consider how the movement appealed to traditional gender roles, to a victimized memory, and to a racialized definition of civic religion. One may wish this peace script was an anomaly—just a momentary relapse into our worst impulses that quickly faded away. However, the Mothers' Movement rhetoric foreshadows elements of Cold War discourse, as well as twenty-first-century articulations of anti-Semitism.

Battles of the Interwar Years

In the wake of World War I, diplomats achieved no lasting peace at the Paris Peace Conference. In the United States, a latecomer to the Great War, the following years saw a wave of resentment toward the status quo. Charismatic figures, from Louisiana governor Huey Long to priest-activist Father Coughlin, railed against perceived enemies domestically and abroad. The harsh economic conditions of the Great Depression only made for easier—and shockingly malleable—appeals to all varieties of demagoguery, fueling calls for political and cultural renewal in often Manichean terms.[5] Reflecting this turbulence and dissatisfaction was a growing literature, itself no less contentious, about the meaning and causes of World War I. Speeches, slogans, and publications, both academic and populist, capitalized on the cruelty and waste of the conflict. Like the fallout from the US Civil War, key actors in the war immediately began writing competing histories of the carnage, squaring off in contests of scapegoating and finger-pointing. These texts—ranging from apologetics to heavy-handed indictments of both the Allies and the Central Powers—circulated alongside more insidious, conspiratorial writings.[6] Rhetorically speaking, the war issue was a goldmine: a rich, inventive resource to advance one's cause. From invoking maternal woe over the needless loss of a son's life to indulging in the more paranoid theories of sinister deals made in secret to control the masses, war rhetoric was as diverse as the communities that used it.

Economic and cultural dislocation also gave way to extremist movements. The Ku Klux Klan, most infamously, rose to prominence in the Midwest and asserted sizable electoral influence in Indiana through their brand of male chivalry, honor, and terroristic anti-Black violence.[7] On the East Coast, both far-Left and far-Right factions grew by exploiting postwar cynicism, impoverishment, and xenophobia.[8] These organizations show the power—and frailty—of peace scripts outside of wartime, each appealing to an idealized, often exclusionary, vision of national culture. Father Coughlin, a popular radio personality and Catholic priest, deserves special attention due to his influence on Elizabeth Dilling. Laid out in his theory of "social justice," the namesake of his periodical, Coughlin propagated a vision of national life that gave way to anti-Semitic views. He saw a dangerous world full of villains: atheists, Marxists, and Jewish people exploiting an already chaotic world and preying upon the innocent. To his followers, Coughlin was a role model who expressed a stern assertion of traditional gender roles needed to protect the sacred (i.e., their interpretation of Christianity's) founding of humanity.[9] Everyone else was, at best, a vulnerable, weak-willed pawn or, at worst, a malicious agent assaulting all that was holy in American culture. It should come as no surprise, then, that Coughlin became a cause célèbre for activists like Dilling.

The rise in anti-Semitism during this period is a key rhetorical context for the Mothers' Movement and reflects the larger trend of undemocratic times that led to the rise of undemocratic peace rhetoric. Of course, the context of World War II did not create anti-Semitism, a hateful ideology with ancient roots. The state of emergency, however, created a climate so hostile to anti-war discourse that the more extreme voices, and typically those with a high degree of cultural privilege, could dominate the conversation. During this period, it was not uncommon for anti-war and isolationist arguments to blur into broader conspiracy theories about the manipulation of global politics and economic markets, which would often exhibit anti-Semitic undertones—if not overt bigotry.[10] Many US citizens were rightfully apprehensive that, as World War II ramped up, the nation might be duped again into entering war. Any Wilsonian idealism about democracy secured through warfare now rang hollow.[11] Leaders, notably President Franklin Delano Roosevelt, were careful to incrementally increase engagement or else risk fueling further suspicions about a sinister plot to enter the war. FDR himself was all too familiar with navigating treacherous waters and evading anti-Semitic attacks.[12] In addition to the KKK, the German Bund fed into the extreme anti-interventionist rancor that assailed FDR. They, too, tied their anti-war rhetoric to a deep distrust or outright hatred of the Jewish faith. Cultural icons such as Charles Lindbergh and Henry Ford fed into this trend by publicizing anti-Semitic sentiments. Such rhetoric often suggested some ill-defined, and thus hard to quickly refute, connection between the war machine and Judaism.[13] In short, anti-Semitic rhetoric found purchase for those invested in exclusionary versions of US society, ushering into the period ugly stereotypes to amplify a not unpopular opinion: the United States must stay out of foreign entanglements.[14]

Upon entering World War II, the Roosevelt administration hoped to avoid the excessive restrictions put on civil liberties that former President Woodrow

Wilson enacted during the previous global conflict. Nevertheless, the field of peace activism was far from robust during this time.[15] For instance, there were several high-profile prosecutions of seditious speech, the denaturalization and deportation of many US citizens, and the mass internment of over one hundred thousand people of Japanese descent. It would be far-fetched to describe this as a period conducive to vigorous democratic dissent. Indeed, even the propaganda measures at the time were unprecedented and, overall, successful in shaping public opinion to support the war. Historian James T. Sparrow describes the United States during World War II as a "warfare state," characterized by the unparalleled reach of the federal government into everyday life, steering public perceptions of the war and redefining the role of the government.[16] It should come as no shock, then, that one of the major anti-war movements during this undemocratic period was itself quite anti-democratic. Nevertheless, the Mothers' Movement co-opted the myths of peace to compose a script that many of its members likely found to be thoroughly "positive" despite its scapegoating and dehumanizing rhetoric. While the script is clearly "negative" by peace theorist Johan Galtung's standard, by adding rhetorical analysis to the process of assessing peace policies we better see how violent appeals can hide behind seemingly peaceful appeals.[17] In this case, the women used a version of Christian nationalism to make their racial and gendered script more palatable.

Glen Jeansonne's detailed work on the Mothers' Movement reveals the depth of their organizing and the key connections they made to the broader isolationist wave. Jeansonne also highlights the special authority these women claimed by tying current events to gender and, most obviously, mining the role of the mother for persuasive effect.[18] Noting the movement's odious fusion of anti-Communism, anti-Semitism, and extreme Christianity, Jeansonne shows the broad reach and popularity of this predominantly white, middle-class, Protestant group, which doggedly opposed FDR's every move. Many scholars have observed the radical changes and opportunities accorded to women by World War II. These new avenues of prosperity and expression also laid new obstacles to gender equality, as some elements of society responded to this development in fiercely retrograde ways.[19] Women who did not directly join the war cause, presumably most members of the Mothers' Movement, would likely be sensitive to this shift—or violation—of the traditional boundaries between the public and the private spheres. It is in this space of reactionary politics that the work of Dilling and Van Hyning ought to be read as a sincere belief that the old way of life, as strictly defined by gender and religious dogma, was receding from history.

Finally, I must acknowledge this chapter's indebtedness to feminist rhetorical scholarship, which comprises one of the most robust and generative areas in the communication discipline.[20] Much work focuses on the struggles women endured and overcame to achieve a semblance of equality and justice. A smaller but no less vibrant portion of the literature focuses on the negative, more extreme segments of women-led movements. Of these, most cover the periods of first-, second-, or third-wave feminism, considering key debates regarding strategy, goals, and identity-formation of women in US life. This chapter looks at a different type of women-led organization: a deeply reactionary movement that illustrates how activists could use traditional definitions of woman- and motherhood to oppose warfare in shockingly violent ways. The Mothers' Movement, a loose assembly of white, upper- and middle-class women primarily living in Midwestern states, found expression in Dilling's *Bulletin* and Van Hyning's *Women's Voice*. In these pages, women could construct a peace script through a process analogous to what Carly S. Woods calls an "argument culture . . . [comprised of] material and symbolic environments where arguments, ideas, and people can thrive together."[21] In the discursive world of the Mothers' Movement, whiteness and femininity combined with appeals to national memory to forge a frightening vision of peace. This peace script, deeply conspiratorial and claustrophobic in style, suggests citizens can achieve harmony, civility, and security only through a radical insistence on an anti-Semitic vision of national life.

Scripting a Motherly Peace: Protecting White Femininity

Gender Crisis

The most frequent appeal across the Mothers' Movement literature is, predictably, to femininity, which they voiced in numerous ways. The protean nature of their gendered rhetoric reflected a serious challenge facing the movement's leaders. Dilling and Van Hyning needed a vision of womanhood that could venture out of the home and into the public sphere to challenge male figures of authority while retaining an aura of traditional female virtue. Gender had to be fixed but flexible. Various tactics met the challenge: the framing and organization of the newsletter, the strategic use of images, and the telling of anecdotes. The last method, in particular, helped animate the gender crisis in personal and often humorous narratives. The stories often involved men in positions of power betraying their gender in some embarrassing way. The women of the Mothers' Movement could thus serve as a corrective force preserving US culture rather than as agents of change. Their stories, as public expressions of their private lives, helped police gender and sexuality while suggesting how proper citizens should behave.[22] Through their words, the women hoped to be a balancing measure, seeking harmony, not discord. Their insistence, gentle yet stern—and in several ways extremist—was thus presented as the fitting conservative response to a gender crisis more elemental than any specific policy position or political issue. We might be reminded here of the Copperhead movement, which similarly employed the peaceful myth that their activism was natural and therefore not disruptive. Instead, like the Mothers' Movement, in their case anti-war rhetoric was simply the performance of a sacred script that maintained gender norms. To adherents in both movements, it was their opponents who enacted a "negative" script that amplified unseemly emotions and dangerous ideologies.

Lyrl Clark Van Hyning's newsletter, which ran into the 1960s, was titled *Women's Voice*.[23] The title suggests the focus of the Mothers' Movement peace script. Rather than foreground any overt political theme, Van Hyning makes gender her organizing principle. Rather than representing a singular "woman," the newsletter instead calls forth the plurality of "women" and distills it into one "voice." Throughout US history, women have faced innumerable obstacles—legal, cultural, and physical—to participating or simply being *present* in public life. "Voice" is thus a useful term because it implies something not merely written or read, two activities that one could do in the privacy of the home away from any public or social context. In contrast, voice is embodied and engaged; it is an act of externalization with resonance, a *speaking-to* heard by others in a shared time and place. Of course, the newsletter circulated and was likely read within the privacy of the home, yet as a peace script, it invited a sense of participation in a collective female voice and, with it, a social space that served as a prerequisite for political action. Through the pages of the newsletter, discrete readers could identify with a collective "voice" as women.

Elizabeth Dilling's newsletter made similar use of gender, appealing to a peace-loving nature intrinsic to motherhood that allowed her to assert a cultural hierarchy. As in Van Hyning's work, gender appeals could obscure the movement's more violent and exclusionary elements, subordinating extreme beliefs to an overriding commitment to gender norms. Unlike *Women's Voice*, Dilling's publication, variously titled the *Patriotic Research Bureau / Bulletin*, acknowledges its political nature while highlighting a more traditional, even passive, approach.[24] Consider the title. A patriot is someone who loves their country. In practice, the descriptor "patriotic" tends to be a self-consummating adjective that needs no explicit object or activity of its own. I am patriotic when I declare my patriotism and, it is thus implied, that I am a loyal citizen who preserves the national order. This sense of "patriotic" works well with Dilling's appeal to femininity because neither calls for an explicit policy or political creed. Instead, the followers of this script seem to emanate from a pre-political realm of devotion, a place of belonging that parallels the idealized maternal role within the home. The phrase "Research Bureau" calls to mind a passive yet objective space where a person mostly accumulates data without biased interpretation or polemics. Such a framing for Dilling's anti-war platform emphasizes a sense of intrinsic peace and nonviolence, casting a superficial fog of harmony over the movement that conceals its more insidious dimensions.

The epistolary style of the *Bulletin* shapes the movement's gendered appeal to a pre-political peace. Dilling typically begins each issue in letter format, addressing her audience as "Dear Friends" before offering a first-person account of her life and current travails. The letter-writing genre, as scholars have noted, has historically been a sanctuary for women. Letter-writing serves as a platform for those who wish to communicate "privately"—an intimate address to a close friend or family member—but retain the potential for "public" significance, both in its content and in its audience.[25] Dilling's letters participate in this tradition, situating discussions of war-related matters squarely within the realm of the "private" and "feminine" domains. Therefore, whenever Dilling discusses her anti-war stance, she appears to move from the private sphere outward, enacting two moves essential to her peace script. First, Dilling's rhetoric suggests that the war issue has *invaded* the interior space of US life, encroaching on the sacred realm of domesticity and motherhood. Second, the *Bulletin*'s arguments now seem as if they were born from the unquestionably proper and peaceful domain of femininity. Dilling occasionally achieves this effect by beginning her letters with personal photographs or acknowledgments of holidays and family milestones, reinforcing a rhetorical connection between the prosaic private realm and the intense, even extremist, political script under construction.[26]

Consider Dilling's December 1943 newsletter, which uses epistolary style to tie the "peaceful" elements of womanhood to her extreme anti-war position.[27] The letter begins with a photograph captioned "Christmas Greetings 1943." The black-and-white image doubles as professional portrait and holiday greeting card, giving visual expression to the Mothers' Movement. Here, Dilling is not the somber, serious figure that her isolationist peers Charles Lindbergh or Father Coughlin projected. Instead, her persona is more traditionally "feminine"—a gentle smile with lipstick and a warm, inviting glance upward complemented by the sartorial choice of a dress, perhaps an outfit for Christmas mass, complete with a faint glimmer of an earring in her left ear. A certain type of reader could reaffirm their own commitment to this American identity—white, middle-class, Christian, "properly" feminine—before wading into the overtly political content. Such an appeal to proper womanhood was the symbolic glue between the harmless world of the home and the brutal dehumanization that defined their "negative" peace. Ultimately, this allowed the script to falsely appear "positive" to many adherents.[28]

After the portrait, a letter begins with two prayers that call for "courage" and "glory in the darkness" for her "dear readers." The political prognosis in this letter, as in so many others, emerges only after the message is carefully encased within the shell of the private sphere, a place of incorruptible femininity and its associated cultural virtues. Grounding both her and the reader in this space, Dilling then wastes no time parsing the causes of the encroaching "darkness" as she begins railing against the Roosevelt administration in a story full of conspiracy and intrigue.[29] In her anecdote, the villains are men of the New Deal, such as the "Injustice Department's" O. John Rogge, Francis Biddle, and Secretary of the Interior Harold Ickes. These men act as foils to Dilling's gender propriety, as they "howl" and act out in attempts to subvert US freedom. These unseemly men are, as Dilling likes to repeat, at odds with America's "Washingtonian principles."[30] She thereby integrates gender and patriotism into her peace script.

The *Bulletin* continues to mix private and public appeals in another representative passage that uses the myths of peace to obscure exclusionary ideas. Dilling notes her "daughter's English course" and education more broadly, a common concern for parents. Yet here, too, is a conflict: another instance of pro-war mania invading the realm of the family and child-rearing. The Dillings chose the school, Northwestern University, partly because its "closeness enables [their daughter, referred to as 'Babe'] to live at home where [Dilling] can help counteract such mental pollution as is compulsory." Dangerous propaganda circulates at schools through figures such as Bertrand Russell, Ernest Hemingway, and Max Eastman, who are pushing "Communistic 'goo' about mixed race relations . . . and 'exaggerated admiration' for Jewry."[31] Here we see how the harmonious nature of the private sphere, reflected in maternal values, is invaded by pro-war propagandists who "advocat[e] world government." Notably, anti-Semitism is expressed as a byproduct of one devoted to a motherly role.

In the Mothers' Movement, we repeatedly see racial, gendered, and religious threats to US peace entangled in a dense thicket of conspiratorial rhetoric that emanates from the maternal realm. From Communists to New Dealers to pro-war hawks, all are part of Dilling's doomsday vision of racial and religious mixing.[32] Railing against all these hypocritical, un-Christian men could appear controversial or too political for a respectable white, middle-class mother. By approaching all issues through the pre-political space of femininity, Dilling's *Bulletin* hits the moral pitch of an innocent and pure pacifism in tune with the harmonies of maternal life. It is from this rhetorical starting point that all outside discord—whether the wailing of effeminate men or the machinations of maniacal bureaucrats—demands Dilling's attention. This is not because she seeks to proclaim her own political beliefs but because, as a mother, she is compelled to guard the sacred realm of domestic life.

Dilling and Van Hyning further adorn their anti-war script with myths of peace through the presentation of mailed-in letters. Numerous inquiries and anecdotes from fellow women activists reinforce the sense of a community emerging from the private, domestic realm of motherhood, which must be respected before all political matters. For instance, in the August 31, 1944, issue of *Women's Voice*, Van Hyning responds to a reader's letter from a woman named Margaret, who asks about the of role of women in achieving peace. Van Hyning responds "that it will be no lasting peace until the women throughout the world teach the children they bear and train to live peaceably with themselves, their family, their neighbors, and naturally this extends to the neighboring nations."[33] In both form and content, Van Hyning activates the gendered nature of the Mothers' Movement to offer the readers a false sense of a natural and pure peace. The article satisfies traditional expectations for feminine expression: an intimate person-to-person chat seeking advice and inviting common ground.[34] Hyning's response uses this gendered expectation to rescript political views as nonpolitical ideas suitable for mothers. Followers of this peace script see a sacred order to things: from the individual woman or mother, to their children, to their neighbors, and then the political realm only as an extension of these other roles. Once again, we see how leaders invoked the role of the mother as a pre-political bedrock of society.[35]

We see gender identity similarly inscribed into the movement's Platform of Principles: "We, the Mothers, Mobilize for America, Inc., Platform of Principles (as set forth in charter granted by the State of Illinois, 1941): 'For civic, educational, patriotic, political, benevolent, charitable and research.' '[D]emocracy'; safeguard against war's destruction; place for mothers."[36] Wordy as it may be, each plays an important role. The platform positions each member as a woman rather than a political agent. More precisely, the readers are mothers whose civic duty naturally extends outward from a sacred pre-political place. The mother's goal is to educate warmly yet sternly; she does this not to alter the world but to safeguard its core values. The reader is thus called upon to be a nurturer of tradition who keeps a "place for mothers." This final phrase cements the notion that being a mother is the key to understanding all movement-related issues, from maintaining respectability to saving democracy to ending the "war's destruction."

The *Bulletin* makes continued use of gendered language to craft its peace script. Dilling favors the anecdote for whimsical, informal retellings of personal experience. These are useful for presenting arguments in a less direct way than an editorial or treatise. Frequently, her anecdotes depict pro-war men as effeminate, once again tying her anti-war stance to a traditional vision of gender identity. For instance, in her 1940 "Christmas Round Table Letter," Dilling tells the story of "two smart, crusading Detroit women . . . [the] blue-eyed blond [Mrs. Rosa Farber] and [the] zippy, brown-eyed little Mrs. Beatrice Knowles." These two voice their dissent, in sharp contrast to a ridiculous man: the "loud-mouthed, war-mongering Claude Pepper, darling of anti-Christian, pro-Red B'nai B'rith."[37] These mothers, who built an effigy of their opponent, are described in Dilling's story as model women standing firm against overly emotional and maniacal men. In another passage, Dilling describes unseemly pro-war men as "traitors . . . [who invite] caskets and taxes." She then frames war hawks in overtly gendered language, referring to them as "some pussycat 'ladies' [who] were criticizing our prospects against Bill 1776," a major defense bill commonly called the "Lend-Lease" bill.[38] It is these types of unmanly "ladies" who stand at the heart of America's problems. To stress her point, Dilling compares these effeminate men to transgressors during the US Revolution: the "American 'society element' who were like 'ladies' [and] curtsied before the ragged band of American fighters."[39] In lambasting pro-war men as "ladies," Dilling's anecdotes keep her peace script focused on gender identity. For Dilling's movement, the war debate concerns many things—often more than a reader can keep track of—but it all revolves around the loss of tradition, seen most clearly in transgressive gender roles that are to be admonished by good mothers. Pro-war thinking is obviously compromised, the thinking goes, because everywhere its proponents appear to be losing their gender identity, acting in ways unbecoming of real men. Women can bolster their feminine bona fides by pointing out these deficits while masking their anti-war stance in an acceptable gender performance.

Dilling repeatedly depicts the pro-war camp as buffoons who want to persecute anti-war women but are not man enough to do it. This allows her to paint the war debate once again as a battle predicated on a gender crisis. Consider Dilling's story of United States attorney William Power Maloney, who prosecuted a group of isolationist women on charges of sedition. She describes him as desperately trying to accuse the women of hysteria (a supposedly "screaming mob of alleged Mothers"). Dilling claims he snidely remarked, "I see the washboards are still out of commission."[40] In their duplicitous, yet ineffectual, attempts to indict the women legally and morally, the men are depicted as the true culprits of desperation and emotional excess. In presenting New Deal men as womanlier than the female activists, the *Bulletin* frames the mothers' activism as the natural policing of gender roles, each member simply bearing witness to these pitiful men.

Dilling continues to mine the gendered differences between pro-war men and anti-war women to insulate her peace script with appeals to a sacred maternal order. Her anecdote regarding William Power Maloney goes on to describe a mother calmly challenging him, who is occasionally referred to as AG "Baloney." In contrast to female activists, Maloney became distraught and then "kicked a swinging door so angrily [that] it flew back and hit him in the face."[41] This anecdote represents how FDR's men diminished their masculinity through desperate pro-war feelings against women. Another New Deal lawyer is characterized as a "rosy, fat, smug" man who shamelessly kowtows to FDR's pro-war agenda.[42] These stories allow Dilling to portray women as targets—even religious martyrs—at the hands of men who are gender aberrations, lacking in bravery and resolution.[43] In one disturbing passage, Dilling addresses allegations that she beat her husband. Her defense is that her husband is simply too masculine and strong ("6 feet 2 inches of steel muscle") for her to have hurt him.[44] Far from an unrelated tangent, her accounting of alleged marital abuse connects directly into the movement's broader vision because it portrays the pro-war party as lunatic: constantly attacking, through lies and allegations, innocent citizens who resolutely maintain the traditional hierarchy of the family. She then reports, as a cautionary tale, that although her husband may be physically strong, his enfeebled mind was once twisted to oppose her anti-war position. Women such as she are the last defense against such wartime mania.[45]

The *Bulletin* contains numerous other anecdotes about New Dealers lacking in manliness, serving as a motif of the Mothers' peace script. One story describes a man who "quit [. . .] working, loafed awhile and has since secured a political New Deal job in Washington, D.C.," implying the administration is quite amenable to lazy men.[46] Another passage considers a minister who—in a thoroughly pejorative sense—Dilling describes as "modern." Rather than traditional religious attire, the "rotund little Bradley" wore "golf attire," walking into an "ornate dining room, waddl[ing] directly to a punch bowl spiked with liquor and starting [to] lap[. . .] it up as adoring ladies surrounded him." It is this kind of unmanly figure—contrasted by the fit, self-possessed, and emotionally unavailable man—who attacks women like Dilling. Such actions render men even more pathetic because they invariably fail. In this instance, she tells how the man "supposedly calls all the 'mothers who protested involvement in the US in this world war . . . 'black cockroaches.'"[47] Through such narratives, the war issue appears in starkly gendered terms. Again and again, Dilling makes this move: critique pro-war men as physically and morally deficient actors who follow the impure will of the New Deal administration. In this scripting of peace, the women position the war debate in a place supposedly more fundamental and less political than the battlefield. From here, their enactment of a "negative" peace is presented as a dramatic battle between real mothers who guard sacred truths and the hypocritical, reactionary men of war.

Paranoid Memory

The movement's vision of femininity worked with memory appeals to offer readers a new history of peace that scripted Christian women as the standard-bearers for national culture. Theirs is an anxious need to remember so as to preserve "true" US culture. Fear triggers these acts of remembering—sparked by some menace, typically a follower of Judaism, who deceives and manipulates innocent citizens in hopes of destroying America. The Mothers' Movement literature supports these memory claims through the frequent citation of texts of nebulous origin, which characterizes their unique brand of historical "research." These documents amplify an abiding sense of persecution that positions readers as true patriots targeted and preyed upon by malefactors and traitors. For instance, a piece attributed to A. A. Depping narrates the US Civil War as a conflict "fomented by a Jewish conspiracy," whose agents allegedly assassinated Abraham Lincoln.[48] The crisis over slavery morphs from a matter of racial equality and emancipation to merely one battle in a centuries-old war between Anglo-Saxon civilization and families such as the Rothschilds, thereby injecting anti-Semitic paranoia into the women's peace script. In another infamous (and falsely attributed) text, readers are told that Benjamin Franklin sounded the alarm on the Jewish threat imperiling the United States, aligning the Mothers' Movement cause with the birth of the nation.[49]

These texts retread the same ground as the infamous anti-Semitic work *The Protocols of Zion* and mask the complexity of historical conflict with an all-encompassing shroud of conspiracy. Admitting to oneself the truth of this conspiracy, no matter how tenuous and absurd, is the scripted path toward peace, and the cultural threats targeted in these works instill a deep sense of fear into the movement's collective memory.[50] Consider Van Hyning's speech titled "The Necessity of a Second Party" given before the Patrick Henry Forum on February 7, 1942. She evokes the memory of great American men— Thomas Jefferson, Alexander Hamilton, and George Washington—to highlight the foppish and unbecoming nature of current leaders. FDR, in contrast to the Founding Fathers, is described as obsequiously leaping "into the sea to meet the incoming British Ambassador; [even] when he made a truce at sea with British representatives; [even] when this man slaughters American boys at the command of Winston Churchill, the Democratic party is dead. *The desecration of the memory* of the great Democrats is the repudiation of the principles of the party."[51] These "men have had their chance," Van Hyning declares, and now "women must take over" to correct the historical wrongs done to "the people whom Jefferson and Jackson rescued."[52] It is through such acts of remembering, performed by mothers, that *true* men who embody the essence of Americanism may "awaken from this mesmerism." Once again, the current debacle is framed as the product of a weakness of will: an unmanly, humiliating inability to see and remember our national culture, which requires the help of strong, but respectable, women who dare to see the truth.[53]

Women of the Mothers' Movement platformed other conspiratorial texts to recast current anti-Semitic fears and prejudices as the central conflict across US history. Dilling's 1934 self-published book, *The Red Network: A "Who's Who" and Handbook of Radicalism for Patriots*, is essentially the master text of her movement, as evidenced by its near-constant citation in the *Patriotic Research Bulletin*.[54] *The Red Network* clearly aligns with the genre of the "conspiratorial," suggesting far-reaching plots by uncommonly organized covert groups. Rather than a traditional narrative or exposé, Dilling's book reads like an encyclopedia or reference guide for scared readers who need quick confirmation that some person or event is sinister.[55] The text is filled with lists of all manner of people, places, and things allegedly tied to one Communist-Judaic world conspiracy hell-bent on destroying US civilization. Dilling's book thus reads like a head-spinning compilation of tenuous connections, vague affiliations, and partial definitions written for true believers. In isolation, no single list is persuasive, but through sheer volume, the book could impress an anxious reader into buying into its aura of comprehensiveness.[56] The organizations and people occupying these lists create an imposing tapestry of actors, motives, and associations that mimics the exhaustiveness of historical research, giving a semblance of objectivity to the movement's paranoid memory. Of course, most parties discussed are said to be explicitly anti-American or "infiltrated" by such forces, suggesting—though not, in fact, *providing*—a frightening wealth of evidence strengthening Dilling's case. She often uses these catalogs to justify the narrative of US culture at war with Marxism, Communism, and Judaism. The goal of the book is to make these ideologies appear absolutely opposed to real, lasting peace because they are grave threats antithetical to America's founding vision.[57]

Dilling's two other reference texts, *The Octopus* and *Roosevelt Red Record*, also act as discursive engines for the movement's rhetoric. Extensively cited in the *Bulletin*, these books amplify an overriding paranoia that sees an impossibly large conspiracy attacking the nation's soul. Members of obscure fraternal orders, banking groups, private industry, international politicians, and immigrants all comprise a world conspiracy engaged in a zero-sum battle for America. Nearly all elements of the Mothers' Movement peace script fit into this framework of world history.[58] Despite a weak evidentiary basis, these texts enable Dilling to portray her fight against peace as only the most recent battle against generational forces of evil. For instance, she constantly inserts FDR into the paranoid memory of the movement's peace script, identifying him as a vital part of the evil network of cunning anti-American agents who seek to violate the Founding Fathers' way of life. Dilling reminds her readers that George Washington "pass[ed] a statute making it a crime for a man" like those in office today to have secretive deals and correspondences.[59] After making such a claim, as with most of her insinuations, Dilling offers multiple citations to her other works. The avid reader, already committed to the peace script, would find such passages persuasive, reinforcing the belief that Roosevelt was, of course, undermining the United States.

In a speech titled "Lincoln," Dilling again taps into a paranoid style to frame her anti-war fight in generational terms. Delivered at a rally in Milton, Massachusetts, she begins by echoing the Gettysburg Address: "Six score and ten years ago was brought forth on this continent a new Soul dedicated to the immortal proposition that all men are created equal in their right to freedom from the bondage of slavery."[60] Dilling thus portrays the current moment and the pursuit of peace to be the result of a long struggle not simply for a "Nation" but for a "Soul." Her fight for peace is not political play, in this script, but rather a spiritual fight for the essence of US culture. Members of the movement gain a sense of duty and honor when their protest is labeled as a spiritual fight stemming from the birth of national civilization. Dilling continues this call to the women of the movement, amplifying her appeal to memory by using generational language: this is a "struggle to stand still, and so, in generation after generation, the same battles, the same defeats, recur against ever rising injustices, the ever rising tyrannies of governments grasped by ambitious dictators who mount over the bodies of a people grown lax and indifferent until they are finally aroused by the violence of events."[61] To "stand still" and preserve US culture requires remembering proper American behavior—in this case, privileging a narrowly defined Christian, conservative, and motherly role—and keeping watchful eye out for its many enemies. While we should rightly judge this a "negative" peace, its adherents likely felt it eminently "positive."[62] A rhetorical analysis of such scripts tells us how appeals to gender, race, and class might create a false sense of moral superiority while perpetuating a profoundly undemocratic vision of America.

The Mothers' Movement makes frequent use of historical figures to compose their peace script and prepare readers for what they see as the impending cultural war. "The Immortal Lincoln," for instance, is reconceived in contemporary terms as bravely staving off conspiratorial powers: "the red forces of disunity and class hatred . . . [that] separate the South and form it into a Soviet State under promised Negro control." In such narratives of US history, epochal moments are reduced from complex events to simple instances of injustice in which violence is perpetrated by unpatriotic (and often nonwhite) actors. The way to carry on Lincoln's fight for "liberty, unity, and justice for our people," as Dilling claims, is best seen when contrasted with these un-American people, whether African Americans, Jewish people, or Chinese citizens, whose cultural deficiency is a recurring theme.[63] These acts of remembering strengthen an overriding sense of paranoia by asserting a cultural battle over national identity: a fight between proper Americans and conniving enemies who can take on the appearance of virtually anyone or anything.

The *Bulletin* repeatedly invokes memory appeals in ways entangled with racial and religious exclusion. Once again, we see a peace script born of undemocratic times that expresses deeply undemocratic dissent. For instance, the newsletter does not present the Lend-Lease Bill (H. R. 1776) as legislation to be debated by policy wonks. Instead, it is treated as an affront to the founding vision of US history: "The dictatorship bill aimed to undo what was won in 1776." Judging by the overall rhetoric of the Mothers' Movement, the Revolutionary War was fought to preserve a place for Christians against a "Judaized" society and the "pro-Red anti-Christian" campaign of B'nai B'rith.[64] In this representative passage, the *Bulletin* cites the Bible to take readers further back in time and remind them that "nation shall rise against nation . . . iniquity shall abound," invoking a vision of radical change long in the making and forged through chaos and conflict among civilizations.[65] References to failed empires, such as Rome, contribute to the movement's epic sense of historical fragility, which inspires activists not toward compassion and inclusivity but toward intense protection of US culture, as they see it, against forces of pure evil.[66] Again, the myths of peace that tell of its inherent nonviolence, its apolitical quality, its approximation to the "natural" and "pure" way of seeing the world are all exploited in the Mothers' Movement peace script.

Discussions of the previous war make up the final piece to Dilling's memory work and drive home her movement's undemocratic peace. Much fearmongering and cultural exclusion could be evoked by referencing World War I, a topic already rife with conspiracy theories. The *Bulletin*, for instance, cynically states that "as in the last war, 'Saving the world for democracy' has been a handy and deceptive slogan. We need to defend California and our own territory in a practical way with SAVE AMERICA FOR AMERICANS as our slogan."[67] What was once "the War to End all Wars" now stands as an uneasy testament to the nation's willingness to fight—successfully, no doubt, but for whose benefit? By depicting the current crisis alongside this "deceptive slogan," Dilling once again reduces historical complexity to stoke lingering resentments. Her argument that citizens must first protect their own country before protecting others' fits well with the rhetorical themes of the peace script, bolstered by George Washington's oft-cited "Farewell Address." Fusing past and present in this way supports the legitimacy of opposing war, even if such memory work depends upon anti-Semitism and vicious attacks on anyone appearing to harbor Communist views.[68] As we will see, the movement's appeal to memory and gender coalesces around an intensely exclusionary and racialized vision of national culture, offering anti-war adherents a disturbing script for their peace activism.

Religion and Racialized Patriotism

Appeals to traditional gender roles and a retelling of US history do not fully capture the core of the Mothers' Movement's script. For the Mothers, a narrow version of Christianity serves as the cultural bedrock that upholds peace while excluding many citizens. The texts under consideration consistently make Judaism the scapegoat and foil to the movement's anti-war purity. By framing Judaism as both a monolithic religion and a race signifier, the movement makes Jewish people into a cultural threat united by a sinister plot to poison the Christian soul of America. The women of the movement thus see themselves as guardians of the spiritual pillars of national culture. Their vision is not of a "civil theology" but of an actual theocracy—a religious nation facing contamination by foreign cultures, religions, and races. On its face, it is clearly a "negative" peace: reactionary, exclusionary, and violent, yet to the millions of white, middle-class, Protestant women who subscribed to the newsletter, it likely seemed not only a lasting, "positive" peace but the only way to survive. Peeling back the rhetorical dynamics of this script can shed light on how deeply rooted anti-Semitism is in US culture, even in peace advocacy.

Consider how Van Hyning scripts peace in starkly religious terms in a public speech. In her untitled address, she equates the country with Christian belief: "The Government of the United States of America is unique among all governments . . . the only government founded on the Christian principle of the worthwhileness of the individual human being. The corner stone of our government, the Declaration of Independence, but puts into practice the teaching of Jesus the Christ . . . The Constitution, the house of refuge, is built upon this principle."[69] What makes the US special, to Van Hyning, is not the granting of religious liberties—at least, not primarily. The nation's exceptionalism stems from a fundamental assent to Christian culture and its eternal principles. It is easy to see from this major premise how it follows that non-Christians (or any Christian who fails to adhere to the movement's rigid interpretation) are un-American and inherently not part of the proper, natural—that is *peaceful*—way of life.[70]

This logic seeps through the pages of the *Bulletin*, whose very subtitle reads, "For the Defense of Christianity and Americanism." To be American is to be Christian in all facets of life. Differences within Christian and non-Christian populations hardly matter. Deviant identities simply blur together, as seen in how Dilling conflates the atheism of Communists with Judaism in her discussion of New Dealers. Consider her 1941 Christmas newsletter, where she speaks of the "Prophecy" of Jesus before decrying the "anti-Christian-Marxian dictatorship now clutching us . . . [as they] struggle to regain the Republic bequeathed us by Christian for[e]bears."[71] The fusion of national memory with Christian faith, as articulated here, ties into Dilling's exclusionary ideal of civic life, which castigates other religions and races with rarely a meaningful distinction. Dilling lumps non-Christian enemies together, asking, "Are We a

Heathen Country. . . . [with] 5,000,000 Jews?" and then targeting "Judaized 'Christians' [who partake] in coast to coast meetings."[72] Her grim perspective depicts America as veering toward cultural collapse due to religious diversity, here reduced to a monolithic enemy.

Dilling continues to stoke fears by tying her anti-war arguments to an apocalyptic image of diversity. She describes how "the savage Mohammedan call of the muezzin as heard in the darkest Asia is mingled with the propaganda of the Hindu, Jew and agnostic. Negro choirs and performers give an inter-racial touch to the meeting. This jumbling of contradictory beliefs leads only to confusion and unbelief and robs Jesus Christ of His rightful place as the light of this World." Without a "Christian revival," the nation is "doomed" to endure such diversity, which she likens to Soviet-style "slavery."[73] The current crisis, referred to as Roosevelt's "Revolution," is not simply about an unjust or wasteful war; it is a metaphysical crisis of faith inseparable from her version of Christian culture, the supposed beating heart of patriotism.[74] Just as religious ritual reaffirms a believer's faith and worldview, Dilling's peace script offers a discursive ritual of exclusion and dehumanization to its adherents.

Anti-Semitism continues to be Dilling's preferred method of critique toward non-Christian culture, serving as a warrant for many of her anti-Roosevelt and anti-war positions. She relentlessly refers to Supreme Court Justice Felix Frankfurter, an appointee of FDR, in terms of his Jewish faith. On these grounds, she deems him part of a coterie of "Red Jews" and other "master-minds" of an "internationalistic Marxism in America and Great Britain." Indeed, anyone associated with the "Lend-Lease dictatorship" is complicit in the religious-based conspiracy.[75] To top off the bigotry, Dilling refers to Roosevelt's New Deal policy the "Jew Deal," and his allies are thus branded not merely political opponents to the Mothers' Movement but "anti-Christ elements." These enemies, framed as Jewish villains, embody an act of extreme scapegoating ironically predicated on the pursuit of peace, revealing again the degree to which anti-war protest can integrate elements of violence.[76]

Throughout Dilling's work, she disparages news agencies for alleged ties to Judaism, a connection that she again presents as proof of a cultural war waged by un-American adversaries. She brands the *Sentinel*, for instance, as "devoted to Jewish interests" and cites an editorial advocating for the death penalty as punishment for those convicted of "seditious utterances and treasonable practices" as proof of Judaism's desire to prohibit all criticism.[77] Dilling distorts the fight to preserve "civil liberties"—an area of focus for many peace activists—into a broad attack on pro-Jewish organizations and advocacy, typically targeting the American Civil Liberties Union, which she suspects of championing free speech to aid the Red revolution.[78] In one anecdote, Dilling portrays herself as a plucky defender of America's soul via an alleged repartee with

Jane Addams, the renowned activist. Addams assured Dilling she was not a member of the Communist Party, to which Dilling retorted, "No, of course not. You can do so much more good from the outside. But you have belonged to every outstanding Red-aid society from the Civil Liberties Union."[79] The Communist element, framed as collaborators working with Judaism to overthrow America, is portrayed as omnipresent in all non-Christian affiliations, creating the sense of a vast network of conspirators opposed to the Mothers' Movement. Yet again, we see how the peace script can exploit scapegoating, fear-mongering, and anti-Semitism.

One way Dilling could mitigate or distract from the unsavory elements of her peace script, especially the rampant anti-Semitism, was through a combination of anti-intellectualism and an insistence on free speech. In a 1943 newsletter, she rails against her opponents' definition of "anti-Semitism" and claims Maloney, now dubbed "Little Baloney," considers any critique of Judaism equivalent to being pro-Hitler.[80] This passage is immediately followed by a conspiratorial take on "organized Political-Judaism" that manipulates US laws to punish the "Gentile majority." In a reversal, she calls for criminalizing "anti-Gentileism [sic]" and compares it to Jim Crow laws and the "race separatism" of the South. By slotting a monolithic Judaism into the clash of war and peace, Dilling fortifies her Manichean image of Jewish people trying to subvert national culture against true Christian men and women who are unafraid to speak out.[81] Consider how she then proceeds into a consideration of the "World State" and an apocalyptic future wherein "The Bible Must Go."[82] By sounding the alarm about the alleged federal control of textbooks and Christian organizations, the Mothers' Movement could link a religious agenda to all governmental actions that are now impinging on the sacred sphere of the home, the church, and the school. Once again, we see the hallmark move of the peace script as instilling a massive feeling of distrust in so-called elites, experts, politicians, and media associations, all of whom are, at best, unwitting agents in the Jewish conspiracy.

Dilling's anti-war argument thrived when it ignored the specifics of World War II. By forgoing details, she easily made the war a simple matter of religious allegiance. It was not about Germany versus France, England or the United States, but Judaism's "new world order" and its auxiliary groups, such as the Anti-Defamation League (ADL), versus real Christians. She repeatedly frames the ADL this way, as "a pro-Communist, anti-Christian, international Jewish secret society which attempts to throttle any Jew or Gentile who displeases it."[83] Due to the sheer repetition of Jewish scapegoating, the Mothers' Movement could make seemingly harmless appeals to Christianity fuel anti-Semitism. For example, when Dilling portrays the struggle between "alien materialistic Marxist-collectivism" and the "Christian American principles which raised the footsore[,] praying Valley Forgers into a Nation, and to an all-time world pinnacle of prosperity and blessing," it is reasonable to assume that a reader fluent in Dilling's work would read into this a coded critique of the Jewish faith.[84]

I must stress how central anti-Semitism was to the movement's peace script, as it worked as a racialized appeal that tied together all other rhetorical dimensions. With suspicion against Judaism the bedrock of the Mothers' anti-war arguments, anti-Semitism could operate as an enthymeme, filling in the gaps of often fragmentary and indirect language across the movement's literature. Even when merely suggested, anti-Semitism should not be considered accidental or marginal but as fulfilling a narrative demand for an all-encompassing yet ever-elusive enemy determined to destroy Christian America. Dilling could be quite direct, however, proclaiming, "If telling the truth in defense of America makes one a 'Nazi' and a 'Copperhead'—so be it!" In persisting in their truth, the movement's adherents are labeled enemies of war when they are, according to their script, the true preservers of peace against cultural enemies who are always tied to Judaism.[85] Thus, we can see the interlocking rhetoric of the Mothers' Movement: an allegedly pre-political space of womanhood that nurtures sacred truths that fuse their version of Christianity with national memory. To recall the foundation of US culture in these pages is to reaffirm one's commitment to a Christianity starkly opposed to an aggressive and duplicitous enemy, cemented in the scapegoated Jewish faith.

Incoherence was no problem for this peace script if the reader already bought into its cultural narrative. Underneath their fearmongering, Dilling and others animated a myriad of extraneous discussions, all haunted by the specter of Judaism. Take one final example that illustrates how deeply encased their anti-Semitism was with the moral veneer of "peace." After chastising certain activist organizations—of course, each with alleged Jewish connections—Dilling defends Father Coughlin, claiming he was revealing "facts" about "atheistic radical Jews" to stave off a flood of Jewish refugees, whom she refers to as "Refujews."[86] She accuses well-known figures like the Rockefellers of inviting "Red 'refujews' and propa[ga]ndists, unwanted in Europe, over to the USA."[87] The organizations that dare to tout themselves as "'Peace' Organizations" actually promote "radical negro and white inter-racial affairs."[88] In this brief passage, we see the peace script in full force: to advocate a lasting "peace" means to oppose Jewish organizations, however ill-defined and unsubstantiated. To be a peace advocate means enforcing an exclusionary Christianity opposed to diversity. Anti-Semitism here operates as a foil to proper Christianity and racial homogeneity. Adorned with the language of patriotism and national memory, the Mothers' Movement's anti-Semitism serves as a master frame, redirecting readers back to the same enemies. Other versions of "peace," as voiced by their opponents, are guises for anti-Christian and anti-American beliefs. "Peace," presented in this script as a pre-political feeling born from the private world of Christian motherhood, is the only hope, even as it ironically amplifies a violent vision of gender, race, and religion.

Conclusion

From Reddit message boards to the 2017 "Unite the Right" rally in Charlottesville, Virginia, to the spouting of anti-Semitic conspiracy theories by celebrities, anti-Semitism has not gone away.[89] Instead, it seems as if the tendrils of hate toward the Jewish faith still grow out of the soil of national culture, giving life to a host of beliefs that, on their face, may seem irrelevant to racial and religious discrimination. We must ask how such bigotry takes root, but also why its adherents so strongly believe parroting such dehumanizing rhetoric is a path toward a peace. This reckoning with US peace does not require a nihilistic dismissal of anti-war activism but rather calls for an accountability for all its variations, democratic and otherwise. Studying the Mothers' Movement peace script can help us see the protean nature of anti-Semitism—its ability to shift and mold into other ideologies, which makes it all the more volatile and frightening.

For the Mothers' Movement, World War II was an opportunity to rearticulate cultural values regarding gender, race, religion, and national memory. Their peace script was built to last because of this adaptability, and Dilling indeed found new controversies to galvanize her moral crusade after the war. In her August 1946 newsletter, she included a telling note on war and peace titled, sensationally, "Satan, Prince of This World." What followed was a brief excerpt from a correspondent named Von Wiegand. Speaking of foreign affairs, the report laments that "the biggest powers—America and Britain—cannot agree even how to make peaceful and govern one little spot in that world."[90] The nature of postwar peace was certainly in dispute worldwide. Nation to nation and community to community, definitions of peace were mobilized, each group trying to reconcile the sobering number of causalities. Many citizens anxiously sought to preserve national civilization, however defined, against further disorder and destruction. While the war crisis was now past, Dilling's movement was ever vigilant in looking for "moral degradation" wherein the "pretense" of "civilized nations" masquerades as modern while "reced[ing] into the Dark Ages."[91] The war had transformed the world, yet Dilling's peace remained fixed on its opposition to any entity, particularly those bureaucratic and global, such as the United Nations, that aligned with any conceivable anti-Christian or pro-Jewish agenda. The struggle for peace was again reduced to a dogged fight for a narrow version of Christian civilization. This was not, however, a culture without its adherents, old and new alike.

For some US citizens, the international order fell into a dichotomy that Mothers' Movement members would recognize. Certainly, a nation that dropped the atomic bomb needed a solid narrative with a clear enemy to defend its moral standing. Among the new evils threatening US culture, Communism would take center stage as an easy foil to Western liberal democracy, capitalism, and, once again, Christianity. Domestically, anti-Communist sentiment helped bolster appeals to "mainstream Americana" wherein rituals of patriotism, celebrations of traditional gender roles, and opposition to non-Christian thought—however defined—were common. The "Baby Boom" generation came of age by generating diverse responses, both positive and negative, to these topics and, in the process, creating new definitions of civic duty, private life, and freedom of expression.

One influential current running through these new debates, with parallels to the Mothers' Movement and its peace script, was the ideology of the "New Right." A broad umbrella encompassing an array of political beliefs, the New Right emerged from deeply conservative organizations, such as the John Birch Society. Many of these groups positioned themselves as the preservers of peace in a frightening postwar world still threatened by uncivilized forces. Peace, yet again, proved fertile ground for nurturing conspiracies and acts of exclusion. In their most extreme expressions, these organizations sought to impose a viciously segregated version of US life supposedly aligned with Christianity. Later, as the "Religious Right" ascended and US warfare proliferated in non-Christian places across the world, questions related to American exceptionalism and American peace would only rise in frequency. We ought to read the Mothers' Movement's script as a rough draft, or a dress rehearsal, for one strand of Cold War rhetoric that still imposes a dark limit to national peace.

5

Rewriting the National Script

Vietnam Veterans against the War

On January 31, 1971, hundreds of Vietnam War veterans crammed into a conference hotel in Detroit. For the next three days, they sat in front of cameras to recount their experiences overseas, speaking of shocking violence perpetrated by themselves and others. The emotional event, known as the Winter Soldier Investigation, was sponsored by the Vietnam Veterans against the War (VVAW), one of the most significant anti-war movements in US history. Months prior, the VVAW grabbed national headlines with a protest "march" to Valley Forge dubbed "Operation RAW" (Rapid American Withdrawal).[1] Hoping to build on this momentum, the group reconvened in the "heartland" of the country to film and then hastily edit their testimony into the anti-war documentary *Winter Soldier*.[2]

Despite limited release and initially scarce media coverage, the documentary event is a crystallization of the movement's identity and their critique of the war—nothing less than a live performance of their peace script. *Winter Soldier* added pressure on legislators to call for renewed action on Vietnam policy, setting the stage for the much-publicized protests in DC two months later.[3] While determining influence is difficult, the documentary coincided with a period of increased VVAW membership, which climbed to nearly ten thousand official members.[4] The documentary screened at film festivals in the United States and Europe, as well as during recruitment events for the organization, until it eventually received a widespread re-release in 2005 that cemented *Winter Soldier* within the public memory of Vietnam protest.[5] The film can be challenging to watch because soldiers reflect on gruesome incidents, yet the activists—some the very perpetrators of these acts—push themselves to face them head on. It is hard to imagine a more direct inquiry into war's violence than one initiated by those at its core, whom the nation adorns with the regalia of military honor. For this reason, the documentary is representative of the VVAW's peace script: a challenging, visceral confrontation with violence that interrogates the individual's role in military conduct. Without giving easy answers, the peace script creates a space for a broader cultural critique. It invites a type of "commonplace witnessing" primed to see the warfare state's contradictions that perpetuate wars.[6]

Figure 5. "An advertisement for Vietnam Veterans against the War in *Playboy* magazine, February 1971." Vietnam Veterans against the War, Washington-Alaska Regional Office Records, Accession no. 5596-001, box 1/1 (University of Washington).

Unlike the "negative" peace movements already discussed in this book, the VVAW offers no clear scapegoat or spectacular diversion. In fact, their peace script rarely isolates a community outside their own, that of the citizen-soldier, upon which to shift the blame. They are thus left with the unbearable realization that they are complicit in the violence they oppose. Therefore, the given path to a "positive" peace is one that questions all that holds them up, everything that gives them a platform. While they do not offer a straightforward program of action, they embody a habit of self-critique required for sustainable peace work, taking stock of the "conceptual cartography" that animates their worldview and compels the United States toward war.[7] The VVAW use intense visuals to achieve this effect and push their script into new stylistic realms. As figure 5 illustrates, no image was more recognizable in discussions of a war's cost than that of the fallen soldier. The returning veteran, however, had special authority to speak to these deaths, question them, and even stare at the image of an American flag draped over a casket and wonder what it meant. Theirs was an exhausted, haunted hope for peace emerging from the depths of the human-made catastrophe they were complicit in. Much of the Vietnam debate in the United States could be described as a struggle to *see* the Vietnam conflict—to discern its lines, boundaries, and edges. *Winter Soldier* represents one such attempt to define, so as to indict, the popular image of the Vietnam War made by those who could not remove themselves from the picture frame.[8]

The VVAW's peace script was defined by its authors, who played dual roles in the conflict: soldiers and agitators, patriots and protesters, criminals and compatriots. Like most VVAW protests, *Winter Soldier* uses these conflicting roles to expose the contradictions within foreign policy, the warfare state, and US patriotism. As veterans, its participants could juxtapose their individual agency with the dehumanizing structure of war. Presenting themselves with the decorations of the citizen-soldier, they could best expose the tensions between liberalist assumptions of individual agency and guilt on one hand and collectivist notions of sacrifice and conformity on the other.[9] They thereby push away the question of culpability—"who is responsible for the war?"—from the individual and toward a larger structural question about war and its place in the national imagination. The VVAW peace script, for all its imperfections, marks a deconstruction of the nation's dominant narratives about its military and use of justified force. As a model for peace-building, theirs embodies the kind of self-reflexivity and attention to persuasion essential to building a lasting, "positive" peace despite evident flaws.[10] As peace scholar David Barash argues, "the movement toward positive peace is not an all-or-nothing phenomenon . . . [it] is likely to be halting and fragmentary, with substantial success along certain dimensions and likely failures along others."[11] The VVAW's script is imperfect; it reflects racial, gendered, and class-based inequalities; it is, on its face, indebted to violence. Yet, more than the other scripts considered here, it leaves the door open for self-critique and challenging the cultural blind spots that arise in peace discourse. If anything, the VVAW activists were willing to scapegoat and dehumanize themselves to foster a more equitable world for all.[12]

In this chapter, I first give an overview of the Vietnam War's visual dynamics. Analyzing visual protest rhetoric, such as *Winter Soldier*, is a chance to engage the cultural narratives that precariously upheld the nation's faith in the war and, eventually, crumbled under the lack of a coherent, visible purpose. Next, I analyze how the VVAW documentary interacts with these narratives to construct its peace script. In particular, VVAW activists use traditional tropes related to soldierly virtue and "martial manhood" to embed their anti-war argument within the logic of warfare. Unlike many anti-war movements at the time, which opposed war from outside the institution, VVAW could not maintain such distance. Using this proximity to their advantage, its members inserted their protest into the optics of soldierly valor, daring the audience and the public at large to reconcile their atrocities with the norms of military reverence. I then consider how the documentary uses color and movement to further frustrate hasty attributions of guilt. Finally, I analyze how the documentary deals with broader tensions regarding race and gender common to the New Left. *Winter Soldier*, as a representation of the VVAW peace script, is a difficult portrait of military culture and nonviolent rhetoric, refusing to dispense blame while confessing to unimaginable violence. It leaves the nature of peace and violence in an uncomfortable yet unavoidable liminal space that opens the door for new scripts of dissent that may, one day, avoid the myths of peace. The VVAW script is not a perfect model of democratic speech, yet its dogged focus on the relationship between the citizen and the war machine models the thinking required for a democracy to survive.

Portraits of War and Witnessing Violence

During the 1950s, 1960s, and 1970s, US activists faced diverse obstacles, ranging from indirect societal pressure to direct government surveillance and repression, all of which impacted the democratic quality of protest. Legal historian Geoffrey R. Stone claims "the Cold War marked perhaps the most repressive period in American history . . . [when] the government initiated abusive loyalty programs, legislative investigation, and criminal prosecutions."[13] The government especially targeted anti-war protest during what has been called an "assault on the Left."[14] Given that the average citizen had so many reasons *not* to protest, it seems all the more remarkable that one of the most vocal organizations against the Vietnam War was veteran-led. To better understand the VVAW peace script, we must consider what sets it apart from those previously examined. Why is it that during this "state of emergency," when undemocratic policies stifled dissent, a group of activists could withstand the heat and proclaim a democratic vision of the future? I believe it is partly because the war pushed these veterans too far, making them do wicked acts in the name of democracy for years, as the death count rose and war crimes circulated in the news. As a result, the myths of peace could not hold. The veil of peace-through-war could longer obscure the reality of the conflict and carnage. Thus, we see a degree of self-reflexivity uncommon to the previous scripts.

The VVAW's rhetoric revolves around an act of witnessing demanded of the citizen and soldier alike. Obviously, the *Winter Soldier* campaign and documentary involved literal testimony. The task was not, however, to simply testify to the horrendous acts each veteran saw or did themselves but to discover a language and style suitable for representing it.[15] Words alone were insufficient because they were too quickly subsumed by a prefabricated discourse. Instead, the VVAW members made both visual and verbal use of their dual roles as soldiers and citizens to offer a subversive image of injustice made with the materials of their collective identity. *Winter Soldier*, accordingly, employs the veterans' visual culture and brings forth inherent tensions through their witnessing: these men are both the doves of peace and the hawks of war; concerned citizens and dedicated soldiers; as fit to indict injustice as to receive punishment for the crime. The VVAW thereby lays bare the rhetorical body and soul of US warfare and its rival demands upon the individual and the group. The result is more a chilling political aesthetic than a concrete policy. Yet, it presents an aesthetic inseparable from the tapestry of US nationalism and public memory, now torn between the reverent appraisal of the citizen-soldier and a discomfiting recognition of the character's deeply flawed, even criminal, nature.

What was the "visual culture" the VVAW made creative use of?[16] Scholars of the Vietnam War underscore the heavily mediated and graphic nature of the conflict, some dubbing it the "first televised war."[17] However, in attempts to understand the visual dimension of the war, scholars have observed a disconnect between actual images of the war and those that anchor it in public memory. For instance, Chester J. Pach Jr. points out that despite the common association of the Vietnam War with brutal images of violence, such as the My Lai massacre, there were very few images released to the public that displayed overt violence.[18] Similarly, Jeremy Lembcke notes that the now infamous image of activists spitting on returning soldiers is equally tenuous once we look for concrete proof of its subject's occurrence.[19] Still, these popular conceptions of the war, illustrate the "visual culture" of the conflict in the United States: how people imagined Vietnam and its relation to national identity. The lasting memory of these disturbing images alongside continued warfare reveals a public still struggling to assign meaning to military excess. Perhaps it is easier to explain away intolerable acts by isolating specific events and attributing guilt to individuals rather than interrogating the historical and structural conditions of the violence itself. In short, the visual culture of Vietnam in US thought reveals an inability to fully *see* the warfare state. At the core of this myopia—present in contemporary debates over war—is a negotiation with liberal-democratic assumptions that privilege timeless, atomistic, individual agency, whether through the citizen or soldier. A bedrock of Enlightenment thought, such focus on the individual can obscure a fuller understanding of war in the United States.[20]

My analysis of *Winter Soldier* seeks to reveal how VVAW activists fought against the atomizing tendency to blame an individual or scapegoat a foreign Other. Instead, they link together dimensions of the Vietnam War and the home front by which to expose the gaps between national culture and military violence; between the individual sacrifice of the soldier and the collective investment in warfare; between the moral call of duty and the societal desire to assign blame. To best describe this, I consider how visual contexts beyond the immediate surface of the documentary, particularly the ideal of the "citizen-soldier," inform the documentary to create an encounter with the paradoxes of warfare, unlike previous peace scripts.[21] The role of the citizen-soldier has long played a key role in US society, evident since the lore of the Revolutionary War. *Winter Soldier* activates its mythic status while shedding light on its most insidious consequences, including its blinders to race, gender, and class.[22]

Attending to the visual dynamics of *Winter Soldier* also contributes to conversations at the intersection of visual rhetoric and dissent. In her history of documentary filmmaking, Betsy A. McClane singles out the Vietnam conflict, stating, "The monumental event affecting the United States' society from the mid-sixties to mid-seventies, and the rallying point for much of the social unrest, was the American War in Vietnam. Documentary filmmakers were very much a part of articulating opinion about the war, particularly for those who opposed it."[23] Bonnie J. Dow similarly stresses the role documentaries play in social movement dynamics, describing their ability to "stabilize [a movement's] meaning" through patterned "rhetorical moves."[24] *Winter Soldier* is a chance to consider the visuality of war and democratic dissent through documentary techniques. The use of color, space, and absence, for instance, work together to expose the gaps and paradoxes of the Vietnam War, redirecting the viewer's attention toward the structural context of Vietnam rather than fixating upon individual soldiers or single acts of brutality. At various moments, the viewer is pushed beyond the documentary's frame through the use of absence—literally through the display of images seemingly unrelated to the action being narrated. At the same time, it pulls a type of identity, usually a version of white masculinity, closer to the screen and thus reproduces a familiar "regime" of sensation that would come to mark schisms within the New Left movement.[25]

These visual aspects of protest are often the most obvious, demanding our attention through ostentatious displays, yet they are also the easiest to dismiss or underestimate. Perhaps this explains why *Winter Soldier* and the VVAW are studied far less than other protest texts and movements of the period. Still, whether through marching on Valley Forge or donning uniforms and medals only to hurl them to the ground, these activists took full advantage of the soldier's symbolism, implanting themselves firmly within the visual tradition of the veteran to radically subvert it. While the documentary, like the movement itself, did not escape problematic tropes of war, violence, and white masculinity, I argue that it ultimately succeeds in revealing many of the contradictions intrinsic to American warfare and democracy. Viewing the fight for peace through the veteran's lens creates a dizzying, kaleidoscopic perspective that bends notions of agency, national identity, and valor into new contexts. While an imperfect peace script, the VVAW's rhetoric is the first detailed in this book to take stock of its own imperfections and place its tarnished symbols at the heart of the war debate. I believe this level of reflexivity and self-critique is necessary for any peace-building project.

The VVAW Peace Script

Rewriting Soldierly Tropes

Winter Soldier (WS) writes its version of peace by invoking the symbolic world of the veteran. By embracing the tropes of "martial manhood," VVAW activists accomplish three rhetorical tasks.[26] First, the visual allusions to military culture—embracing emblems of bravery, loyalty, and violence—create a recognizable scene for those watching a documentary centered on veterans. Instead of eschewing these elements and alienating viewers, WS invites and occasionally celebrates martial manhood. However, these visual references to the soldierly ideal also help reveal the ambiguity of the Vietnam War, asking the viewer, "Who, or what, is responsible for the conflict and the repugnant violence taking place in Vietnam?" WS's use of familiar soldierly virtues also helps evade quick accusations that only individual soldiers were cowardly or that the current cohort of soldiers lacked the valor or grit of the honorable World War II generation preceding them. Thus, the documentary defers the question of culpability for war crimes, pushing away from the shocking images to provoke the viewers to investigate what lies beyond the screen. Finally, WS's activation of soldierly tropes allows the movement to exploit the metonymy and synecdoche of the soldier as either an individual representative of the more extensive war system or as a simple cog in the war machine.[27] The veterans' identity is clearly constituted by their role in the military system. By embedding themselves within the structure of warfare, VVAW activists use individual testimonies as entries into larger structural questions.

Unlike many peace movements, the VVAW directly integrates the language of warfare. For instance, John Kerry's famous speech before Congress, which the documentary includes, stresses how the activists are protesting out of a sense of soldierly duty: he says that we must "undertake one last mission—to search out and destroy the last vestige of this barbaric war, to pacify our own hearts, to conquer the hate and fear that have driven this country these last ten years and more."[28] Kerry's speech finds its rhythm and moral resonance through the rhetoric of combat and martial duty, connecting it, counterintuitively, to the VVAW's anti-war cause. As referenced in the speech, the movement adopted "Winter Soldier" as a subsidiary name for the organization to invoke Thomas Paine's call for *true* patriotism. Kerry describes how "the term Winter Soldier is a play on words of Thomas Paine's in 1776 when he spoke of the Sunshine Patriots and summertime soldiers who deserted at Valley Forge because the going was rough. We who have come here to Washington have come here because we feel we have to be winter soldiers now."[29] In the documentary of the same name, the veteran-activists continually embrace the iconography and language of patriotic duty essential to the citizen-soldier. They thereby challenge the audience to reconcile their dissent, their war crimes, and their anger with traditional notions of military honor as voiced by a Founding Father.

The documentary begins with a reference to soldierly honor, framing the entire movement as deeply concerned with patriotic values and national security.[30] The opening shot of a black-and-white title card is narrated by an assertive female voice quoting Thomas Paine.[31] The stark image, along with the narrator's voice filled with gravitas, visually and sonically alludes to older short films made by the US government to inform the public about previous wars. The VVAW style reaches further back past these state-sponsored documentaries in their repeated reference to Paine's *Common Sense*: their scripting of peace emerges out of a long line of revolutionary soldiers. This introduction thereby situates the movement as iconoclastic but not in the sense typical of the 1960s and 1970s countercultures. Instead, the veterans' rebellion is part of the tradition of patriots who predate the nation's birth. This move suggests to the viewer that what they are about to see is not a deviation or rejection of the conventions of valor and self-sacrifice but rather a documentation of its current form. "Winter Soldier," now in the words of both Thomas Paine and John Kerry, represents a fuller realization of sacrifice and obligation from those most dedicated to the nation and who persist when everything seems hopeless—when the cause has been so distorted as to disfigure the veteran. This acknowledgment is more fundamental than any policy or sustained argument and crucial to their "positive" peace script. They are willing to make themselves a scapegoat, to interrogate their investments in a "negative" peace, all in the hopes of creating a better future for all.

The next scene brings the viewer to the origin of the citizen-soldier identity as two activists restage their military registration. Both men have long hair and wear civilian clothes, which creates a productive incongruity. No longer looking like a stereotypical soldier, they nevertheless have more military experience than most Americans and force the viewer to reconcile the two roles of veteran and hippie. Sitting at a table, a veteran follows the standard script, asking one of the "recruits" standing nervously before him for his biographical information. In the hands of another peace movement, this scene could have been a chance to subvert and critique the notion of the "soldier" at its birth. For the VVAW, the opening scene forefronts empathy toward the enlisted and those who now dissent. The familiar scene, now made strange, commands the viewer to imagine, along with the activists, what it would feel like to sign up to serve one's country. Together, they put themselves up for sacrifice, foregoing their individuality to become part of the military system. From this space of respectability, the next moment is especially jarring. One soldier lists off war atrocities while the other confirms, with a wry, confident smile, that he has also witnessed such acts—for instance, prisoners of war thrown out of an airplane—and laughs as if acknowledging a common joke in his battalion when he says that the men who did it were from "Philly."[32] Unlike other anti-war movements, these activists cannot summarily critique or gloss over the violence of the Vietnam War. The VVAW's members must testify to the violence because they were there and, in some cases, committed these acts. To see their perspective, one must dare to follow the script of the citizen-soldier, of the brave and brash veteran who commands deadly force for the sake of their country. In playing that role, in this case, one is forced to feel both hero and villain as inseparable.

The opening minutes of *Winter Soldier* continue to display norms of "martial manhood" rather than reject them, composing the VVAW peace script with the symbols of war. For instance, when the man at the registration table asks the other veteran for his highest rank, his response of "Marine Captain" receives a war cry of "Woo!"[33] It is significant that the first mention of a war crime is surrounded by enthusiastic performances of soldierly behavior recognizable to many citizens. The documentary thereby ties the topic of war crimes to a scene of GI camaraderie where the men brag about their rank and compare acts of valor. It connects the worst of America to its best with no easy response from the pro-war or anti-war side. By capturing a discussion of war crimes through the language of martial manhood, WS gives the viewer little room to respond with outright condemnation of the soldiers for lacking courage, manliness, or patriotism. Exuding an aura of honor and duty, these opening sequences force those hoping to answer questions regarding the Vietnam War to go beyond the traditional framework of individual blame.

The next scene builds upon this theme to solidify a peace script defined by a tension between individual agency and collective duty. Like the previous scene, we see one veteran registering another for "service" in the panel, asking for name, rank, and tour of duty. The scene includes other men greeting each other: almost all white, bearded, and wearing fatigues. To some, they might look like hippies, yet their gruff manner and embrace of the military uniform signifies an enduring reverence for "martial manhood." This image tells the viewer that there has not been a cultural overhaul in the military: these men are not cowards who shirked their duties and ran from the call of duty. Later in the scene, one man boasts about how his regiment aggressively sought to "set an example that we weren't fucking around."[34] This type of interaction sets the stage for the testimonies to come: brusque, caustic, and often profane discussions of warfare. The descriptions of war atrocities, delivered in an often-stoic way, place these veterans within the sonic and visual culture of soldierly virtue, challenging its coherence from within. The VVAW peace script gains its drama from precisely this tension between the recognition of the honorable veteran and the moral recoil at their accounts of abhorrent acts of violence. The path toward peace is made possible only through an interrogation of the system that brought these men to this point and allowed their peace script its unique protagonist.

The testimonies proceed with witnesses speaking in the language of the soldier while indicting it. VVAW activist Nathan Hale, for instance, describes scenes of torture in a mostly emotionless way, as if delivering a daily report or memo.[35] At the forty-three minute mark, another veteran lists off insults, ranging from "sweet pea" to "pussy," that superior officers would call soldiers. Notably, the documentary shows him laughing as if in agreement with the gendered insults, as if he still inhabits or is shaped by the military culture that produced him.[36] WS shows other soldiers reminiscing over the "competition between squads" during the war, while others stoically describe their regiments' "body counts."[37] By activating the visual and verbal tropes of "martial manhood," each instance creates a push-and-pull effect that leaves the viewer unable to satisfy their desire to assign blame. The scenes pull in viewers accustomed to patriotic veterans, only to shock them with their confessions. *Winter Soldier* forecloses the argument that the war's atrocities are the result of a lack of bravery, a loss of manliness (whatever that might mean), or the fault of a select few soldiers who deviated from military norms. The violence is part and parcel of the military system; it animates the discursive terrain of soldierly valor and gives the VVAW's peace script its legibility. Those who profess patriotism use the script to interrogate, even deconstruct, their own identity, a rhetorical act required for a lasting, positive peace.

Winter Soldier constantly plays with the soldier's symbolism to force viewers to interrogate their beliefs about war and patriotic duty.[38] Most anti-war activists simply could not tap into the complexities of this dynamic like the VVAW. But what makes the citizen-soldier role so revered? In warfare, the individual citizen can become part of something greater through the role of the soldier. Insofar as they commit to that symbolic role, they are promised assimilation into what society holds in highest regard. The soldier, thereby, represents the gold standard of citizenship—a manifestation of all that is right about Americans, the embodiment of proper thought and action. Yet, the soldier is at odds with the idealization of individualism found in much US discourse because, although society often lauds specific soldiers and their sacrifice, each specific soldier forgoes their individuality and agency for the greater good. This valorization of conformity at the heart of the citizen-soldier is a clear deviation from, if not outright contradiction to, the otherwise liberalist, individualistic narratives of US citizenship and capitalism. In the case of *Winter Soldier*, the citizen-soldier's ability to be both the ideal individual as well as the representative of the larger war system—that is, their metonymic function—challenges viewers to interpret the structure and meaning of warfare itself.

The overriding question posed by the VVAW peace script is, if "martial manhood" is the framework by which we see and praise individual soldiers, then what framework do we reference when a soldier does something clearly immoral but nevertheless in line with the veteran role? *Winter Soldier* forces this question upon the viewer, making them look at the structure and limits of their own beliefs. For instance, when a soldier describes horrific scenes from war, such as the decimation of entire villages, the murder of women and children, and rape, these are presented not as the acts of a deviant or renegade soldier but as extensions of the war system.[39] Through their adherence to the role of "citizen-soldier," the soldiers are displayed as loyal servants to the war system, which now seems horrific. They bear witness to their individual sacrifices, asking the camera, "What sense is there to the system that demanded the loss of our humanity?" Peace is not simply an imperative in their script, as it is for many others. Peace is not merely a conclusion one arrives at through a chain of reasoning. Peace for the VVAW requires a visceral apprehension of one's intolerable, yet socially sanctioned, role in perpetuating violence.

The VVAW's rhetoric thereby acts as a model for peace-building because it obstructs facile attempts to depersonalize or dismiss acts of violence without regard to the larger system. In WS, you are part of the corrupt game if you recognize its players. It is the system of war that bestows meaning upon these individuals, and the veterans, by playing the masculine and gruff soldier, make the revered military system daringly speak to the prospects of peace in the face of their atrocities. While the gears of war are difficult to capture, as evidenced by the peace movements throughout this book, WS gets closest to the military system by eliminating other avenues of interpretation. It proclaims, "We are all the citizen-soldier, for better or worse, and we reject the violence we committed in the name of an honor we still believe is possible." In a broader view, the narratives of the Cold War—whether "the Domino Effect" or "American exceptionalism"—could only survive if the individual characters of the story appeared to fit together and act in a recognizable way. Vietnam marked a moment when the eyes could no longer convince the mind. *Winter Soldier* is a visual instantiation of this symbolic tension, bringing war rhetoric to bear upon peace in a subversive way.

Testimony beyond Black-and-White

The VVAW's peace script, expressed through the visual style of *Winter Soldier*, frustrates any desire for the purity of war. By relying on black-and-white footage, the documentary draws out—and then implodes—the moral spectrum of warfare and military violence. The color scheme gives the appearance of a straightforward, binary moral order. The scenes compel us to believe there is no gray area in these horrific retellings. Such black-and-white imagery can operate as a visual metaphor for the battle over "good" and "evil," or "right" and "wrong." When these testimonies deviate from the expected norms of soldierly valor—typically in the form of war crimes—the documentary makes jolting cuts to vibrant colored photographs of the Vietnam War, throttling the viewer with an overwhelming sense of disconnect. This jarring shift from colorless to oversaturated color visually separates the individual soldier's world from the larger world of warfare.

Winter Soldier repeatedly uses color in a similar manner: to foreground a cut-and-dry scene for the testimonies that present matter-of-fact narratives. At the moment of intolerability, the documentary throws the viewer into the kaleidoscopic world of the Vietnam War. The realm of absolute violence that other peace scripts either avoid or condemn from afar is here displayed as a crushing, visceral field of action that implicates the viewer. The question of culpability—the heart of the "Vietnam Question" posed by this documentary—is asked and then interlaced with shocking images of war. *Winter Soldier* thus forces the audience to bear witness alongside the veterans as they collectively search for the meaning of war, a pursuit cut off from simple cut-and-dried, black-and-white explanations of individual guilt and now pushed toward the chaotic reality of armed conflict.

Consider the third scene of the documentary. Here black-and-white depictions of veteran testimony are visually pierced by colored photographs of the Vietnam War for the first time. One veteran describes how "people were in the village; they wanted time to get their goods out and shit, but we just burned down the village."[40] The camera zooms in on the veteran's face, underscoring his individuality and encasing his matter-of-fact comments in a black-and-white frame before a colored photograph of a Vietnamese village ruptures the screen. WS presents this picture as an archival fragment from the field of battle that haunts the soldier's testimony and, by proxy, haunts the broader culture that makes the soldier recognizable in US society. As the veteran's narration continues over the colored photograph, the documentary hits viewers with a jolting image that only partially shows what the veteran is describing—there is no perfect empirical artifact to explain away the trauma and violence of war. This jarring visual shift from black-and-white to color, and to an image that imperfectly represents what the veteran says, redirects the viewer's attention from the individuality of the soldier to the larger context of war. The veteran safely remains in the simple black-and-white frame where he dutifully testifies to what he saw and did. The rapid cut to the color image dramatically pushes the viewer away from identification with the individual soldier and forcefully throws them into the shocking world of the Vietnam War with no clear faces or individual actors to absorb our gaze and no perfect image to subsume or explain the narration. The use of the familiar to show the strange—to express peace through war—is the rhetorical essence of the VVAW script.

The documentary uses such juxtaposition and dissonance to induces the viewer to search for missing information within the color photographs by showing a disconnect between what is testified, usually specific actions by specific people, and the presentation of a static, indecipherable image. We can understand this rhetorical phenomenon through theorist Ariella Azoulay's concept of visuality. *Winter Soldier* demands an ethical engagement with the viewer in a way that parallels what Azoulay calls the "civil contract": an imperative to interpret the color images sprung before the viewer as relief from the individual veteran's unbearable testimony of war crimes. Like the soldiers left with traumatic memories to process, the viewer is hit with incomplete images and archival fragments of the war and its actors, left to reconcile the traces of meaning with their preexisting beliefs.[41] *Winter Soldier*'s visual logic leaves no clear sense of who the victims or perpetrators are in the Vietnam War. Simple black-and-white distinctions, standard attributions of guilt, or any common knee-jerk reaction to horrible violence perpetrated by individuals are all challenged by the images of the dutiful soldier describing the horrors of war as stark images of Vietnam cut across the scene, carrying the viewer deep into the fog of war.

Winter Soldier also expresses its disorienting rhetoric through close-ups. One of the most intimate moments of the documentary uses all the rhetorical tools mentioned thus far to undermine individual culpability. The documentary captures VVAW member Scott Kamil in a black-and-white close-up as he describes an innocent woman killed by a US sniper. Kamil never makes eye contact with the camera and instead looks off into the distance. This lingering, ruminative shot of Kamil's face is then punctured by a jarring color photograph that only loosely relates to what he describes.[42] Kamil's face then returns to the screen and recounts more acts of violence and brutality, such as knocking out teeth. As the camera inches closer and closer to his face, the shot transforms into an intense "confessional" scene, with Kamil's face dominating the screen. At this moment, he recounts his personal journey in one of the few instances of biographical narrative given during the documentary.[43] Consider the visual journey thus far: from the up close, personal, black-and-white testimony to a color photograph of chaotic war and then back to an even closer, intimate shot of Kamil's face. This movement, one representative of the VVAW's peace rhetoric, forces the viewer to reconcile the dutiful soldier with the immoral events of the Vietnam War. The war becomes the unbearable structure upon which all else depends for meaning—the script points toward a "positive" peace achieved through the serious interrogation of the nature of violence.

The VVAW frequently used such imagery to interrogate the tension between the individual and collective, between the "I" and the "we," the soldier and the nation. Kamil's narration is the most personal moment of the entire documentary. It is noteworthy, therefore, that the scene recounts his journey from a state of individualism to a state of conformity, once again complicating the attribution of blame through any traditional liberalist framework. He describes how he was a troublemaker as a kid, sadly recounting his experience as a high school outcast who turned to drugs until he simply "had to go into [military] service."[44] Kamil then cites one of the more common reasons to join the war: to "see what kind of person I really was." As the viewer follows Kamil's relatable story, the camera hangs on him in an unrelenting close-up. Like other testimonies, this intimate narration highlights the veteran's individuality, only to be disrupted by the war and the violence it demands.

The documentary repeatedly interrupts these personal, close-up testimonies with interspersed shots of chaotic military action to question the ties between individual behavior and the system that reinforces it. War, as witnessed by those who conduct it, is undignified in its demand for absolute conformity and lethal action. *Winter Soldier* gives this common observation a unique visual style uncommon in US anti-war protest. For instance, in the black-and-white frame of Kamil's personal story, he repeatedly describes degrading training at boot camp that was an attack on his individuality.[45] As he describes his loss of personal agency, his clean face is juxtaposed with dirty, sweaty faces of anonymous soldiers in full color. At this moment, the black-and-white individuality of Kamil is subsumed by the military system that demands, as Kamil describes, that you either "piss your pants or get your ass kicked."[46] Any agency attributed to the veteran in the documentary is now transferred to the larger military system, which can only be approached in fits and starts, in intermittent and always incomplete encounters with its shocking traces and fragments, as reflected in the saturated photographs.

For every recognizable element of the VVAW—their fatigues, their slang, their masculinity—there is some element of the awful or strange to trigger a reexamination of the war's broader context by the viewer. For every black-and-white, clear-cut representation of military culture, there is a splintering slice of colorful, jarring images of the Vietnam War. A fissure of national identity is thus made manifest and given visual form through the soldiers' testimony. Consider another soldier's narration of a horrific story—the stabbing of an innocent Vietnamese—which includes a jolting image of an anonymous soldier pointing a gun at what looks to be a prisoner of war. Over this image, the veteran warns, "Don't ever let your government do this to you." Then, instead of showing the individual soldier testifying in black-and-white, the documentary shows a colorful shot of the soldier in Vietnam smiling.[47] The VVAW peace script, through these techniques of color, proximity, and juxtaposition, refuses to let the violence of war settle in either the realm of the individual soldier or the system of warfare. The path to peace requires a constant negotiation between the two, making the viewer question the relationship between discrete acts of violence and national culture.

These startling shifts of color and movement reflect the documentary's tireless tacking back and forth between the individual and the collective, connecting war's violence to both. The VVAW performs their peace script through these shifts: from black-and-white to color, from movement to static shots, and from close-ups of discrete people to the chaotic structure of war. These moves subvert traditional logics of blame by suggesting the individual soldier is partly a victim—*not* someone who asserted their full agency but someone who followed orders—while also admitting war crimes. Whatever feelings a viewer has toward the military, veterans, war, and peace, the documentary challenges them. The inexplicability of the Vietnam War, if anything, is presented as the source of atrocities while also directly implicating national identity and pride. Most viewers who apprehend this peace script feel the call to interrogate their complicity in this violence, if they recognize its characters.

Seeing the Symbols of White Masculinity

If there is one lesson to learn thus far, it is that few visions of peace can completely avoid violence. Peace-building projects, therefore, must be self-reflexive and consider all the ways citizens perpetuate violent systems, ideas, and values. A rhetorical analysis of peace scripts can sensitize us to how well-meaning people may, nevertheless, tie their peace to exclusionary systems. The VVAW members attempt such a reflection on their relationship to violence—the way in which they are its literal agents—more than the movements previously considered. However, I have not yet discussed the degree to which the documentary addresses two areas of violence and division: racialized and gendered violence. At first glance, the language of the citizen-soldier and "martial manhood" resembles some of what we might today label "toxic masculinity."[48] Such concepts can help peel away the intersection of white, male heterosexuality that, in the US context, has long been a site of privilege. The presumed "natural" US citizen, who requires the least qualification or defense when appearing in public life, is typically a straight, white, heterosexual man. Attributes such as aggression, violence, lack of empathy, ruthless competition, and abrasiveness, seen periodically in the VVAW and *Winter Soldier*, all work together to create a social role similar to the "toxic masculine" type.

The military is one institution among many that has historically fortified this gender role. Here, duty-bound young men learn lethal skills and are encouraged, through acts of bravery and violence, to become the archetypal "man." As mentioned previously, *Winter Soldier* plays up these tropes to garner a degree of familiarity and rhetorical force with the viewer. While I believe the testimony, which features men crying and offering emotional support to each other, contributes somewhat to subverting the violent norms of masculinity, the movement and much of the documentary are racially homogenous. However, one scene in the documentary challenges this racial identity, adding depth to the film and demonstrating the difficult conversations required for a "positive" peace.

About one hour into the documentary, a Black veteran accuses a group of white VVAW members of not seeing the racial dimensions of the Vietnam War. The white veterans uncomfortably circle him as they become defensive. In response to the accusation—"It's racism. It's racist."—a white veteran aggressively responds, "What the hell do you think I'm fucking here for?" to which the Black veteran counters, the "reason we go into [the] army is a different reason. Being Black is a deep thing." He tells him that Black veterans have fewer opportunities than white soldiers. The VVAW "forgot about racism . . . that's why you ain't got no Black people behind you."[49] This scene does not absolve or rectify the racial blind spot of the movement, but it does help expose it. Just as the veteran testimonies uncomfortably hang in the air, this encounter is left for the viewer to experience and reconcile.

This exchange does important rhetorical work for the VVAW peace script, adding a wrinkle to its complex presentation of the war issue. First, the interaction commands significant critical force because of the exact moment it occurs in the documentary. Happening near the middle point, it comes after *Winter Soldier* had already established that the veterans are dutiful and brave, if frustrated, exemplars of the citizen-soldier ideal. Thus, their tense exchange with the Black veteran indicts not only the veteran-activists but the citizen-soldier ideal they represent. The long-standing inability to see the racialized aspects of these social roles is here made explicit. Second, the scene reveals the racial dimensions that animate the larger question about the Vietnam War, which has so far focused on broad political values but not race. By speaking to the limitations of white leadership, the scene illustrates, without giving easy answers, how the structural problems of Vietnam are tied to domestic issues of race.[50] Highly imperfect and roiled in contradiction, the VVAW peace script, nevertheless, suggests an intersectional rebuttal to the war machine that brings to the viewer's attention the topics of gender and race.

The scene continues to indict the VVAW, exposing limitations to their peace rhetoric that few movements dare to acknowledge. The Black veteran, who noticeably does not wear fatigues like the white activists, describes the "whitewashing" taking place at the event and then notes how the "high visibility" of being Black "keeps you down all the time."[51] Much of WS, in fact, features problematic footage of nonwhite actors. The overwhelming casualties of the Vietnam War—innocent Southeast Asian men, women, and children—receive intermittent and unfocused attention. They are the nameless, faceless, and voiceless victims whose pain and suffering are, at times, overshadowed by the veterans' own grief. While images of suffering Vietnamese people eventually proved unacceptable to much of the US public, it clearly took years for the unjust treatment of nonwhite bodies in Vietnam to matter in a substantive way. Even then, the Vietnamese victims often needed white bodies to mediate and represent their cause, as seen in the VVAW. While *Winter Soldier* offers no easy solutions, it does extend some hope: that within the symbolic world of even the most staunchly "American" narrative lies the potential to reconsider the nation's future and its racial blind spots. Every "American" value—particularly those that sustain the citizen-soldier—can be a mirror by which to critique oneself and the system we all inhabit.

Additional documents from the VVAW suggest that there were efforts to expand their peace script from a narrow isolationist vision to a broader stand against race, gender, and class-based inequalities. For example, in a 1972 speech abroad, Brian Ross Adams stresses the "racist" conflicts confronting the activists. As seen in other addresses, pamphlets, and protest events, Adams references the VVAW's work to aid the working-class and fight veteran poverty, noting the "ignorance, racism, compulsive consumption, and apathy [that] have been manipulated by a crass profit-oriented system."[52] VVAW activists tried—and their peace script did not foreclose the possibility—to connect the veteran experience with issues of racism and poverty, uniting their fight against all types of "alienation."[53]

The VVAW occasionally tried to offer a peace script amenable to citizens across the standard divisions of the New Left. While they came up short in some ways, their insistence on structural inequalities while retaining the ethos of patriots stands out in the pantheon of peace rhetoric. It also shows the potential for peace to be a unifying space for bearing witness to violence both domestically and abroad without fracturing into division. Multiple VVAW correspondences demonstrate their focus on poverty and other issues not immediately related to the Vietnam War. One representative passage exclaims that the organization will fight against division within the United States, "not allow[ing] Americans to be polarized against one another."[54] Another memo describes diverse protest sites for the VVAW—college campuses, Veteran's Day Parades, and Thanksgiving events—and stresses the need for permeable boundaries to their movement: It "encompasses all people, crossing all ethnic and religious groups, labor, third world, peace groups, politicians, and any other group. This letter, while being almost apolitical, is important in that it can garn[er] the necessary broad-based support that an action like this requires. It also leaves much room for regional interpretation and implementation."[55] This passage exemplifies the movement's desire not to impose specific agendas or identities upon membership. In many ways, the VVAW were combatting the cultural division that was commonplace during the Nixon administration while also addressing the war overseas.

Other documents surrounding *Winter Solider* illustrate the movement's attempt to expand its peace script to encompass more than the perspective of white American men. Various items list "fight racism" and "fight sexism" as explicit objectives.[56] One document, titled "The Enraged Ones," mentions "labor unions, GIs, and the black community."[57] Another calls for the movement to keep pressure on "men and women of all nationalities, students, workers, veterans, communists, socialists, and potheads."[58] Additional material suggests the VVAW was in contact with the Third World Women's Alliance.[59] The third official objective of a VVAW platform stresses the need to unite with "women for peace, so that the men and women having first-hand knowledge of the military . . . can effectively voice their opinions."[60] The VVAW appeared to observe, contact, and, in at least one instance, possibly lend direct support to a string of naval protests led by Black soldiers stationed in Southeast Asia.[61] Far from an intentionally divisive or exclusionary movement, the VVAW consistently appealed to a unified fight against the racist, sexist, and class-based dimensions of the war machine.[62]

To be clear, the VVAW was not always successful. Theirs is a peace script with much talk, some action, and mixed results. It is also important to note that many members did not consider themselves either strictly anti-war or absolute pacifists. As seen in *Winter Soldier*, they voiced their appeals through the language of patriotism to forge a flexible and reflexive opposition to nondemocratic, imperialist policies that hurt citizens of the world. A representative public statement describes how "Kent State, Augusta and Jackson, Miss . . . Newark, Watts, Miami, and Detroit riots" are all connected to struggles in Vietnam.[63] The VVAW's attempt to connect the Vietnam conflict to diverse issues, narratives, and social roles helped fuel a powerful, visceral peace script that required self-criticism, regardless of whether its followers or the public always listened.

Conclusion

Roughly one hundred years after the Copperhead movement, we've returned to another peace script that relies on appeals to manliness and violence, albeit in a markedly different way. Fifty years later and we still hear appeals to masculinity across the political spectrum: from Joe Biden and Donald Trump trading physical threats, to media pundits like Jordan Peterson lamenting the loss of traditional "manhood," to the extreme fringes of the Alt-Right that violently assert toxic masculinity in a world "gone soft."[64] Even far Left groups, like the "Redneck Revolt," embrace elements of stereotypically masculine culture, such as an enthusiastic embrace of the Second Amendment.[65] Rhetorical studies can help us peel back the layers of these discourses and explain why a given community may find them persuasive. *Winter Soldier* represents one instance where a peace script presented traditional masculine tropes while calling its entire culture into question.

The VVAW's rhetoric, in this way, was less a policy of peace than an unrelenting look at the Vietnam War and at the casket of collective sacrifice it left behind. They dared to ask what it says about US society. Historian Christian Appy notes the fracturing of national culture after the war that occurred because, among other things, there was no solid answer to the moral ambiguities that citizens faced during the Vietnam War. This cultural fracture, brought on by the apprehension of incompatible actions and ideals, was in many ways a visual event: images and vivid descriptions of the war's intolerable violence circulated to an unprecedented degree, and *Winter Soldier* is an understudied part of this phenomenon. In the vacuum of national discourse following the war, some political leaders and citizens repackaged the belief of American exceptionalism into a new narrative of victimhood.[66] Others simply lost faith in the promise of democracy as guaranteed by the US government. Either way, the country remained largely unpersuaded by peace as the Cold War showed few signs of stopping. Nevertheless, to some citizens, the war caused a rupture of meaning that required a new peace script to express, if not to absolve, the nation's sins.

One such script remains crystallized in the *Winter Soldier* documentary. Through its visual juxtaposition of individual agency and the structure of the war, along with an embrace of the visual tropes of the citizen-soldier, the documentary reveals tensions intrinsic to national identity that allowed the war to reach such an excruciating climax. For Vietnam War protesters, the repulsion elicited by war images was one rhetorical tool among many, but for veterans protesting the war, it was also a means to interrogate their own complicity, as well as the concepts of individualism, collective violence, social responsibility, and the fabric of national identity that inspired them to fight in the first place. The VVAW peace script, while imperfect, involves a degree of self-reflection rarely seen in major anti-war movements. WS offers no scapegoats to offload the responsibility for war's crimes against humanity. Instead, it makes central the task of seeing one's role in a violent system, expressed through acts of witnessing that invite the viewer to take on the roles of perpetrator, bystander, and victim. By challenging its own symbolic world, WS is a model for the self-reflexivity needed to foster a sustainable, "positive" peace.

The VVAW's focus on national identity and the violence it demands continues as a central concern for today, no less so for the military than for citizens. How does the war machine continue? What language, images, and appeals to the martial spirit linger? Leaders were rightly seeking answers to these questions in the wake of Vietnam. One survey conducted by the US government during the Vietnam War surmised that possibly 25 percent or more active-duty soldiers participated in some form of obstruction or dissent.[67] Understandably, the government was worried about issues of morale, desertion, and loyalty.[68] One solution that has typified US warfare ever since is to focus on the professionalization of the military, instituting new measures that partly divide service men and women from civil society.[69] The result, intentional or not, is a loss of the connective thread that made the citizen-soldier—the John Kerrys of the world—popular. Either way, it was a response, in many ways, to the VVAW script and the radical potential it suggested for anti-war dissent.

The core lesson from the VVAW is that, try as some might, war and culture cannot be separated, and to deny their overlap all but guarantees peace scripts will continue to miss the mark. Even the most mundane facets of military bureaucracy usher in new types of cultural exchange, behavior, and discourse. Law, public policies, and foreign diplomacy surely play a role, but so does culture and its symbolic materiel of gender, race, and class. As we repeatedly see, when the military mobilizes and the government activates a "state of emergency," those in opposition craft their dissent with whatever resources they have at their disposal, for better or worse. Thus, debates over US war will continue to involve issues off the battlefield, just as race, sexual orientation, and religious freedom were all implicated in the war on terror.[70] We would do well, therefore, to consider the VVAW's flexible and self-reflexive peace script, however imperfect it is, because it refuses to completely abandon symbols of democracy, nationalism, and patriotism, appeals that still garner tremendous attention, while rendering them unable to absolve people of guilt and our complicity with violence near and far.

Conclusion

The Remnants of "Negative" Peace
and the Future of War

If people frame war and peace through the cultural toolbox available to them, we ought to make sure these tools are not weapons of mass destruction. At the time of writing, there are over two dozen violent conflicts spread across the globe, leaving no hemisphere untouched.[1] If there is one lesson from this book, it is that to understand the conditions necessary for a peaceful tomorrow, we must take stock of the peace scripts of yesterday. We must ask what narratives, identities, motives, and values animated versions of peace that proved persuasive for a given time and place. To this end, consider Francis Fukuyama's infamous hypothesis that, as the Soviet Union collapsed and Communism appeared on its last legs, a new era might arrive absent of major ideological struggles—that history might be, in a word, "over."[2] Fukuyama has since revised his theory, but the concept is emblematic of the myths of peace, suggesting that violence is unnatural and will eventually dissipate on its own. Like all peace scripts, this also reflects a specific culture or interpretive community that privileges certain characters, ideas, and values over others. The twenty-first century, about a quarter of the way through, has already shown warfare is not ceasing, as we've witnessed horrific violence in places like the Democratic Republic of Congo, Darfur, Iraq, Ukraine, and, of course, Afghanistan, which marks the longest war in US history. The causes of these conflicts are diverse and complex, but we clearly must do more work to arrive at a persuasive and "positive" peace.[3] We cannot forget that, although our old scripts are imperfect, they can still guide us toward lasting peace because, as David Barash describes, a perfect peace may "never [be] fully achieved; it can only be approached."[4] Critical studies of peace rhetoric can help sensitize activists and scholars alike to how new injustices may arise through anti-war discourse.

In this effort, I have followed the work of communication scholars who contend that war is a special occasion to gauge the quality of democracy and dissent within a nation.[5] To disregard anti-war rhetoric, even of those who simply employ the acts of dehumanization and scapegoating common to their pro-war opponents, risks missing how the end of one war sets the conditions for future conflicts—even conflicts seemingly unrelated to warfare.[6] While many of these movements might be considered failures by their own metric, no less by those of today, each offers a portrait of public sentiment at the time as it concerns definitions of war and peace. This book has emphasized how deeply such discourse concerns, even *fixates upon*, issues of race, gender, and class. Bringing this critical-cultural focus to bear on the study of war and peace can draw new connections across diverse scholarship that is rarely in conversation with traditional studies of warfare, such as decolonial rhetorical studies, theories of gender and sexuality, environmental rhetoric, and even new materialism. This book is just one step on that path, which leads down countless directions to rediscover and rejuvenate the study of war rhetoric in hope of directly contributing to peace-building projects.

A rhetorical analysis of peace discourse also helps make sense of current "emergency" rhetoric by illuminating how cultural identities, practices, and values get tied to official policies, laws, and rights. As legal scholars have noted, the period of warfare—or more broadly any "state of emergency"—typically triggers some reformatting or reframing of rights.[7] The peace script directly takes part in this process. For instance, the Copperheads added a racialized subtext to an otherwise common defense of the Constitution. More recently, the Patriot Act during the war on terror ushered in new restrictions on civil liberties that also sparked debates over the meaning of "national security," "freedom," and "US culture."[8] Just as the peace scripts in this book integrated their own cultural hierarchy into war debates, studies suggest that more recent responses to the Iraq War policies also fell, to varying degrees, along racial, gendered, and class-based lines.[9] Discussions of war abroad cannot escape cultural concerns at home.

US peace scripts, no matter how meager, can have dire consequences. Some global conflicts over the last thirty-odd years certainly would have benefited from principled US participation rather than haphazard responses born out of ignorance, indifference, or antipathy. President Bill Clinton, for instance, expressed regret over not offering timely assistance during the Rwandan Genocide, which spun out into the Second Congo War, the worst military conflict since World War II.[10] Current conflicts in Syria and Ukraine, not to mention the treatment of Uyghurs in China, could all profit from some ethical and assertive peace vision. Yet, the loss of life continues, and US citizens continue to reflect a narrow understanding of global affairs.[11] Thus, we must take stock of our peace scripts, no matter how insufficient they may be, to offer citizens a greater sense of the argumentative terrain upon which we must persuade people to end needless violence in the twenty-first century, to ultimately "break free of [. . .] the governing framework of disdain and damnation" that too often characterizes US discourse.[12] Glancing at the rhetoric of the 2020 and 2024 presidential campaigns, it appears that the national peace script has lurched toward an ill-defined isolationism, seen in both Donald Trump's and Joe Biden's words, although not actions, as they insist the country avoid entanglements abroad.[13] If I had to characterize the prevailing attitude toward peace in the United States, I would liken it to a dull sword slashing at all things that look like "interventionism." We are a culture that has grown weary of military involvement yet incapable of living outside "wartime," as a pattern of conflict, repression, and violence continues.[14] In closing, let me briefly underscore the key advantages of and future directions for the peace script approach.

Peace Script: Advantages

The two primary advantages of the peace script are conceptual and historical. Like many tools of rhetorical criticism, the peace script aims to balance the generalizable with the highly specific. For every myth of peace, countless instances exist of its use in response to some situation deemed violent. By isolating the concept to the "emergency context," as I did in this book, we can more easily compare peace scripts across time and space, constrained only by the specific exigence of war mobilization. Furthermore, scholars can compare a relatively small but highly significant data set by limiting ourselves to the available *public* texts of major anti-war groups during or after wartime. I do not claim that these, or any, archival documents are perfect replicas of peace advocacy at a given time, nor that they represent what most citizens thought about war and peace. Nevertheless, these public texts, limited and biased as they may be, remain the best empirical starting point to consider the kinds of arguments and appeals the public would have heard during these brief yet transformative moments in history. The pamphlets, newsletters, and speeches that make up this book's evidentiary basis may occasionally strike the reader as odd, but this mostly reflects what we have chosen to remember—and forget—as a nation. The dissonance between our expectations and the voices we discover from the past is all the more reason to ask what, precisely, gave these voices a degree of power and persuasive force.

The peace script approach can also aid in studying social movement rhetoric. By approaching the emergency context of warfare as a period of "collective action" with competing scripts of war and peace, I hope to offer a finer sense of how wartime is partly shaped by the grassroots fight over resources, networks, and political opportunities in conjunction with shifting cultural frames.[15] We see, for instance, how central the study of class and socioeconomic privilege is to anti-war history. Maintaining a position of peace, however defined, belongs to actors and organizations that can sustain attention and control resources during repressive, resource-scarce periods of wartime emergency.[16]

The peace script cues us into the symbolic dynamics of these organizational struggles. It can help explain why movements and their typically affluent leaders may be tied to antiquated notions of peace that restrict the war debate to the cultural milieu that bestowed them the wealth and influence required to fight for peace. The "peace script," in short, tells us that peace is a product of cultural contestation that is inseparable from the dynamics of war and democracy that constitute modern nation-states.[17] To understand peace ultimately requires an identification of what counts as acceptable dissident discourse in a body politic.

This approach takes the interpretive tools of rhetorical studies and offers them to scholars outside communication and English departments to complement interdisciplinary studies of anti-war social movements. Traditional categories of persuasion, such as ethos, logos, and pathos, are still relevant but used less as measures of eloquence than as tools to assess better other rhetorical dynamics, such as collective memory, narrative, and identity formation. Taken as a whole, the rhetorical interpretation of anti-war discourse helps us see how "peace" rhetoric emerges from a field of debate with new definitions related to harmony, restraint, and civility. We begin to see a new language emerge that reclaims—sometimes to further distort—the myths of peace. The peace script concept, by formalizing our object of study and limiting it to a given time and place, makes it easier to compare each instance of anti-war dissent with other social movements. We could thus ask how anti-war narratives, identities, and arguments merge into networks beyond the emergency context and even beyond peace activism itself, looking for overlaps with suffrage, temperance, or civil rights movements, for instance. The result is not a new theory or universal concept of "peace" but a blueprint for tracing peace discourse by remaining sensitive to the particularity of nations, communities, grassroots actors, and types of conflict.

For instance, a rhetorical analysis of peace scripts, with its sensitivity to cultural discourse *within* a nation, can help explain the "most widespread, most destructive, and the most characteristic form of organized human violence:" civil wars.[18] As historian David Armitage expertly shows, civil wars—understood as conflict between members of the same national community—have become the most prevalent type of armed conflict. We must be careful what conclusions we draw from this observation, yet several commonsense assumptions have enormous implications for the study of peace. First, what counts as a "civil war" is partly a rhetorical matter, and when a conflict is or is not labeled as such we must ask how that creates specific conditions for reconciliation. Secondly, civil wars, by their very name, suggest some inner turmoil, some element of cohesion and goodwill that has since shattered. A nation's cultural makeup is a central element that comes under scrutiny during a civil war, and we can better grasp it through the peace script approach. The rise in civil wars shows how urgently a nation needs to have its own internal tradition of peacebuilding to defend against the extreme types of intrastate violence. Taking "the rhetorical" as a key variable in the construction of a "positive" peace can help bring to light—so as to assuage—the deep-seated cultural biases that fester long after a war and force us to ask who might be written out of a given peace script. We can glimpse these dynamics most clearly in "negative" scripts that dramatize conflict in ways that reestablish cultural hierarchies.

The advantages for rhetorical history follow from these conceptual benefits. Instead of a priori imposing a definition of "peace," the peace script directs us to the practice of close reading. Thus, we base our interpretation of peace less on a philosophical ideal than on an interpretation of texts in context. Like studies of "nationalism," we discover that "peace" results from situationally specific structures, opportunities, and events that, through the agency of rhetors, take on new meanings. There are patterns that emerge, such as the myths of peace. However, these patterns gain their significance, or "hermeneutic depth," when we track their articulations in relation to some other variable, whether the available public texts or the "emergency context."[19] We thereby begin to see how each community constructs its definitions and debates about peace by fusing cultural themes at a given time. A rhetorical history guided by this approach shows how peace emerges as a highly pragmatic appeal, cobbled together in response to perceived threats of lethality, brandishing whatever symbols are available to stave off impending destruction. Furthermore, a grassroots focus on rhetorical history makes room for smaller-scale approaches that might look more like cultural or microhistories than traditional top-down histories. These smaller stories of conflict, as seen in this book, add nuance to the significant shifts in world history that usually dominate public memory and the scholarly study of history, protest, and rhetoric.

What does the peace script ultimately tell us about the rhetorical history of the United States? First, much peace-related dissent bears the trace of racialized, gendered, and class-based inequalities. This book illustrates how race, particularly whiteness, serves as an engine for much peace talk. Therefore, any exhaustive history of US race relations cannot be separated from the national record of war and dissent in all its glory and shame. On one hand, the intertwined history of whiteness and peace has a degree of common sense: during states of emergency, only those with sizable socioeconomic privilege can comfortably afford to act in opposition to oppressive measures and a climate inhospitable to dissent.[20] White-majority peace movements are thus the rule rather than the exception. From Clement Vallandigham to Henry Ford to VVAW leadership, white men tend to dominate these movements and control their material and symbolic resources. Certain cultural touchstones—the "tycoon of industry" or the "salt-of-the-earth Midwestern folk"—become part of influential peace campaigns. That these cultural resources, which make up the available tools of rhetorical discourse for a given community, are indebted to whiteness is a matter both arbitrary and significant for the history of rhetoric and social justice. It is arbitrary because it need not be so; nothing about peace demands whiteness. It is significant because, as this book illustrates, peace scripts can be vehicles to justify or translate whiteness into new discursive terrain, activating the myths of peace to enforce new borders that gather whiteness on one side—the side of "peace." To study the history of peace scripts is thus to partly write a history of how whiteness mutates alongside society's defense of life and allowance of death.

Between the lethal and the peaceful lies a vast, disputed territory in which we also see a history of gender. Much scholarship has established connections between war and masculinity, yet comparatively few studies ask how gender and peace work together to justify violent visions of society. Simply theorizing this connection achieves little when we consider the tremendous variation of such rhetoric across time and space. The peace script can acknowledge conceptual parallels while zeroing in on the context-specific expressions of peace at a given moment. Accordingly, we can compare how each peace script uses gendered rhetoric. Staking some assertive, powerful, and even violent gender identity, whether masculine or feminine, may be as familiar to peace as to war. Rhetorical scholars of US public address can work from this observation to consider how discourse *between* wars has similar investments in a martial spirit, even if expressed through an ostensibly peaceful disposition across gender identities.

Pitfalls and Future Considerations

The study of peace falls into many of the same trappings as the study of war. For starters, given the omnipresent nature of warfare, how do we choose one period of study over another? Furthermore, focusing on *public* texts clearly favors major peace movements over the smaller organizations that may offer a diversity of voices more hopeful and inclusive than those in this study. These two issues are connected, pointing to a basic methodological impasse that, I believe, cannot be avoided. There is nothing determinate nor necessary about the major peace movements under consideration in this study. I do not wish to claim that they comprise the sum total of national thought on peace and anti-war advocacy. Nevertheless, they represent the more vocal and sustained public voices during periods popularly considered as "wartime" and thus were peace arguments likely to have been read or heard during episodes of military violence.

The rhetoric of these five movements could help complement a more extensive historiography of war and peace rhetoric, as well as cue us to the continued need for considering race, gender, and class alongside peace advocacy. To expand on this, future studies ought to compare the larger movements with the smaller ones. The lesser-known, marginalized movements that disappear during states of emergency might indicate what voices and scripts of peace were possible but neglected or suppressed, which in turn could grant greater clarity to the persuasive dynamics of the groups covered in this book. Additionally, studying the five organizations in this book once the wars concluded and nations started debating postwar peace would add much perspective to my findings. Finally, in comparing these movements, we might better understand how intergroup dynamics played a role in forming dominant peace scripts, an overlooked area of study.

Rehearsing and Rehashing the Peace Script

In the fall of 1969, Vice President Spiro Agnew gave his thoughts on anti-war activism, chastising what he saw as its "spirit of national masochism." According to Agnew, these protesters were not real men but "an effete corps of impudent snobs who characterize themselves as intellectuals." In a passage that the Vietnam Veterans against the War would reprint in their pamphlets, Agnew concluded, "We can afford to separate [protesters] from our society—with no more regret that we should feel over discarding rotten apples in a barrel."[21] For the vice president and his colleagues, conducting a war abroad also meant conducting one at home. Those who mount critiques of war must often overcome such social stigma, usually some variation of the "traitor" label. Perhaps it comes as little surprise, then, that peace scripts during wartime occasionally respond with a cocktail of cultural appeals just as volatile as those employed by pro-war hawks.

As this book shows, peace is no static object to be simply seized and wielded in the name of harmony. While there are myths of peace—a common set of assumptions and themes that impact how peace is interpreted and communicated—they don't come prefabricated or set in stone. Each social movement in this book creatively, and sometimes opportunistically, used assumptions about peace to script their version with respect to their cultural milieu. Peace, as such, belongs to the realm of the contingent, the makeshift, and the pragmatic. This is all to say: peace is thoroughly *rhetorical* and thus subject to all the dynamics of persuasion, both heavenly and hellish. When peace rhetoric happens during an "emergency" context—the purview of this book—the results often mirror the reactionary quality of pro-war discourse.[22] Military theorist Carl von Clausewitz argued that war is simply an extension of politics, pointing to an overlap between warfare and social discourse.[23] We could, at times, also view peace as an extension of war as it draws its own defensible borders. In short, peace always bears war's signature, rarely able to achieve an absolute rejection of violence save through tremendous effort and careful self-reflection. Ultimately, the idea of the peace script implies that citizens compose appeals to war and peace along a spectrum of violence—cultural, moral, political, legal, economic, and, of course, physical—that different communities find more or less persuasive.

To tell this story, I have considered the rhetorical dynamics of five major US anti-war movements during what could be called the "US Century of War": the Copperhead movement (Civil War), the Anti-Imperialist League (Spanish-American and Philippine-American War), Henry Ford's Peace Expedition (World War I), the Mothers' Movement (World War II), and the Vietnam Veterans against the War (Vietnam War). To be clear, I have not argued that these organizations' archival documents—pamphlets, speeches, newsletters, etc.—are representative of peace rhetoric in toto. Nor do they tell us what each adherent to a given movement definitely thought. But they do suggest the types of anti-war appeals frequently made to the public by major organizations during periods of radical change. A central question throughout has been, "How does the dominant anti-war advocacy of a given time use cultural appeals of race, gender, and class to protest war and, occasionally, legitimatize other kinds of violence during war?"

Ultimately, if we ignore the potential for peace advocacy to justify violence, we ignore a central obstacle in the pursuit of social justice—and the important role of failure in the struggle. As each script offers new heroes, villains, and values for readers to embrace as essential to peaceful living, so too are concepts of equality, justice, freedom, and citizenship implicated. Arriving at a "positive" peace on the first go is likely impossible, but that doesn't mean we are left with no recourse and should simply give up and admit failure. Using Galtung's "positive" peace as an ethical standard to judge peace scripts, we can move past merely denigrating a script or social movement as "negative" and instead cultivate a generative attitude toward hidden biases and assumptions, even within ourselves.[24] Moving past a zero-sum approach to "positive" peace means that we can be vulnerable and self-reflexive about our shortcomings. Similarly, each movement under consideration in this book, to varying degrees, could be labeled a failure despite dominating the field of peace advocacy for a moment in time. Each was full of grassroots activists who aspired to give a persuasive answer to what, for better or worse, makes the United States stand out among the rest of the world—what makes the nation a just, fair, equitable, and harmonious place. At the same time, the script tells readers which people are unequal, disharmonious, or uncivil. At its extreme, it tells us whose existence is inherently violent. What's required is the humility to admit our shortsightedness and a willingness to be self-reflective. At its best, a peace script can become a lens to see how the pursuit of nonviolence is so often permeated with our own biases—but never irretrievably so.

Any anti-war movement that hopes to dominate peace debates must navigate this moral terrain, one made more treacherous when the nation is at war. The five movements in this book, largely neglected in communication and rhetorical studies, are keys to understanding how societal norms, definitions, and identities are brought to bear on matters of life and death through war debates. By saying "no" to a given military conflict, these movements offer scripts of civility and self-restraint that may, nevertheless, contain exclusionary elements. Just as Agnew saw the Vietnam War as a referendum on masculinity and patriotism, so too might peace activists frame war as a symptom of a larger cultural crisis.

At the heart of this book, and any period of turmoil, is the question, "What vision of culture must be protected from harm to guarantee peace?" Understandably, people look to the past, drawing on tradition to forge new defenses of old ways of living. The rescripting of gender, race, and class that will shape the twenty-first century will have unpredictable expressions and consequences. Nevertheless, if this study is any guide, they will combine with appeals to compassion, harmony, and nonviolence to, for better or worse, shape both "positive" and "negative" peace scripts. These appeals—what I've called the myths of peace—are indebted to a national history of anti-war advocacy. We must hope new scripts correct the errors of past attempts. Each new script risks privileging some cultural identity or hierarchy over others; some will be more self-reflexive than others. In the end, they will help define what type of society is desirable and what kind of violence is permissible for even a fleeting moment of peace.

Notes

Introduction

1. Ishaan Tharoor, "Why Was the Biggest Protest in World History Ignored?" *Time*, February 15, 2013.

2. "Grannie Joins Global Anti-War Protests," *Guardian* (Charlottetown, Prince Edward Island), February 15, 2003.

3. "Women Stage Anti-War Protest outside US Embassy in Guyana," *BBC Summary of World Broadcasts*, February 16, 2003; "Peace Cries Ring; Millions in U.S., around World Protest a War in Iraq," *San Diego Union-Tribune*, February 16, 2003.

4. "Cities Jammed in Worldwide Protest of War in Iraq," CNN, February 16, 2003.

5. Hilary Douglas and Andrea Perry, "Britain on the Brink: Demonstrators Flood through London and Glasgow as Anti-War Crowds Take to Streets All over the World to Protest at Impending War; Millions on March in a Tide of Peace," *Sunday Express*, February 16, 2003.

6. "Authoritarianism and Anti-Semitism in the Anti-War Movement?" *Tikkun* 18, no. 3 (2003): 39.

7. Kenneth Burke's theory of "dramatism" similarly asserts that humans operate according to various dramas and stories that we repeatedly tell ourselves. See Burke, *A Grammar of Motives* (Berkeley: University of California, 1945). "Peace scripts," in this way, give us certain dramatic opportunities to express ourselves in relation to war. Scholars of social movements similarly describe how certain "frames," or "schemata of interpretation," are used to help activists identify their role, the key issues, and the best policies to advocate. See David A. Snow et al., "Frame Alignment Processes, Micromobilization, and Movement Participation," *American Sociological Review* 51 (1986): 464.

8. See Allan W. Austin, *Quaker Brotherhood: Interracial Activism and the American Friends Service Committee, 1917–1950* (Urbana: University of Illinois Press, 2012); John M. Craig, "The Woman's Peace Party and Questions of Gender Separatism," *Peace and Change* 19, no. 4 (1994): 373–98.

9. Geoffrey R. Stone, *Perilous Times: Free Speech in Wartime* (New York: W. W. Norton, 2004).

10. For an in-depth look at the persecution of one segment of pacifists during World War I, see Duane C. S. Stoltzfuls, *Pacifists in Chains: The Persecution of Hutterites during the Great War* (Baltimore: John Hopkins University Press, 2013).

11. Stone, *Perilous Times*.

12. Robert Ivie, "Hegemony, Instabilities, and Interventions: A Special Issue on

Discourses of War and Peace," *Journal of Multicultural Discourses* 11, no. 2 (2016): 125–34; see also Ivie and Oscar Giner, *Hunt the Devil: A Demonology of US War Culture* (Tuscaloosa: University of Alabama Press, 2015).

13. For a representative text, see Patricia Roberts-Miller, *Rhetoric and Demagoguery* (Carbondale: Southern Illinois University Press, 2019). Roberts-Miller discusses wartime speech many times to elaborate on the concept of "demagoguery."

14. Robert Ivie, *Dissent from War* (Bloomfield, CT: Kumarian Press, 2007), 78, 49. See also Kenneth Burke's classic analysis of wartime rhetoric in "The Rhetoric of Hitler's Battle," *Southern Review* 5 (1939): 1–21. Burke understood war's symbolic importance, noting the potential "remoralization" of war societies by reaffirming shared values and common purpose. Burke, "War and Cultural Life," *American Journal of Sociology* 48, no. 3 (1942): 404–10.

15. Martin Luther King Jr., "Beyond Vietnam," speech delivered on April 4, 1967, at Manhattan's Riverside Church, available from the University of Hawaii (web).

16. Johan Galtung, *Peace by Peaceful Means: Peace and Conflict, Development and Civilization* (London: Sage, 1996).

17. David Barash, *Approaches to Peace: A Reader in Peace Studies* (Oxford: Oxford University Press, 2010), 146.

18. Galtung, *Peace by Peaceful Means*.

19. See Robert David Johnson, "Anti-Imperialism and Good Neighbour Policy: Ernest Gruening and Puerto Rican Affairs, 1934–1939," *Journal of Latin American Studies* 29, no. 1 (1997): 89–110.

20. Johnson, "Anti-Imperialism," 95–108.

21. Barash, *Approaches to Peace*, 161.

22. Barash, *Approaches to Peace*, 2.

23. George W. Bush, "Address to a Joint Session of Congress and the American People," September 20, 2001, White House Archives (web); Barack Obama, "Remarks by the President on the Way Forward in Afghanistan," June 22, 2011, White House Archives (web); Obama, "Afghanistan Strategy Speech," December 1, 2009, available at BBC (web).

24. See Craig Whitlock, *The Afghanistan Papers: A Secret History of the War* (New York: Simon and Schuster, 2021) to best see how the public rhetoric of the war did not match the realities of the conflict.

25. See the Republican Party shift in military engagement here: "Opposition to Syrian Airstrikes Surges," Pew Research Center, September 9, 2013.

26. Barash, *Approaches to Peace*, 2.

27. Johnson, "Anti-Imperialism," 109.

28. See Daniel Immerwahr, *How to Hide an Empire* (New York: Farrar, Straus and Giroux, 2019); Erin Blackmore, "The U.S. Forcibly Detained Native Alaskans during World War II," *Smithsonian Magazine*, February 22, 2017.

29. Barash, *Approaches to Peace*, 66–67.

30. For instance, see Jean-Jacques Rousseau, *The Social Contract and Other Later Political Writings*, ed. and trans. Victor Gourevitch (Cambridge, UK: Cambridge University Press, 1997).

31. See Keren Wang, *Legal and Rhetorical Foundations of Economic Globalization: An Atlas of Ritual Sacrifice in Late-Capitalism* (New York: Routledge: 2020).

32. Colum Lynch, "Exclusive: Rwanda Revisited," *Foreign Policy*, April 5, 2015; Joe Bavier, "Congo War-Driven Crisis Kills 45,000 a Month," *Reuters*, January 22, 2008.

33. "China Responsible for 'Serious Human Rights Violations' in Xinjian Province," *UN Human Rights Report*, August 31, 2022; see also Llewellyn King, "How NIMBYism Is Strangling America," *Washington Chronicles*, August 30, 2024.

34. See Martin Luther King Jr., "Letter from Birmingham Jail," speech delivered on April 16, 1963, available at King Institute, Stanford University (web).

35. Hannah Arendt's conception of the public sphere is relevant here, as she describes citizens entering a space of contingency and freedom where the activities of rhetoric play a key role. See *The Human Condition* (New York: Harcourt Brace Jovanovich, 1951).

36. Gene Sharp, *The Politics of Nonviolent Action* (Boston: Porter Sargent, 1973). See also Sharp, "198 Methods of Nonviolent Action," Brandeis University (web).

37. Ellen W. Gorsevski, *Peaceful Persuasion: The Geopolitics of Nonviolent Rhetoric* (Albany: State University of New York Press, 2004), 5, 178–88.

38. The significance of anti-war rhetoric within a democratic republic depends on the model of the nation-state that a given scholar presumes at the start of their analysis. If, for example, warfare is taken as the primary activity of the state, then the rest of political life could reasonably be assumed to bear some relationship to the nature of state violence. Charles Tilly, in one of his master surveys of historical data, argues that the essential nature of the nation- state—its reach, its organizational features, its legitimacy—is dependent on warfare. European nation-states, he argues, can all be explained by "continuously varying combinations of concentrated capital, concentrated coercion, preparation for war, and position within the international system." Sidney Tarrow expands upon Tilly's project, arguing that social movement activity is a key variable in the material and symbolic formation of the nation-state: each step of the war-making process is informed by civil unrest, and the pains a state goes to control this unrest leaves permanent marks upon the state apparatus. Tilly, *The Formation of National States in Western Europe* (Princeton, NJ: Princeton University Press, 1975), 14; Tarrow, *War, States, and Contention: A Comparative Historical Study* (Ithaca, NY: Cornell University Press, 2015), 48–50.

39. Aristotle, *Rhetoric*, trans. W. Rhys Roberts (Mineola, NY: Dover, 2004), I.2, 1355b26f.

40. Ivie, *Dissent from War*.

41. Mark Vail, "The 'Integrative' Rhetoric of Martin Luther King, Jr.'s 'I Have a Dream' Speech," *Rhetoric and Public Affairs* 9 (2006): 590; see also Robert Ivie, *Democracy and America's War on Terror* (Tuscaloosa: University of Alabama Press, 2006).

42. Ivie highlights the role of "identification" and "division" in his work, particularly as it regards the development of war and peace-building strategies. See *Democracy and America's War on Terror*, 8.

43. Gorsevski, *Peaceful Persuasion*; Ivie, *Dissent from War*.

44. Ivie, *Democracy and America's War on Terror*; Kenneth Burke, *A Rhetoric of Motives* (Berkeley: University of California Press, 1969).

45. Roger Stahl, *Militainment, Inc.: War, Media, and Culture* (New York: Routledge, 2010); Paul Achter, "Rhetoric and the Permanent War," *Quarterly Journal of Speech* 102, no. 1 (2016): 79–94.

46. Ivie and Giner, *Hunt the Devil*, 140–42.

47. Kim Lane Scheppele, "Law in a Time of Emergency: States of Exception and the Temptations of 9/11," *Journal of Constitutional Law* 6, no. 5 (2004): 1001–83; Scheppele, "The Rise of Authoritarian Democracies," Center on National Security, March 12, 2020.

48. Stone, *Perilous Times*.

49. Giorgio Agamben, *State of Exception* (Chicago: University of Chicago Press, 2005), 22.

50. Mary L. Dudziak, *War Time: An Idea, Its History, Its Consequences* (New York: Oxford University Press, 2012), 8, 25–31.

51. Alfred W. McCoy, *Policing America's Empire: The United States, the Philippines, and the Rise of the Surveillance State* (Madison: University of Wisconsin Press, 2009).

52. Jeremy Engels and William O. Saas, "On Acquiescence and Ends-Less War: An Inquiry into the New War Rhetoric," *Quarterly Journal of Speech* 99, no. 2 (2013): 225–32.

53. Stone, *Perilous Times*.

54. Robert L. Ivie, "Democratic Dissent and the Trick of Rhetorical Critique," *Critical Studies, Critical Methodologies* 5, no. 3 (2005): 278.

55. Ivie, "Democratic Dissent."

56. Robert L. Ivie, "Hierarchies of Equality: Positive Peace in a Democratic Idiom," in *The Handbook of Communication Ethics*, ed. George Cheney, Steve May, and Debashish Munshi (New York: Routledge: 2011), 378.

57. See Tarrow's discussion of emergency script and its implications for democratic governance in *War, States, and Contention*, 160–67, 244–59; Charles T. Lee, *Ingenious Citizenship: Recrafting Democracy for Social Change* (Durham, NC: Duke University Press, 2016), 81.

58. Ivie, *Dissent from War*, 155.

59. Ivie, "Hierarchies of Equality," 381.

60. Ivie, *Dissent from War*, 109.

61. See Timothy Barney, "The Sight and Site of North Korea: Citizen Cartography's Rhetoric of Resolution in the Satellite Imagery of Labor Camps," *Quarterly Journal of Speech* 105, no. 1 (2019): 1–24; Engels and Saas, "On Acquiescence and Ends-Less War"; Ivie, "Hegemony, Instabilities, and Interventions"; Stephen H. Browne, *The Ides of War: George Washington and the Newburgh Crisis* (Columbia: University of South Carolina Press, 2016); Jenell Johnson, "The Limits of Persuasion: Rhetoric and Resistance in the Last Battle of the Korean War," *Quarterly Journal of Speech* 100, no. 3 (2014): 323–47; Jessy J. Ohl, "In Pursuit of Light War in Libya: Kairotic Justifications of War that Just Happened," *Rhetoric and Public Affairs* 20, no. 2 (2017): 195–222; Allison M. Prasch, "Maternal Bodies in Militant Protest: Leymah Gbowee and the

Rhetorical Agency of African Motherhood," *Women's Studies in Communication* 38, no. 2 (2015): 187–205; Stephen J. Heidt, "Presidential Power and National Violence: James K. Polk's Rhetorical Transfer of Savagery," *Rhetoric and Public Affairs* 19, no. 3 (2016): 265–396; Paul Stob, "Sacred Symbols, Public Memory, and the Great Agnostic: Robert Ingersoll Remembers the Civil War," *Rhetoric and Public Affairs* 19, no. 2 (2016): 275–305; David Zarefsky, "Consistency and Change in Lincoln's Rhetoric about Equality," *Rhetoric and Public Affairs* 1, no. 1 (1998): 21–44; David Campbell, *Writing Security: United States Foreign Policy and the Politics of Identity*, rev. ed. (Manchester: Manchester University Press, 1998); Robert Ivie and Oscar Giner, "Hunting the Devil: Democracy's Rhetorical Impulse to War," *Presidential Studies Quarterly* 37, no. 4 (2007): 580–98; Jeremy Engels, *Enemyship: Democracy and Counter-Revolution in the Early Republic* (East Lansing: Michigan State University Press, 2010), 15; Abby M. Dubisar, "Embodying and Disrupting Antiwar Activism: Disrupting YouTube's 'Mothers Day for Peace'," *Rhetoric Review* 34, no. 1 (2015): 56–73; Christopher J. Gilbert, "The Press of War Imagery," *Rhetoric Society Quarterly* 47, no. 2 (2017): 206–14; Mark D. Harmon, "This Is Not Goldfish Swallowing: Newsreels Encounter Protests against the Vietnam War," *Visual Communication Quarterly* 17, no. 4 (2010): 200–212; Billie Murray, "For What Noble Cause: Cindy Sheehan and the Politics of Grief in Public Spheres of Argument," *Argumentation and Advocacy* 49, no. 1 (2012): 1–15.

62. Barbara Biesecker, "No Time for Mourning: The Rhetorical Production of the Melancholic Citizen- Subject in the War on Terror," *Philosophy and Rhetoric* 40, no. 1 (2007): 147–69; Roger Stahl, "A Clockwork War: Rhetorics of Time in a Time of Terror," *Quarterly Journal of Speech* 94, no. 1 (2008): 73–99.

63. Stephen Heidt, *Resowing the Seeds of War* (East Lansing: Michigan State University Press, 2022).

64. Vail, "'Integrative' Rhetoric," 582.

65. Ivie, "Hegemony, Instabilities, and Interventions," 127.

66. See Ivie's discussion of critical studies and reflexive peace studies in "Hierarchies of Equality," 380–81.

67. Ivie, "Hierarchies of Equality."

68. Ivie, "Hierarchies of Equality."

69. Ivie, "Hierarchies of Equality."

70. My rhetorical approach to social movements is inspired by the hermeneutic theory of social movements articulated by Alberto Melucci, *Challenging Codes* (Cambridge, UK: Cambridge University Press, 1996).

71. Robert S. Cathcart, "Movements: Confrontation as Rhetorical Form," *Southern Speech Communication Journal* 43, no. 3 (1978): 233–47; Karma R. Chávez, "Counter-Public Enclaves and Understanding the Function of Rhetoric in Social Movement Coalition-Building," *Communication Quarterly* 59, no. 1 (2011): 1–18. See also Darrell Enck-Wanzer, "Trashing the System: Social Movement, Intersectional Rhetoric, and Collective Agency in the Young Lords Organization's Garbage Offensive," *Quarterly Journal of Speech* 92, no. 2 (2006): 174–201.

72. Kirt H. Wilson, "Interpreting the Discursive Field of the Montgomery Bus Boycott: Martin Luther King Jr.'s Holt Street Address," *Rhetoric and Public Affairs* 8,

no. 2 (2005): 299–326; Thomas W. Benson, *Posters for Peace: Visual Rhetoric and Civic Action* (University Park: Pennsylvania State University Press, 2016).

73. Christina R. Foust, Amy Pason, and Kate Zittlow Rogness, eds., *What Democracy Looks Like: The Rhetoric of Social Movements and Counterpublics* (Tuscaloosa: University of Alabama Press, 2017). See also Nathan Crick, ed., *The Rhetoric of Social Movements: Networks, Power, and New Media* (London: Routledge, 2020); Michael Warner, *Publics and Counterpublics* (Brooklyn: Zone Books, 2002); Robert Asen and Daniel C. Brouwer, eds., *Counterpublics and the State* (Albany: SUNY Press, 2001); Daniel C. Brouwer and Robert Asen, eds., *Public Modalities: Rhetoric, Culture, Media, and the Shape of Public Life* (Tuscaloosa: University of Alabama Press, 2010).

74. See Lisa M. Corrigan, *Black Feelings: Race and Affect in the Long Sixties* (Jackson: University Press of Mississippi, 2020); Ersula J. Ore, *Lynching: Violence, Rhetoric, and American Identity* (Jackson: University Press of Mississippi, 2019); Kirt H. Wilson, *The Reconstruction Desegregation Debate: The Politics of Equality and the Rhetoric of Place, 1870–1875* (East Lansing: Michigan State University Press, 2002); Lisa Corrigan, "On Rhetorical Criticism, Performativity, and White Fragility," *Review of Communication* 16, no. 1 (2016): 86–88; Robin DiAngelo, "White Fragility," *International Journal of Critical Pedagogy* 3, no. 3 (2011): 54–70; Alexander G. Weheliye, *Habeas Viscus: Racializing Assemblages, Biopolitics, and Black Feminist Theories of the Human* (Durham, NC: Duke University Press, 2014), 3–4; and Robert Young, *White Mythologies* (London: Routledge, 1990). See also Karma R. Chávez, "The Body: An Abstract and Actual Rhetorical Concept," *Rhetoric Society Quarterly* 48, no. 3 (2018): 242–50; Paul Elliot Johnson, "The Art of Masculine Victimhood: Donald Trump's Demagoguery," *Women's Studies in Communication* 40, no. 3 (2017): 229–50; Casey Ryan Kelly, "The Wounded Man: Foxcatcher and the Incoherence of White Masculine Victimhood," *Communication and Critical/Cultural Studies* 15, no. 2 (2018): 161–78; and Matthew Houdek, "Racial Sedimentation and the Common Sense of Racialized Violence: The Case of Black Church Burnings," *Quarterly Journal of Speech* 104, no. 3 (2018): 279–306.

75. Lisa A. Flores, "Between Abundance and Marginalization: The Imperative of Racial Rhetorical Criticism," *Review of Communication* 16, no. 1 (2016): 4–24.

76. Weheliye, *Habeas Viscus*. See also Judith Butler, *Precarious Life: The Powers of Mourning and Violence* (New York: Verso Press, 2006).

77. Natalia Molina, *How Race Is Made: Immigration, Citizenship, and the Historical Power of Racial Scripts* (Berkeley: University of California Press, 2014). For a more general rhetorical perspective, see Kenneth Burke, "Literature as Equipment for Living," in *The Philosophy of Literary Form: Studies in Symbolic Action* (Berkeley: University of California Press, 1973), 293–304.

78. DiAngelo, "White Fragility."

79. Casey R. Kelly, *Apocalypse Man: The Death Drive and the Rhetoric of White Masculine Victims* (Columbus: Ohio State University Press, 2020).

80. Thomas K. Nakayama and Robert L. Krizek, "Whiteness: A Strategic Rhetoric," *Quarterly Journal of Speech* 81, no. 3 (1995): 291–309.

81. See Robert Ivie and Oscar Giner, "Waging Peace: Transformations of the

Warrior Myth by US Military Veterans," *Journal of Multicultural Discourse* 11, no. 2 (2016): 199–213.

82. Claire Sisco King, "It Cuts Both Ways: *Fight Club*, White Masculinity, and Abject Hegemony," *Communication and Critical/Cultural Studies* 6, no. 4 (2009): 366.

83. Kimberlé Crenshaw, "Demarginalizing the Intersection of Race and Sex: A Black Feminist Critique of Antidiscrimination Doctrine, Feminist Theory and Antiracist Politics," *University of Chicago Legal Forum* 1 (1989): 139–67. See also Patricia Hill Collins, "Intersectionality's Definitional Dilemmas," *Annual Review of Sociology* 41, no. 1 (2015): 2.

84. Karma R. Chávez and Cindy L. Griffin, eds., *Standing in the Intersection: Feminist Voices, Feminist Practices in Communication Studies* (Albany: SUNY Press, 2012), 4; see also the special issue of *Communication and Critical/Cultural Studies* 15, no. 4 (2018) on #rhetoricsowhite; Eduardo Bonilla-Silva, *Racism without Racists: Colorblind Racism and the Persistence of Inequality in America*, 4th ed. (New York: Rowman and Littlefield, 2014), 25; Karma R. Chávez, "Beyond Inclusion: Rethinking Rhetoric's Historical Narrative," *Quarterly Journal of Speech* 101 (2015): 162–72; Charles W. Mills, *Black Rights/White Wrongs: The Critique of Racial Liberalism* (New York: Oxford University Press, 2017); Raka Shome, "Postcolonial Interventions in the Rhetorical Canon: An 'Other' View," *Communication Theory* 6, no. 1 (1996): 40–59.

85. Houdek, "Racial Sedimentation."

86. Peter Silver, *Our Savage Neighbors: How the Indian War Transformed Early America* (New York: W. W. Norton, 2008); Frederick C. Leiner, *The End of Barbary Terror* (New York: Oxford University Press, 2006). For a broad survey of anti-indigenous violence, see Roxanne Dunbar-Ortiz, *An Indigenous People's History of the United States* (Boston: Beacon Press, 2014).

87. See Ari Kelman, *A Misplaced Massacre: Struggling over the Memory of Sand Creek* (Cambridge, MA: Harvard University Press, 2013).

88. See Maurice Halbwachs, *On Collective Memory*, trans. Lewis A Coser (Chicago: University of Chicago Press, 1992).

89. James M. Volo offers a hypothesis for war's attracting widespread public attention. Wars are likely to be passed over or easily accepted if they are "quick, decisive, cheap, and relatively bloodless." See *A History of War Resistance in America* (Santa Barbara, CA: Greenwood Press, 2010), viii.

90. Amy Greenberg, *A Wicked War: Polk, Clay, Lincoln, and the 1846 US Invasion of Mexico* (New York: Alfred A. Knopf, 2012).

91. We could view the period following the Civil War as an acceleration and amplification of processes and institutions that Anthony Giddens associates with "modernity," namely "surveillance, military power, industrialism, and capitalism." See *The Consequences of Modernity* (Stanford, CA: Stanford University Press, 1990), 51.

92. Jennifer L. Weber, *Copperheads: The Rise and Fall of Lincoln's Opponents in the North* (Oxford: Oxford University Press, 2006), 3.

93. Stephen Kinzer, *The True Flag: Theodore Roosevelt, Mark Twain, and the Birth of American Empire* (New York: Henry Holt, 2017), 225.

94. Tarrow, *War, States, and Contention*, 120.

95. The Woman's Peace Party is perhaps the most significant of these organizations that, due in large part to the repression following US entry into war alongside their relatively extreme marginalization, shifted away from anti-war issues toward civil liberties.

96. Erez Manela, *The Wilsonian Moment: Self-Determination and the International Origins of Anticolonial Nationalism* (New York: Oxford University Press, 2007).

97. James T. Sparrow, *Warfare State: World War II Americans and the Age of Big Government* (New York: Oxford University Press, 2011).

98. "1948 Presidential Election," 270 to Win (web).

99. For a recent historical interpretation that emphasizes the declensionist narrative, see Daniel T. Rodgers, *Age of Fracture* (Cambridge, MA: Harvard University Press, 2011).

100. Galtung, *Peace by Peaceful Means*, 2.

101. Immanuel Kant, *Perpetual Peace: A Philosophical Treatise*, trans. Mary Campbell Smith, available at Project Gutenberg, January 14, 2016 (web).

102. There is a body of rhetoric scholarship that focuses on the topic of "violence" from both theoretical and historical perspectives. See Jay P. Childers, "Transforming Violence into a Focusing Event: A Reception Study of the 1946 Georgia Lynching," *Rhetoric and Public Affairs* 19, no. 4 (2016): 571–600; Jeremy Engels, "Forum: The Violence of Rhetoric," *Quarterly Journal of Speech* 99, no. 2 (2013): 180–81; Megan Foley, "Of Violence and Rhetoric: An Ethical Aporia," *Quarterly Journal of Speech* 99, no. 2 (2013): 191–99; Heidt, "Presidential Power and National Violence"; Claire Sisco King and Joshua Gunn, "On a Violence Unseen: The Womanly Object and Sacrificed Man," *Quarterly Journal of Speech* 99, no. 2 (2013): 200–208; Kristan Poirot, "Gendered Geographies of Memory: Place, Violence, and Exigency at the Birmingham Civil Rights Institute," *Rhetoric and Public Affairs* 18, no. 4 (2015): 621–47; Alyssa A. Samek, "Violence and Identity Politics: 1970s Lesbian-Feminist Discourse and Robin Morgan's 1973 West Coast Lesbian Conference Keynote Address," *Communication and Critical/Cultural Studies* 13, no. 3 (2016): 232–49; and Nathan Stormer, "On the Origins of Violence and Language," *Quarterly Journal of Speech* 99, no. 2 (2013): 182–90. I consider violence, defined as any form of harm upon or suffering by an individual or group, inevitable within political society. The proliferation of violence across society, however, demands we create distinctions to identify its various forms. Critical race scholars offer parallel distinctions when they describe various kinds of racism, such as "biological racism; intentional racism; unconscious racism; microagressions; nativism; institutional racism; racism tinged with homophobia or sexism." See Richard Delgado and Jean Stefancic, *Critical Race Theory*, 2nd ed. (New York: New York University Press, 2012), 30. Slavoj Žižek similarly identifies three types of violence: subjective or experiential violence, objective violence (which includes linguistic forms such as hate-speech), and systemic violence caused by political and economic structures. See also Judith Butler, *Frames of War: When Is Life Grievable* (London: Verso, 2009), 165.

Chapter 1

An earlier version of this chapter, shared here with permission, was included in *Rhetoric Society Quarterly*. See Dominic Manthey, "A Violent Peace and America's Copperhead Legacy," *Rhetoric Society Quarterly* 50, no. 1 (2020): 3–18.

1. Clement L. Vallandigham, *Speeches, Arguments, Addresses, and Letters of Clement L. Vallandigham* (New York: J. Walter, 1864), 201.
2. Vallandigham, *Speeches*, 202.
3. Vallandigham, *Speeches*, 203.
4. Vallandigham, *Speeches*, 204.
5. Vallandigham, *Speeches*, 204–5. He says the failed insurrection proves that there is no "irrepressible conflict" and that the "conspiracy was the natural and necessary consequence of the doctrines proclaimed every day, year in and year out, by the apostles of Abolition" (204).
6. The name was originally an attack on anti-war activists, comparing them to a poisonous snake, but by 1862 activists appropriated the term to signify the positive aspects of "Lady Liberty," who was on the penny called at the time a "copperhead." See Jennifer L. Weber, *Copperheads: The Rise and Fall of Lincoln's Opponents in the North* (Oxford: Oxford University Press, 2006), 3.
7. I am not arguing that all Democrats or anti-war activists united in these beliefs, rather that Copperheadism as a peace script could activate these interlocking appeals to adapt to different contexts and policy positions.
8. David Barash, *Approaches to Peace: A Reader in Peace Studies* (Oxford: Oxford University Press, 2010), 66–67.
9. Geoffrey R. Stone, *Perilous Times: Free Speech in Wartime* (New York: W. W. Norton, 2004), 29–43.
10. William A. Blair shows how diverse and diffuse definitions of "treason," "loyalty," and the like were during the Civil War in *With Malice toward Some: Treason and Loyalty in the Civil War Era* (Chapel Hill: University of North Carolina Press, 2014), 14–18. See also Giorgio Agamben, *State of Exception* (Chicago: University of Chicago Press, 2005), 22; Dominic J. Manthey, "A Vision of Violence in General Orders No. 100," *Rhetoric and Public Affairs* 23, no. 1 (2020): 47–76.
11. Stone, *Perilous Times*, 108–33.
12. Stone, *Perilous Times*, 113; 120.
13. Stone, *Perilous Times*, 124.
14. Manthey, "Vision of Violence." In my work analyzing Lincoln's General Order no. 100, the first modern legal declaration of war, we can see the worrisome precedent given to the state to control the populace in wartime predicated on the idea that a quick, brusque war is the best war.
15. Mark E. Neely, *Lincoln and the Democrats* (Cambridge, UK: Cambridge University Press, 2017).
16. See Charles F. Irons, *The Origins of Proslavery Christianity: White and Black Evangelicals in Colonial and Antebellum Virginia* (Chapel Hill: University of North Carolina Press, 2008); Larry E. Tise, *Proslavery: A History of the Defense of Slavery in America, 1701–1840* (Athens: University of Georgia Press, 1987); Sean Wilentz, *No Property in Man: Slavery and Anti-Slavery at the Nation's Founding* (Cambridge, MA: Harvard University Press, 2018).
17. Neely, *Lincoln*; Weber, *Copperheads*.
18. Johan Galtung, *Peace by Peaceful Means: Peace and Conflict, Development and Civilization* (London: Sage, 1996).

19. David H. Bennett, *The Party of Fear: The American Far Right from Nativism to the Militia Movement* (Chapel Hill: University of North Carolina Press, 1995).

20. Robert H. Churchill, *To Shake Their Guns in the Tyrant's Face: Libertarian Political Violence and the Origins of the Militia Movement* (Ann Arbor: University of Michigan Press, 2012), 134.

21. Churchill, *To Shake Their Guns in the Tyrant's Face*, 133.

22. Churchill, *To Shake Their Guns in the Tyrant's Face*.

23. *Copperhead Conspiracy in the Northwest: An Exposé on the Treasonable Order of the "Sons of Liberty." Vallandigham, Supreme Commander* (New York: John A. Gray and Green, 1864), 1.

24. *Copperhead Conspiracy in the Northwest*, 3.

25. *Copperhead Conspiracy in the Northwest*, 8.

26. *The Record of Hon. C. L. Vallandigham on Abolition, the Union, and the Civil War* (Cincinnati: J. Walter, 1863), 91, emphasis added (hereafter cited as *Record of Vallandigham*).

27. *Record of Vallandigham*, 59–91, emphasis added.

28. As previously mentioned, William A. Blair discusses how terms like "loyalty" and "treason" were put to varied Civil-War-era uses depending on their users' previously determined end goals.

29. See Jeremy Engels, *Enemyship: Democracy and Counter-Revolution in the Early Republic* (East Lansing: Michigan State University Press, 2010); Alison Olson, "The Pamphlet War over the Paxton Boy," *Pennsylvania Magazine of History and Biography* 123, no. 1/2 (1999), 31–55; Amy S. Greenberg, *A Wicked War: Polk, Clay, Lincoln, and the 1846 U. S. Invasion of Mexico* (New York: Vintage Books, 2012), 36–55; James M. Volo, *A History of War Resistance in America* (Santa Barbara, CA: Greenwood, 2010).

30. For a survey of the major masculinity definitions across US history, see E. Anthony Rotundo, *American Manhood: Transformations in Masculinity from the Revolution to the Modern Era* (New York: Basic Books, 1993).

31. Thomas Jefferson et al., "Declaration of Independence," July 4, 1776.

32. Amy Greenberg, *Manifest Manhood and the Antebellum American Empire* (New York: Cambridge University Press, 2005), 12.

33. Susan Zaeske, "'The South Arose as One Man': Gender and Sectionalism in Antislavery Petition Debates, 1835–1845," *Rhetoric and Public Affairs* 12, no. 3 (2009): 344.

34. Greenberg, *Manifest Manhood*, 12. See also Lorien Foote, *The Gentlemen and the Roughs: Violence, Honor, and Manhood in the Union Army* (New York: New York University Press, 2010) and Joshua A. Lynn, "A Manly Doughface: James Buchanan and the Sectional Politics of Gender," *Journal of the Civil War History* 8, no. 4 (2018): 591–620.

35. After the Mexican-American War, the wish fulfillment of western expansion only exacerbated the issue of slavery. Politicians proposed various solutions, of which most crucial to the Copperheads was the Crittenden Compromise. See, for instance, *Record of Vallandigham*, 98. See also Jonathan Earle and Diane Mutti Burke, eds., *Bleeding Kansas, Bleeding Missouri: The Long Civil War on the Border* (Lawrence: University Press of Kansas, 2013)

36. Charles B. Dew, *Apostles of Disunion: Southern Secession Commissioners and the Causes of the Civil War* (Charlottesville: University of Virginia Press, 2001), and Seymour Drescher, *Abolition: A History of Slavery and Antislavery* (Cambridge, UK: Cambridge University Press, 2009). Consider Jonathan A. Glickstein's *American Exceptionalism, American Anxiety: Wages, Competition, and Degraded Labor in the Antebellum United States* (Charlottesville: University of Virginia Press, 2002) and its discussion of how Northern economic attacks on slavery—"we cannot compete with it!"—could still stoke racial fears of white subordination to black labor of any variety.

37. Tyler Anbinder, *Nativism and Slavery: The Northern Know Nothings and the Politics of the 1850s* (New York: Oxford University Press, 1992). Anbinder argues that "there can be no doubt that in the west, the slavery issue killed the Whig party. New anti-slavery coalitions formed in nearly all of these states before they felt the full impact of Know Nothingism. In the east, on the other hand, the Whig party might have struggled on for another year if Know Nothingism had not emerged in 1854" (100).

38. Weber describes the Copperheads in this regard as "naysayers and obstructionists" with no "concrete program to achieve peace" (*Copperheads*, 216). While they were certainly obstructionists, I argue that reading their rhetoric closely and considering it as a reflection of their "moral vision" can show how an ideology so impractical and obstructionist was, to the many it mobilized, the only concrete and righteous path forward. The consequence of this worldview, and the violence it justifies as civilized, far outlives the Civil War. See James M. Jasper, *The Art of Moral Protest: Culture, Biography, and Creativity in Social Movements* (Chicago: University of Chicago Press, 1997).

39. Frank L. Klement, *Copperheads in the Middle West* (Chicago: University of Chicago Press, 1960); Klement, *Dark Lanterns: Secret Political Societies, Conspiracies, and Treason Trials in the Civil War* (Baton Rouge: Louisiana State University Press, 1984); Klement, *The Limits of Dissent: Clement L. Vallandigham and the Civil War* (New York: Fordham University Press, 1998); Klement, *Lincoln's Critics: The Copperheads of the North* (Shippensburg, PA: White Mane Books, 1999).

40. Weber, *Copperheads*, 1–2.

41. Jonathan W. White, "Copperheads," Essential Civil War Curriculum, accessed April 3, 2018 (web).

42. *Record of Vallandigham*, 6.

43. *Record of Vallandigham*, 8.

44. *Record of Vallandigham*, 21.

45. *Record of Vallandigham*, 23.

46. *Record of Vallandigham*, 31, emphasis added; also p. 57.

47. *Record of Vallandigham*, 60.

48. *Record of Vallandigham*, 69, 70.

49. *Record of Vallandigham*, 202.

50. *Record of Vallandigham*, 94. See also 111, 118–19, 128, 134, 143, 153; Vallandigham, *Speeches*, 520, 526.

51. *Record of Vallandigham*, 118–19. For similar instances, see 128: the ideal of "a man who, through evil and through good report, has adhered, with the faith of a

devotee and the firmness of a martyr, to the principles and policy of that grand old party of the Union"; see also pages 134, 143, 153; Vallandigham, *Speeches*, 520, 526.

52. Vallandigham, *Speeches*, 88–89.

53. Vallandigham, *Speeches*, 492.

54. Vallandigham, *Speeches*, 494.

55. G. M. D. Bloss, ed., *Life and Speeches of George H. Pendleton* (Cincinnati: Miami Printing, 1868), 32.

56. Bloss, *Life and Speeches of George H. Pendleton*, 76.

57. Daniel W. Voorhees, *Speeches of Daniel W. Voorhees of Indiana: Embracing His Most Prominent Forensic, Political, Occasional, and Literary Address*, ed. Charles S. Voorhees (Cincinnati: Robert Clarke, 1875), 55.

58. Voorhees, *Speeches of Daniel W. Voorhees*, 49–50.

59. Voorhees, *Speeches of Daniel W. Voorhees*, 55, 55–56.

60. Voorhees, *Speeches of Daniel W. Voorhees*, 120. See also 120–21.

61. Voorhees, *Speeches of Daniel W. Voorhees*, 62.

62. Engels, *Enemyship*.

63. For a history of this idea, see Clark McPhail's *The Myth of the Madding Crowd* (London: Routledge, 1991).

64. Bloss, *Life and Speeches of George H. Pendleton*, 30.

65. Bloss, *Life and Speeches of George H. Pendleton*, 32.

66. Bloss, *Life and Speeches of George H. Pendleton*, 30.

67. Bloss, *Life and Speeches of George H. Pendleton*, 34.

68. Bloss, *Life and Speeches of George H. Pendleton*, 51. See also 36, 50–51.

69. Bloss, *Life and Speeches of George H. Pendleton*, 85. See also 66, 76, 82.

70. *Record of Vallandigham*, 215.

71. *Record of Vallandigham*, 8.

72. *Record of Vallandigham*, 9.

73. *Record of Vallandigham*, 10. See also 12–14.

74. *Record of Vallandigham*, 17–18. See also 25–34, where he repeats again that slavery is a matter of private morality, not of federal concern.

75. *Record of Vallandigham*, 47, 61, 75.

76. *Record of Vallandigham*, 160 (introduction by editor on Mt. Vernon speech). See also 174–76, his tale of fanatic mob mentality; Vallandigham, *Speeches*, 485–86.

77. *Papers from the Society for the Diffusion of Political Knowledge* (New York: Society for the Diffusion of Political Knowledge, 1863–1864), 2. See also 59, 103–7, 108.

78. *Papers from the Society*, 3.

79. *Papers from the Society*, 11–12.

80. *Papers from the Society*, 46.

81. *Papers from the Society*, 50.

82. Robert H. Churchill calls this the "roots of modern patriotism," in *To Shake Their Guns in the Tyrant's Face: Libertarian Political Violence and the Origins of the Militia Movement* (Ann Arbor: University of Michigan Press, 2012), 107–44.

83. See *Record of Vallandigham*, 41, on the "Anglo-Saxon race, and the habit of self-command and of obedience."

84. *Papers from the Society*, 11–14; see also 15–16.
85. *Papers from the Society*, 31.
86. *Papers from the Society*, 31–32.
87. *Record of Vallandigham*, 9. Emphasis added.
88. *Record of Vallandigham*, 10. For other Jackson references, see 124, 196; *Papers from the Society*, 109.
89. *Record of Vallandigham*, 15.
90. *Record of Vallandigham*, 144.
91. *Record of Vallandigham*, 10, 131.
92. *Record of Vallandigham*, 11.
93. *Record of Vallandigham*, 11. Emphasis added.
94. *Record of Vallandigham*, 54. Emphasis added.
95. *Record of Vallandigham*, 54–56.
96. *Record of Vallandigham*, 61, 62–63.
97. *Record of Vallandigham*, 66.
98. Vallandigham, *Speeches*, 519–20.
99. *Record of Vallandigham*, 32.
100. *Record of Vallandigham*, 144–46. Sometimes the unmanly Abolitionists are compared unfavorably to the French. *Record of Vallandigham*, 227. Also see mentions of Austria and Russia as civilizational foils, in Vallandigham, *Speeches*, 488; *Papers from the Society*, 113.
101. *Record of Vallandigham*, 69.
102. *Record of Vallandigham*, 77–78, for a discussion of how England, for all its ills, still serves as an indicator of where civilization is heading.
103. *Papers from the Society*, 30–34. See also 63–65.
104. Vallandigham, *Speeches*, 344–45.
105. Vallandigham, *Speeches*, 522.
106. Vallandigham, *Speeches*, 347.
107. Vallandigham, *Speeches*, 480.
108. Bloss, *Life and Speeches of George H. Pendleton*, 43.
109. Bloss, *Life and Speeches of George H. Pendleton*, 32.
110. Bloss, *Life and Speeches of George H. Pendleton*, 61–62. See also 73–74; *Papers from the Society*, 107–8.
111. Bloss, *Life and Speeches of George H. Pendleton*, 73–74, again compares the current behavior to that of England, whose denizens historically did not even act as uncouth as the men at present. Thus, the thinking went, if we continued to act irrationally the United States risked returning to monarchies in the style of Louis XVI, Napoleon, or Louis Phillippe.
112. Voorhees, *Speeches*, 27.
113. Voorhees, *Speeches*, 28.
114. Voorhees, *Speeches*, 65.
115. Voorhees, *Speeches*, 28–38. See mentions of Egypt and Greece, among others, 38–53.
116. See also Voorhees, *Speeches*, 69–82, 88, 101–2, 133–38, 172.

117. Voorhees, *Speeches*, 98.

118. Once word of Lincoln's Emancipation Proclamation began to circulate, Copperheads ramped up their defense of the antebellum status quo, articulating a new defense of racial violence in the civilizational discourse of white supremacy.

119. *Papers from the Society*, 51.

120. *Papers from the Society*, 52.

121. *Papers from the Society*, 54.

122. *Papers from the Society*, 150.

123. *Papers from the Society*, 150.

124. *Papers from the Society*, 151. Morse continues to stress their "indolence."

125. *Papers from the Society*, 156.

126. The *Chicago Times*, a staunchly Copperhead newspaper, occasionally echoed such rhetoric in its pages, at times defending slavery and identifying "miscegenation and social equality" as grave threats to US culture. See Churchill, *To Shake Their Guns in the Tyrant's Face*, 118.

127. *Record of Vallandigham*, 70–72.

128. *Record of Vallandigham*, 86.

129. *Record of Vallandigham*, 189. See also 115, 130, 150–51.

130. *Record of Vallandigham*, 163.

131. *Record of Vallandigham*, 185, 176.

132. *Record of Vallandigham*, 189; 191, 198, 209.

133. Vallandigham, *Speeches*, 512.

134. Bloss, *Life and Speeches of George H. Pendleton*, 53–56.

135. Bloss, *Life and Speeches of George H. Pendleton*, 78.

136. Voorhees, *Speeches*, 34.

137. Voorhees, *Speeches*, 36–37; he then goes on to mention Scandinavia, Britain, the pharaohs, and Southern Europe.

138. J. Walter and Company, "Publishers' Notice," in *Record of Vallandigham*, 3.

139. Voorhees, *Speeches*, 35–41.

140. Voorhees, *Speeches*, 44, 41.

141. Voorhees, *Speeches*, 44, 41.

142. Voorhees, *Speeches*, 41–42.

143. Voorhees, *Speeches*, 54.

144. Vallandigham, *Speeches*, 186.

145. Vallandigham defied "treason" laws, most infamously in a speech at Mount Vernon, Ohio, and was exiled to the Confederacy, then to Bermuda, and finally to Ontario by a military tribunal. See Weber, *Copperheads*, 95–101.

146. See Kirt H. Wilson, *The Reconstruction Desegregation Debate: The Policies of Equality and the Rhetoric of Place, 1870–1875* (East Lansing: Michigan State University Press, 2002); W. E. B. Du Bois, *Black Reconstruction* (London: Routledge, 2017).

147. Weber, *Copperheads*, 215–15, 120–22, 131.

148. In James Vallandigham, *A Life of Clement L. Vallandigham* (Baltimore: Turnbull Brothers, 1872), 439.

149. J. Vallandigham, *Life of Clement L. Vallandigham*.

150. J. Vallandigham, *Life of Clement L. Vallandigham*.

151. J. Vallandigham, *Life of Clement L. Vallandigham*, 442.

152. See David W. Blight, *Race and Reunion: The Civil War in American Memory* (Cambridge, MA: Harvard University Press, 2001); Caroline E. Janney, *Remembering the Civil War: Reunion and the Limits of Reconciliation* (Chapel Hill: University of North Carolina Press, 2013).

153. Felix Harcourt, *Ku Klux Kulture: America and the Klan in the 1920s* (Chicago: University of Chicago Press, 2017).

154. Nancy MacLean, *Behind the Mask of Chivalry* (New York: Oxford University Press, 1994).

155. Matthew Houdek, "Racial Sedimentation and the Common Sense of Racialized Violence: The Case of Black Church Burnings," *Quarterly Journal of Speech* 104, no. 3 (2018): 279–306.

156. C. V. Vitolo-Haddad, "The Blood of Patriots: Symbolic Violence and 'the West,'" *Rhetoric Society Quarterly* 49, no. 3 (2019): 280–96.

Chapter 2

1. Ivan Musicant, *Empire by Default: The Spanish-American War and the Dawn of the American Century* (New York: Henry Holt, 1998). Musicant suggests that the occupation of the Philippines was less the result of active imperialist desire than the consequence of tough decisions with no perfect outcomes. While this may have been the experience of many adherents of expansion, the extended history of American occupation, seen from the point of view of those occupied, tells its own story. See David J. Silbey, *A War of Frontier and Empire: The Philippine-American War, 1899–1902* (New York: Hill and Wang, 2007); Angel Velasco Shaw and Luis H. Francia, eds., *Vestiges of War: The Philippine-American War and the Aftermath of an Imperial Dream, 1899–1999* (New York: New York University Press, 2002). See also David F. Trask, *The War with Spain in 1898* (New York: Free Press, 1981). Trask is more critical of American policy, describing its inception as a "failure of diplomacy" (30–71), although he similarly concedes that imperialism was "neither planned nor even anticipated before the brief conflict with Spain" (483).

2. Gary Scott Smith, *Religion in the Oval Office: The Religious Lives of American Presidents* (New York: Oxford University Press, 2015), 183.

3. Smith, *Religion in the Oval Office*.

4. For a prominent example of the religious argument for the colonizing project, see Josiah Strong, "On Anglo-Saxon Predominance, 1891," in *The New Era: Or, The Coming Kingdom* (New York: Baker and Taylor, 1893).

5. Achille Mbembe, "Necropolitics," *Public Culture* 15, no. 1 (2003): 25.

6. Frederic Bancroft and William A. Dunning, eds., *The Reminiscences of Carl Schurz*, vol. 3, *1863–1869* (New York: McClure, 1908); Francesca Bordogna, *William James at the Boundaries: Philosophy, Science and the Geography of Knowledge* (Chicago: University of Chicago Press, 2008).

7. Natalia Molina, *How Race Is Made in America: Immigration, Citizenship, and the Historical Power of Racial Scripts* (Berkeley: University of California Press, 2014).

8. In one of the stronger criticisms, Jackson Lears portrays Progressive activists as largely middle-class professionals who, though clamoring for "rebirth," often settled for piecemeal change well within the system of capitalist exploitation. See his *Rebirth of a Nation: The Making of Modern America, 1877–1920* (New York: Harper Perennial, 2009). This period saw a wave of anti-immigration, anti-environment, and racist reforms; see Richard White, *The Republic for Which It Stands: The United States during Reconstruction and the Gilded Age, 1865–1896* (Oxford: Oxford University Press, 2017); Ray Ginger, *Age of Excess: The United States from 1877 to 1914* (New York: Macmillan, 1975); H. Wiebe, *The Search for Order, 1877–1920* (New York: Hill and Wang, 1967); Drew Gilpin Faust, *This Republic of Suffering: Death and the American Civil War* (New York: Vintage, 2008); and Molly McGarry, *Ghosts of Futures Past: Spiritualism and the Cultural Politics of Nineteenth-Century America* (Berkeley: University of California Press, 2008).

9. Fabian Hilfrich, *Debating American Exceptionalism: Empire and Democracy in the Wake of the Spanish-American War* (Basingstoke, UK: Palgrave Macmillan, 2012). Hilfrich foregrounds the debate over "exceptionalism," but here I take a closer look at the racialized ideas of civilization and nationalism that undergird AIL rhetoric.

10. While earlier notions of race shaped these appeals, the AIL shows how debates over imperialism generate new forms of racialized rhetoric. Eric Rauchway, "Willard Straight and the Paradox of Liberal Imperialism," *Pacific Historical Review* 66, no. 3 (1997): 363–97. Rauchway argues that "imperialism preceded and decisively shaped racism, and that liberalism (of a distinctly American variety) gives rise to and abets imperialism" (368).

11. The work of Robert Hariman demonstrates how context-specific ideas and elements of style shape the historical development of political thought. See his *Political Style: The Artistry of Power* (Chicago: University of Chicago Press, 1995).

12. The policing methods developed in the Philippines by US soldiers, for instance, would return to the States and be used upon civilians. See Alfred W. McCoy, *Policing America's Empire: The United States, the Philippines, and the Rise of the Surveillance State* (Madison: University of Wisconsin Press, 2009).

13. Trask, *War with Spain*.

14. C. Roland Marchand, *The American Peace Movement and Social Reform, 1889–1918* (Princeton, NJ: Princeton University Press, 1972).

15. Mary L. Dudziak, *War Time: An Idea, Its History, Its Consequences* (New York: Oxford University Press, 2012).

16. Herbert H. Haines, "Radical Flank Effects," in *The Wiley-Blackwell Encyclopedia of Social and Political Movements*, December 15, 2022 (web).

17. Bonnie M. Miller, "The Incoherencies of Empire: The 'Imperial' Image of the Indian at the Omaha World's Fairs of 1898–1899," *American Studies* 49, nos. 3–4 (2008): 55–56.

18. "Fifty Lusty Filipinos," *Omaha World-Herald*, June 25, 1899.

19. "Midway Gleanings," *Omaha World-Herald*, August 31, 1898.

20. Lears, in surveying this period, describes AIL members as "patrician intellectuals from the Northeast." See *Rebirth of a Nation*, 217.

21. Scholars have long debated the merits, motivations, accomplishments, and consequences of the Populist and Progressive movements. See J. Michael Hogan, ed., *Rhetoric and Reform in the Progressive Era: Rhetorical History of the United States* vol. 6 (East Lansing: Michigan State University Press, 2002); Alan Brinkley, "Richard Hofstadter's *The Age of Reform*: A Reconsideration," *Reviews in American History* 13, no. 3 (September 1985): 462–80; Allen F. Davis, "The Progressives, Once More, with Conviction," *Reviews in American History* 11, no. 3 (1983): 404–8; Robert D. Johnston, "The Possibilities of Politics: Democracy in America, 1877 to 1917," in *American History Now*, ed. Eric Foner and Lisa McGirr (Philadelphia: Temple University Press, 2011), 96–124; and Robert C. McMath Jr. et al., "'Agricultural History' Roundtable on Populism," *Agricultural History* 82, no. 1 (Winter 2008): 1–35. A social movement approach can help explain this period. Focusing on "social movement sectors," "industries," and "organizations" shifts attention away from totalizing narratives concerning "Progressivism" or "Populism" and instead takes a contingent and relational perspective on activism existing in a web of resources, allies, opportunities, networks, mobilizing structures, and cultural frames. See Sidney G. Tarrow, *Power in Movement: Social Movements and Contentious Politics*, 3rd ed. (Cambridge, UK: Cambridge University Press, 2011). While the Temperance movement, Knights of Labor, and the movement for poverty reform, for instance, may share some basic characteristics, their differences are of equal significance, and to neglect them risks obscuring the rhetorical texture of political thought at the time. Activists responded to similar issues but with vastly different sets of resources, political opportunities, and associational linkages, or what we might call "repertoires" of contestation that tied each group to discrete activist trajectories.

22. See John D. Buenker, "Moral Reform Movements," in *Encyclopedia of American Social Movements*, ed. Immanuel Ness (New York: Routledge, 2004), 886.

23. In addition to informal discrimination, this period saw legislation passed targeted at non-European immigration, such as the Chinese Exclusion Act of 1882, the Geary Act of 1892, and the Literacy Law of 1917. See Richard Gribble, "The Immigration Restriction Debate, 1917–1929," *Journal of Church and State* 60, no. 3 (2018): 398–425.

24. Paul Kahan, *The Homestead Strike: Labor, Violence, and American Industry* (New York: Routledge, 2014).

25. Marchand, *American Peace Movement*.

26. Robert Ivie, *Dissent from War* (Bloomfield, CT: Kumarian Press, 2007).

27. See Gary Cross, *A Social History of Leisure since 1600* (State College, PA: Venture Publishing, 1990).

28. Regarding fears that enervation was associated with being "overcivilized," see Lears, *Rebirth of a Nation*, 7, and Martin Green, *The Vernon Street Warrens: A Boston Story, 1860–1910* (New York: Charles Scribner's Sons, 1989), 4.

29. Louis A. Perez Jr. describes how historiography of the conflict excludes the colonial subjects, which extends even into accounts of protest against colonization. See *The War of 1898: The United States and Cuba in History and Historiography* (Chapel Hill: University of North Carolina Press, 1998).

30. Green, *Vernon Street Warrens*, 156–57.

31. Green, *Vernon Street Warrens*, 157.

32. As the name "gilded" suggests, the period's tantalizing promise of prosperity was undercut by soaring wealth inequality, calling forth new grievances and protests. Ginger, *Age of Excess*; Lears, *Rebirth of a Nation*; White, *Republic for Which It Stands*.

33. For a more positive evaluation of the Mugwumps, see David M. Tucker, *Mugwumps: Public Moralists of the Gilded Age* (Columbia: University of Missouri Press, 1998).

34. For a more local study, see Geoffrey Blodgett, *The Gentle Reformers: Massachusetts Democrats in the Cleveland Era* (Cambridge, MA: Harvard University Press, 1966). More recently, some have reappraised Mugwump activism, lauding its vision of moral liberalism. See Tucker, *Mugwumps*; White, *Republic for Which It Stands*; Lears, *Rebirth of a Nation*; Ginger, *Age of Excess*.

35. E. Berkeley Tompkins, *Anti-Imperialism in the United States: The Great Debate, 1890–1920* (Philadelphia: University of Pennsylvania Press, 1970), 127–34. Tompkins also notes the mixed messaging surrounding race (109–10).

36. See Copperhead leader Clement Vallandigham's "New Direction" speech. In James Vallandigham, *A Life of Clement L. Vallandigham* (Baltimore: Turnbull Brothers, 1872), 439–42.

37. For a survey on the range and ambivalence of social Darwinism, see Richard Hofstadter, *Social Darwinism in American Thought* (Boston: Beacon Press, 1944); see also Peter Dobkin Hall, "Social Darwinism and the Poor," Social Welfare History Project, February 10, 2014 (web).

38. See discussion of "liberal imperialism" in John Milton Cooper Jr., *The Warrior and the Priest: Woodrow Wilson and Theodore Roosevelt* (Cambridge, MA: Harvard University Press, 1985); Walter LaFeber, *The New Empire: An Interpretation of American Expansion, 1860–1898* (Ithaca, NY: Cornell University Press, 1998); Tony Smith, *America's Mission: The United States and the Worldwide Struggle for Democracy in the Twentieth Century* (Princeton, NJ: Princeton University Press, 1994); and William Appleman Williams, *The Tragedy of American Diplomacy* (New York: Norton, 1988).

39. David Starr Jordan, *The Question of the Philippines: An Address Delivered before the Graduate Club of Leland Stanford Junior University on February 14, 1899* (Palo Alto, CA: John J. Valentine, Esq., 1899).

40. Trask, *War with Spain*, 475.

41. See H. W. Brands, *American Colossus: The Triumph of Capitalism, 1865–1900* (New York: Anchor Books, 2011).

42. Caroline E. Janney, *Remembering the Civil War: Reunion and the Limits of Reconciliation* (Chapel Hill: University of Chapel Hill, 2013), 223–31. See also Kirt H. Wilson, *The Reconstruction Desegregation Debate: The Politics of Equality and the Rhetoric of Place, 1870–1875* (East Lansing: Michigan State University Press, 2002).

43. See Raka Shome, "Postcolonial Interventions in the Rhetorical Canon: An 'Other' View," *Communication Theory* 6, no. 1 (1996): 40–59; Danielle Endres, "The Rhetoric of Nuclear Colonialism: Rhetorical Exclusion of American Indian Arguments in the Yucca Mountain Nuclear Waste Siting Decision," *Communication and*

Critical/Cultural Studies 6 (2009): 39–60; Mary E. Stuckey and John M. Murphy, "By Any Other Name: Rhetorical Colonialism in North America," *American Indian Culture and Research Journal* 25, no. 4 (2001): 73–98; Jason Edward Black, "Native Resistive Rhetoric and the Decolonization of American Indian Removal Discourse," *Quarterly Journal of Speech* 95 (2009): 66–88; Jason Edward Black, "Plenary Rhetoric in Indian Country: The Lone Wolf v. Hitchcock Case and the Codification of a Weakened Native Character," *Advances in the History of Rhetoric* 11/12 (2008): 59–80; Jason Edward Black, "Remembrances of Removal: Native Resistance to Allotment and the Unmasking of Paternal Benevolence," *Southern Communication Journal* 72 (2007): 185–203; Jason Edward Black, "Native Authenticity, Rhetorical Circulation, and Neocolonial Decay: The Case of Chief Seattle's Controversial Speech," *Rhetoric and Public Affairs* 15 (2012): 635–45; Derek T. Buescher and Kent A. Ono, "Civilized Colonialism: Pocahontas as Neocolonial Rhetoric," *Women's Studies in Communication* 19 (1996): 127–53; Darrel Enck-Wanzer, "Decolonizing Imaginaries: Rethinking 'the People' in the Young Lords' Church Offensive," *Quarterly Journal of Speech* 98 (2012): 1–23; Darrel Allan Wanzer, "Delinking Rhetoric, or Revisiting McGee's Fragmentation Thesis through Decoloniality," *Rhetoric and Public Affairs* 15 (2012): 647–57.

44. Charles De Benedetti, "Peace History, in the American Manner," *History Teacher* 18, no. 1 (1984): 94–95.

45. Michael Patrick Cullinane's survey of the Anti-Imperialist League fairly appraises the diverse uses of "liberty" and other key terms, noting how notions of race and superiority could seep into anti-imperialist discourse. While he focuses mostly on the positive elements of their rhetoric, I consider how the negative dimensions added pitfalls to the AIL script that could have obstructed its progressive elements. See Michael Patrick Cullinane, *Liberty and American Anti-Imperialism, 1898–1909* (New York: Palgrave Macmillan, 2012). See also Eric T. L. Love's analysis of race's complicated role in imperialist debates, *Race Over Empire: Racism and US Imperialism, 1865–1900* (Chapel Hill: University of North Carolina Press, 2004).

46. "Platform of the American Anti-Imperialist League," in *Speeches, Correspondence and Political Papers of Carl Schurz*, vol. 5, ed. Frederic Bancroft (New York: Knickerbocker Press, 1913), 77n1.

47. Charles Francis Adams, *"Imperialism" and "The Tracks of Our Forefathers": A Paper Read by Charles Francis Adams before the Lexington, Massachusetts, Historical Society, Tuesday, December 20, 1898* (Boston: Dana Estes, 1899).

48. Adams, *"Imperialism" and "The Tracks of Our Forefathers."*

49. Adams, *"Imperialism" and "The Tracks of Our Forefathers."*

50. Adams, *"Imperialism" and "The Tracks of Our Forefathers."*

51. Adams, *"Imperialism" and "The Tracks of Our Forefathers."*

52. Richard White describes the increased push after the Civil War to conceptualize the United States as a single, unified entity in *Republic for Which It Stands*, xvii.

53. Edward C. Pierce, "The 'Single Tribe' Fiction, Liberty Tracts no. 14," Chicago: American Anti-Imperialist League, Folder Anti-Imperialist League, Chicago, 1899–1901, Swarthmore Peace Collection, Swarthmore, Pennsylvania, United States.

54. Pierce, "'Single Tribe' Fiction."

55. Pierce, "'Single Tribe' Fiction."

56. Edward Atkinson, "The Cost of an Anglo-American War," *American Periodicals*, March 1896, 74.

57. George S. Boutwell, *Bryan or Imperialism: Address by the Hon. George S. Boutwell, Delivered at the National Congress of Anti-Imperialists at Indianapolis, Ind., August 15–16, 1900* (Boston: New England Anti-Imperialist League, 1900).

58. Boutwell, *Bryan or Imperialism*, 11.

59. Boutwell, *Bryan or Imperialism*.

60. Boutwell, *Bryan or Imperialism*, 11–12.

61. Boutwell, *Bryan or Imperialism*, 18.

62. George S. Boutwell, *Imperialists or Republicans?: Mr. Boutwell's Speech before the Essex Institute, Salem, January 9, 1899* (Washington, DC: Anti-Imperialist League, 1899), 12.

63. Boutwell, *Imperialists or Republicans?* 12.

64. George S. Boutwell, *The President's Policy: War and Conquest Abroad, Degradation of Labor at Home* (Chicago: American Anti-Imperialist League, 1900), 3, 9.

65. George S. Boutwell, in William Jennings Bryan, *Republic or Empire* (Boston: New England Anti-Imperialist League, 1900), 17.

66. Carl Schurz, "Our Future Foreign Policy," address at Saratoga, NY, August 19, 1898, in Bancroft, *Speeches, Correspondence and Political Papers*, vol. 5, 481.

67. Schurz, "Our Future Foreign Policy."

68. Schurz, "Our Future Foreign Policy," 483, 485.

69. Schurz, "Our Future Foreign Policy."

70. Schurz, "Our Future Foreign Policy," 504, 511–12; Schurz, "The Issue of Imperialism," in Bancroft, *Speeches, Correspondence, and Political Papers*, vol. 6, 1–34; Schurz, "For Truth, Justice and Liberty," in Bancroft, *Speeches, Correspondence, and Political Papers*, vol. 6, 215–50.

71. Samuel Gompers, "Imperialism—Its Dangers and Wrongs: A Speech by Samuel Gompers, President of the American Federation of Labor," delivered October 18, 1898, available at Thirteen.org (web).

72. Moorfield Storey, "Statement of Hon. Moorfield Storey, of Boston, Mass., before the Committee of Insular Affairs, House of Representatives (888A)," April 6, 1906, 153.

73. Storey, "Statement of Hon. Moorfield Storey," 171.

74. See also Storey, *What Shall We Do with Our Dependencies? The Annual Address before the Bar Association of South Carolina* (Boston: Geo. H. Ellis, 1903).

75. William Jennings Bryan, "Imperialism," delivered August 8, 1900, available via Voices of Democracy (web).

76. William Jennings Bryan, "America's Mission," in *Speeches of William Jennings Bryan* (New York: Funk and Wagnalls, 1913), 15–16, emphasis added.

77. See also William Graham Sumner, "The Conquest of the United States by Spain," January 16, 1899, in *On Liberty, Society, and Politics: The Essential Essays of William Graham Sumner*, ed. Robert C. Bannister (Carmel, IN: Liberty Fund, 1992), 272.

78. David Starr Jordan, *The Question of the Philippines: An Address Delivered before*

the Graduate Club of Leland Stanford Junior University on February 14, 1899 (Palo Alto, CA: John J. Valentine, Esq., 1899), 26.

79. Jordan, *Question of the Philippines*, 24.

80. Joseph Henry Crooker, "The Menace to America," Chicago: American Anti-Imperialist League newsletter (1900), 3–4.

81. Adams, *"Imperialism" and "The Tracks of Our Forefathers."*

82. Adams, *"Imperialism" and "The Tracks of Our Forefathers."*

83. Adams, *"Imperialism" and "The Tracks of Our Forefathers."*

84. Brands, *American Colossus*.

85. Atkinson, "Cost of Anglo-American," *American Periodicals*, March 1896, 75.

86. Atkinson, "Cost of Anglo-American," 82.

87. Atkinson, "Cost of Anglo-American," 83–88.

88. Boutwell echoes "producerist" sentiments in his *Address to the Laboring and Producing Classes of the United States* (Chicago: American Anti-Imperialist League, 1900).

89. Boutwell, "Address to the Laboring and Producing Classes."

90. Boutwell, "Address to the Laboring and Producing Classes."

91. Boutwell, *Bryan or Imperialism*.

92. See Boutwell, *President's Policy*, 3–13.

93. Boutwell, *Republic or Empire?*

94. Boutwell, *Republic or Empire?* 21; Boutwell, *The Enslavement of American Labor* (Boston: New England Anti-Imperialist League, 1902).

95. Schurz, "Issue of Imperialism." Schurz suggests in the introduction that his essay is meant to be a guide for AIL members to advocate their cause.

96. Carl Schurz, "Militarism and Democracy," *Annals of the American Academy of Political and Social Science* 13, no. 12 (1899): 77–103.

97. Grover Cleveland, "Founder's Day Address," in *Addresses, State Papers and Letters*, ed. Albert Ellery Bergh (New York: Sun Dial Classics, 1909), 423.

98. Cleveland, "Founder's Day Address," 424. The prospect of more minority (or nonwhite) citizens allows for a seemingly more benevolent approach to America's own heterogeneity, yet it is framed here in a way that prioritizes a homogenizing process required for entry into American culture. This previewed critiques of "racial uplift" initiatives, such as those by Booker T. Washington, as compromising a group's racial identity in favor of assimilation. See also Eric Foner, *Give the Liberty! An American History* (New York: W. W. Norton, 2008), 659.

99. See Bryan, *Republic or Empire?* 17, 47, 67–68.

100. Bryan, *Republic or Empire?* 67.

101. Bryan, *Republic or Empire?* 85. See also 191–200, 234–35.

102. Bryan, *Republic or Empire?* 413.

103. AIL members also stressed the onerous taxation brought about by the war, sometimes as a proxy for critiquing federal taxes and intervention more broadly. See Edward Atkinson, *The Cost of a National Crime* (Boston: Rockwell and Churchill Press, 1898). Here Atkinson expounds upon the ills of federal excess, citing figures and possible expenditures that lend themselves to critiques of tariffs and other forms of government interference in the economy.

104. Adams, *"Imperialism" and "The Tracks of Our Forefathers."* Emphasis added.

105. Boutwell, "Enslavement of American Labor," 7. Emphasis added.

106. Schurz, "Our Future Foreign Policy," 481–83. Emphasis added.

107. Schurz, "Our Future Foreign Policy," 482. Emphasis added.

108. Andrew Carnegie, "Americanism versus Imperialism: II," *North American Review* 168, no. 508 (1899): 363. Emphasis added.

109. Jordan, "Question of the Philippines," 26–43.

110. Boutwell, "Enslavement of American Labor," 7. Emphasis added.

111. Mark Twain, easily the most recognizable AIL member today despite minimal participation, did not succumb to the movement's overtly racist elements, instead aiming his satiric wit at America's moral hypocrisy. See Jim Zwick, *Mark Twain's Weapons of Satire* (Malden, MA: Blackwell, 1992).

112. "Platform of the American Anti-Imperialist League."

113. "Platform of the American Anti-Imperialist League."

114. Jordan, "Question of the Philippines," 26–43.

115. Adams, *"Imperialism" and "The Tracks of Our Forefathers."*

116. Adams, *"Imperialism" and "The Tracks of Our Forefathers."*

117. References to "Muhammad" were common, aimed to contrast the Christian Anglo-Saxon superior quality of self-restraint, in Adams, *Imperialism and "The Tracks of Our Forefathers"*; Bryan, *Republic or Empire?* 9.

118. George F. Edmunds, *The Insular Cases* (Boston: Anti-Imperialist League, 1901), 10.

119. Boutwell, *Imperialists or Republicans?*

120. Boutwell, *Imperialists or Republicans?* 14.

121. Boutwell, *President's Policy*, 13. Emphasis added.

122. Boutwell, *Republic or Empire* (Boston: New England Anti-Imperialist League, 1900, 18.

123. Schurz migrated from Germany following the 1848 revolutions, which greatly influenced his political thinking.

124. Schurz, "National Honor," in Bancroft, *Speeches, Correspondence, and Political Papers*, vol. 5, 453–54. Emphasis added.

125. Schurz, "National Honor," 454. Emphasis added.

126. Schurz, "National Honor," 455. Emphasis added. Schurz also invokes Lincoln's memory in "Thoughts on American Imperialism," in Bancroft, *Speeches, Correspondence, and Political Papers*, vol. 5, 496. See also 512–13.

127. Schurz, "Issue of Imperialism," 1–36.

128. Schurz, "To Charles Francis Adams, Jr. New York, Jan. 1, 1899," in Bancroft, *Speeches, Correspondence, and Political Papers*, vol. 6.

129. Schurz, "Issue of Imperialism," 36.

130. See also, Schurz, "The Policy of Imperialism," in Bancroft, *Speeches, Correspondence, and Political Papers*, vol. 6, 108.

131. Schurz, "For the Republic of Washington and Lincoln," in Bancroft, *Speeches, Correspondence, and Political Papers*, vol. 6, 188.

132. Other AIL members couch their anti-war rhetoric in appeals to America's

moral exceptionalism, stressing the "homogenous" nature of the great nation. See Moorfield Storey, "The Neutralization of the Philippines as a Peace Measure," in *Advocate of Peace* 70, no. 1 (1908): 20; Storey, "Statement of Hon. Moorfield Storey," 152–53.

133. "Soldier's Letters," pamphlet (Anti-Imperialist League, 1899), in *The Anti-Imperialist Reader: A Documentary History of Anti-Imperialism in the United States*, vol. 1, ed. Philip S. Foner and Richard Winchester (New York: Holmes and Meier, 1984), 316–23.

134. "Soldier's Letters."

135. "Soldier's Letters"; Storey, "What Shall We Do with Our Dependencies?" 41–58. See also Sumner, "Conquest of the United States by Spain."

136. Carnegie, "Americanism versus Imperialism: II," 366.

137. Carnegie, "Americanism versus Imperialism: II," 367. Emphasis added.

138. Carnegie, "Americanism versus Imperialism: II," 369.

139. Carnegie, "Americanism versus Imperialism: II," 370. Emphasis added.

140. Cleveland, "Founder's Day Address," 403. Similarly, most congressional anti-imperialist addresses in Bryan's edited collection are not anti-war in the slightest—they only caution against the loss of America's exceptionalism that would be made possible by engaging with inferior races, with many members citing the lingering Civil War memory as justification to avoid further intervention both near and far. See Bryan, *Republic or Empire?* See also Frederick W. Gookin, "A Liberty Catechism" (Chicago: Central Anti-Imperialist League, October 1899), in box 1, folder: Anti-Imperialist League, Bound Volume of Pamphlets/Tracts, 1899, Swarthmore Peace Collection, Swarthmore, Pennsylvania, United States, 3–15; J. Laurence Laughlin, "The Philippine War," in *Liberty Tracts*, no. 1: The Chicago Liberty Meeting Held at Central Music Hall, April 30, 1899 (Central Anti-Imperialist League, Tacoma Building, Chicago: 1899); Laughlin, "Patriotism and Imperialism," in *Liberty Tracts*, no. 2 (Chicago: Central Anti-Imperialist League, 1899), 12, 16.

141. "Proclamation on Declaring a National Emergency Concerning the Novel Coronavirus Disease (COVID-19) Outbreak," White House, March 13, 2020 (web).

142. Simon Tisdall, "Trump Is Playing a Deadly Game in Deflecting Covid-19 Blame to China," *Guardian*, April 19, 2020. See also Richard Haass, "The Pandemic Will Accelerate History Rather than Reshape It," *Foreign Affairs*, April 7, 2020.

143. Billy Perrigo, "White Supremacist Groups Are Recruiting with Help from Coronavirus—and a Popular Messaging App," *Time*, April 8, 2020.

144. Nick Martin, "Give Me Capitalism or Give Me Death," *New Republic*, March 25, 2020.

145. Craig Timberg and Allyson Chiu, "As the Coronavirus Spreads, so Does Online Racism Targeting Asians, New Research Shows," *Washington Post*, April 8, 2020.

146. Johan Galtung, *Peace by Peaceful Means: Peace and Conflict, Development and Civilization* (London: Sage, 1996).

147. Jane Addams, "Democracy or Militarism," in *The Chicago Liberty Meeting, Liberty Tract no. 1* (Chicago: Central Anti-Imperialist League, 1899), 35–39.

148. Addams, "Democracy or Militarism."

149. Addams, "Democracy or Militarism," emphasis added.

150. Addams, "Democracy or Militarism," emphasis added.

151. This address is one of her few extant contributions to the AIL, specifically.

152. Wilson would face similar obstacles to articulate post–World War I peace. See Erez Manela, *The Wilsonian Moment: Self-Determination and the International Origins of Anticolonial Nationalism* (New York: Oxford University Press, 2007).

Chapter 3

1. "Henry Ford's Peace Ship Brings $67,500 as Junk," *Chicago Daily Tribune*, September 4, 1933.

2. "Ford's Peace Ship on Way to War Zone," *Gazette Times*, December 5, 1915.

3. It is noteworthy how previous anti-war activists deployed public memory to make their activities seem quintessentially "American," whereas Ford opted for a starkly memory-free movement that easily traversed national borders but exposed peace advocacy to countermemories.

4. See Pearl James, *Picture This: World War I Posters and Visual Culture* (Lincoln: University of Nebraska Press, 2009), 21: "We reject the idea that instantaneous intelligibility has, as its necessary corollary, unambiguous simplicity."

5. Consider Guy Debord's seminal work *Society of the Spectacle*, trans. Fredy Perlman and Jon Supak (Detroit: Black and Red, 1970), which incorporates salient insights from Marxist theory to critique mass media and capitalist ideology. Debord's initial conceptualization of spectacle was largely concerned with the phases of capitalism, commodification, and consumerism. For a case study on the overlap of consumer culture, technology, and global politics, see also Margaret Creighton, *The Electrifying Fall of Rainbow City: Spectacle and Assassination at the 1901 World's Fair* (New York: W. W. Norton, 2016). Many scholars also note the combination of rising literacy, the proliferation of news and cultural publications, and rapidly changing conditions of industrial capitalism as formative to the rise of the visual culture, labeling the period as the birth of "modernity." See Robert Hariman and John Louis Lucaites, *The Public Image: Photography and Civic Spectatorship* (Chicago: University of Chicago Press, 2016); Jonathan Crary, "Modernity and the Problem of the Observer," in *Techniques of the Observer: On Vision and Modernity in the Nineteenth Century* (Cambridge: MIT Press, 1990): 1–24; see also Carl F. Kaestle et al., *Literacy in the United States: Readers and Reading since 1880* (London: Yale University Press, 1991).

6. See the work of Ariella Azoulay, particularly *The Civil Contract of Photography* (New York: Zone Books, 2008) and *Civil Imagination: A Political Ontology of Photography*, trans. Louise Bethlehem (London: Verso, 2015); Jacques Rancière, *The Emancipated Spectator*, trans. Gregory Elliot (London: Verso, 2009); Hariman and Lucaites, *Public Image*.

7. For a more detailed account of how political spectacles act as powerful sources of meaning while still being barren of essential meaning, see Murray Edelman's *Constructing the Political Spectacle* (Chicago: University of Chicago Press, 1988).

8. Matthew Jackson, "The Enthymematic Hegemony of Whiteness," *JAC* 26, no.

3 (2006): 601–41; Krista Ratcliffe, "In Search of the Unstated," *JAC* 27, no. 1 (2007): 275–90.

9. Thomas K. Nakayama and Robert L. Krizek, "Whiteness: A Strategic Rhetoric," *Quarterly Journal of Speech* 81, no. 3 (1995): 291–309.

10. Geoffrey R. Stone, *Perilous Times: Free Speech in Wartime* (New York: W. W. Norton, 2004).

11. Curtis C. Simpson III, "The Logan Act of 1799: May It Rest in Peace," *California Western International Law Journal* 10, no. 2 (1980): 369–70.

12. Stone, *Perilous Times*, 137.

13. Stone, *Perilous Times*, 137–44.

14. See J. Michael Hogan, ed., *Rhetoric and Reform in the Progressive Era: Rhetorical History of the United States*, vol. 6 (East Lansing: Michigan State University Press, 2003).

15. Roger Possner, *The Rise of Militarism in the Progressive Era, 1900–1914* (London: McFarland, 2009).

16. See John Steele Gordon, *An Empire of Wealth: The Epic History of American Power* (New York: Harper Perennial, 2004); Ray Ginger, *Age of Excess: The United States from 1877 to 1914* (New York: Macmillan, 1975); Jackson Lears, *Rebirth of a Nation: The Making of Modern America, 1877–1920* (New York: Harper Perennial, 2009).

17. Steven Watts, *The People's Tycoon: Henry Ford and the American Century* (New York: First Vintage Books, 2005), 111. See also Greg Grandin, *Fordlandia: The Rise and Fall of Henry Ford's Forgotten Jungle City* (New York: Metropolitan Books, 2009).

18. Ford Motor Company, "The Model T: A Timeless Legacy," accessed November 16, 2024 (web).

19. James, *Picture This*.

20. C. Roland Marchand, *The American Peace Movement and Social Reform, 1889–1918* (Princeton, NJ: Princeton University Press, 1972).

21. Business: consider Andrew Carnegie's organization, Endowment for International Peace, *A Manual of the Public Benefactions of Andrew Carnegie* (N.d.: Washington, DC, 1919), 281–86. Science: David Starr Jordan, prominent academic, eugenicist, and member of the Anti-Imperialist League, continued peace activism into the early twentieth century. See Marchand, *American Peace Movement*, 104. Culture: Mark Twain, although a comparatively inactive member of the Anti-Imperialist League, was among its most popular figures.

22. Marchand, *American Peace Movement*. For a broader survey of the transnational formation of Progressive Era policy, see Daniel T. Rodgers, *Atlantic Crossings: Social Politics in a Progressive Age* (Cambridge, MA: Harvard University Press, 1998).

23. Marchand, *American Peace Movement*, 74.

24. Marchand, *American Peace Movement*, 74.

25. Marchand, *American Peace Movement*, 381–90.

26. Michael Kazin, *War against War: The American Fight for Peace, 1914–1918* (New York: Simon and Schuster, 2017), ii.

27. Kazin, *War against War*, 4. See also Alan Axelrod, *Selling the Great War: The Making of American Propaganda* (New York: St. Martin's Press, 2009).

28. The 2014 Hong Kong pro-democracy movement, for instance, achieved global popularity through digital means but was violently repressed. The George Floyd movement, one of the largest global protests, also has had only limited impact on police reform and attitudes.

29. Indeed, the American public could hold complex, even contradictory, feelings, such as the "Two Germanys" ideology, which posited the poor folks of Germany were hapless victims of the autocratic, militant elites of Germany who waged an atrocious war. Thus, one could hate Germany but feel sympathy for the Germans. As more incidents of German aggression came to public attention, and the impression that the war would end soon faded, a growing anti-German consensus emerged. Michael S. Neiberg, *The Path to War: How the First World War Created Modern America* (New York: Oxford University Press, 2016), 4, 9–38.

30. Woodrow Wilson, "Joint Address to Congress Leading to a Declaration of War against Germany (1917), available at National Archives (web).

31. Woodrow Wilson, "State of the Union Address (December 7, 1915)," available at the American Presidency Project (web). Wilson tightly wrapped his pro-preparation stance in the fabric of American public memory by acknowledging the country's historical hesitancy to intervene to intervene abroad, an issue made tricky by Democrats' long association with anti-war sentiment.

32. Few scholarly works exist on Henry Ford's anti-war movement; those that do mostly focus on behind-the-scenes squabbling. See Barbara S. Kraft, *The Peace Ship: Henry Ford's Pacifist Adventure in the First World War* (New York: Macmillan, 1978) and Burnet Hershey, *The Odyssey of Henry Ford and the Great Peace Ship* (New York: Taplinger, 1967). See "Ford Favors Allies," *Philadelphia Inquirer*, December 7, 1915.

33. "Newspaper Specials," *Wall Street Journal*, August 24, 1915.

34. "Newspaper Specials," *Wall Street Journal*, September 21, 1915.

35. "Ford Opposes Loan to Allies," *Philadelphia Inquirer*, September 25, 1915.

36. "Roosevelt Likens Ford to Old Fashioned Chinaman," *Chicago Daily Tribune*, October 21, 1915.

37. "Ford Urges Wilson to Start Peace Talk," *Gazette Times*, November 24, 1915.

38. "Ford Will Send Ship to War," *Philadelphia Inquirer*, November 25, 1915.

39. "Ford Will Send Ship to War."

40. The legalistic focus on process at the time also suggests how Ford's emphasis on a peace meeting may have appeared enough of a plan for some readers. See Marchand, *American Peace Movement*.

41. "Ford Will Send Ship to War." Emphasis added.

42. See Max Weber, "The Nature of Charismatic Authority and Its Routinization," in *Theory of Social and Economic Organization*, trans. A. R. Anderson and Talcott Parsons (New York: Free Press, 1947).

43. "Ford Aids Peace Move by Women," *New York Times*, November 27, 1915.

44. "Ford Asks Bryan," *New York Times*, November 26, 1915.

45. "Ford Hires Liner in Peace Crusade," *New York Times*, November 25, 1915.

46. "Ford Hires Liner in Peace Crusade."

47. See "Governor Willis Undecided," *New York Times*, November 26, 1915; "Wanamaker May Go on Ford Peace Trip," *Philadelphia Inquirer*, November 26, 1915.

48. See "Ford Asks Bryan to Be First Mate on His Peace Ship," *New York Times*, November 26, 1915.

49. "The Expedition of the Notables," *Gazette Times*, November 26, 1915.

50. "Ford Now Planning an Overflow Ship," *New York Times*, November 29, 1915.

51. Ohio Governor Frank B. Willis, like most politicians, declined Ford's mission. See "Ford Aids Peace Move by Women," *New York Times*, November 27, 1915; see "Wanamaker Is Skeptical," *New York Times*, December 1, 1915.

52. "Ford Hopes Troops Will Start a Strike: Believes Men Will Climb Out," *New York Times*, November 30, 1915; "Ford Aids Peace Move by Women." See also "Grotesque," *New York Times*, December 1, 1915.

53. "Ford Gets His Ship," *New York Times*, November 28, 1915; see also "Ford Asks Bryan.".

54. "Ford Gets His Ship." Emphasis added.

55. "Ford Gets His Ship."

56. "Courts May Stop Ford's Peace Mission Voyage," *Gazette Times*, November 27, 1915.

57. "Ford Asks Bryan." Emphasis added.

58. "The Expedition of the Notables," *Gazette Times*, November 26, 1915.

59. "Ford Aids Peace Move by Women." See also "Pleas Received and Filed," *New York Times*, November 28, 1915; "Ford Hopes Troops Will Start a Strike."

60. "Ford Fireworks," *Irish Times*, November 29, 1915.

61. "Ford Defies His Critics: Issues Long Statement before Leaving Detroit for New York," *New York Times*, December 2, 1915.

62. "Ford Hopes Troops Will Start a Strike."

63. "Ford Favors Allies: Makes Will," *Philadelphia Inquirer*, December 4, 1915. Ford calls the newspaper and magazine writers the "most important part of the mission," stating that he "leave[s] the fate of the mission in their hands."

64. "Ford Favors Allies."

65. "Peace Ark Starts," *New York Times*, December 5, 1915; see also "Ford's Peace Ship on Way to War Zone."

66. "Peace Ark Starts."

67. "Peace Ark Starts."

68. "Peace Ark Starts."

69. Alena Zupancic, *The Odd One In: On Comedy* (Cambridge: MIT Press, 2008), 8.

70. "Ford's Peace Ship on Way to War Zone"; see also "Ford Peace Mission Starts Its Voyage at a Lively Gait," *Philadelphia Inquirer*, December 5, 1915, which details further how Bryan "dodged" the kissing bride, Ford's befuddlement when asked for a "message," and how he was supposedly just going over to Europe "for a damn good time and a rest."

71. "Ford Favors Allies."

72. "Peace Ark Starts."

73. "Peace Ark Starts."

74. "Peace Ark Starts."

75. "Ford Peace Mission Starts Its Voyage at a Lively Gait"; A. E. Hartzel, "Germans May Arrest Ford's Peace Party," *Gazette Times*, December 6, 1915; "Roosevelt Scores Ford Peace Junket and Wilson Policy," *Philadelphia Inquirer*, December 6, 1915; "England May Detain the Ford Pilgrims," *New York Times*, December 6, 1915.

76. C. F. Aked, "Into the Unknown," *Philadelphia Inquirer*, December 7, 1915.

77. "Departing Pacifists Worry," *New York Times*, December 9, 1915.

78. "Even Have War on Ford's Peace Ship," *Philadelphia Inquirer*, December 9, 1915.

79. H. W. J., "Pepper and Salt," *Wall Street Journal*, December 10, 1915.

80. "Ship of Fools," *Spectator*, December 11, 1915; "An American Car Maker's Antics: The Trip of 'Ford's Ark' to Europe," *North-China Herald and Supreme Court and Consular Gazette*, December 11, 1915.

81. "Editorial Comment," *Philadelphia Inquirer*, December 13, 1915; in *Pittsburgh Gazette*, from *Milwaukee Sentinel*, December 16, 1915; "Sad State of Affairs," *Gazette Times*, December 22, 1915. See also "Ford's Ark," *Shanghai Times*, December 18, 1915; "Some Topics of the Week," *Philadelphia Inquirer*, December 19, 1915.

82. "Talks with Mr. Ford: A Quaint Crusader," *Times of India*, January 3, 1916.

83. Listing in *Philadelphia Inquirer*, December 13, 1915.

84. Aked, "Into the Unknown."

85. Aked, "Into the Unknown." Emphasis added.

86. Aked, "Into the Unknown." See also "Ford Seeking Congress' Aid," *Chicago Daily Tribune*, December 7, 1915; "Departing Pacifists Worry."

87. "Row on Ford Ship over Expulsions," *New York Times*, December 20, 1915; "Squabbles Mark Peace Ark's Voyage," *Philadelphia Inquirer*, December 20, 1915.

88. "Ford Finds Peace Elusive," *New York Times*, December 21, 1915.

89. Mrs. Ford disputed rumors of Ford falling ill, which ironically would have made his decision seem more reasonable. See "Ford Abdicates; Sails for Home: Leaves $270,000 Check for the Peace Party," *New York Times*, December 25, 1915.

90. "Ford Offers Party $2,000,000 Backing," *New York Times*, December 28, 1915; "First Photographs Made Aboard Ford Peace Ship," *Philadelphia Inquirer*, December 28, 1915.

91. "Ford Party in Dispute, Mrs. Boissevain Leaves: Indicts Party as Having No Plans and Being Directed by an Undemocratic Few," *New York Times*, December 26, 1915; Charles P. Stewart, "Peace Party Split Again," *Chicago Daily Tribune*, December 26, 1915.

92. "Henry Ford Back, Admits an Error, Denies Deserting: Disabused of Idea That the War Was Caused by Militarists or Munition Men: Now Blames the People," *New York Times*, January 3, 1916.

93. "Ford Ship Arrives in Christiansand," *New York Times*, December 19, 1915.

94. From the *Aftenposten*, as reported in "Ford Finds Peace Elusive."

95. "Peace Party to Cross Germany in Locked Cars," *Chicago Daily Tribune*, January 4, 1916.

96. "Ford Pacifists Go through Germany," *Gazette Times*, January 4, 1916.

97. The *Dagbladet*, quoted in "Dr. Aked Ill?" *New York Times*, January 1, 1916, 3.

98. "Flash! Bang! Peace Party Is Forgotten," *San Francisco Chronicle*, December 22, 1915.

99. "Henry Ford Back, Admits an Error."

100. Henry Ford Back, Admits an Error."

101. See "Ford Ship Arrives at Christiansand: Peace Party Rent by Discord on Eve of First Landing in Europe: Curfew Crusade Blocked: Reported Attempts at Espionage Also Serves to Enliven the Voyage . . . Proprietors Refuse to Reserve Rooms," *New York Times*, December 19, 1915; Carolyn Wilson, "War on Ford's Peace Ship: Want to Expel Reporters at Christiania," *Chicago Daily Tribune*, December 20, 1915.

102. "The Ford Expedition: Being Morally Right Time Is on the Side of Those Who Strive for Peace," *San Francisco Chronicle*, December 22, 1915.

103. "Ford Deserts Pacifists at Christiania," *Gazette Times*, December 24, 1915; see also "Henry Ford Is Reported to Be Ill," *San Francisco Chronicle*, December 24, 1915.

104. As cited in "Ford Finds Peace Elusive"; see also "Ford Peace Meeting Barred by Denmark: Papers in Christiania Surprised That Manufacturer Had No Definite Plan Mapped Out," *Philadelphia Inquirer*, December 21, 1915.

105. "The Dove of Peace Breaks Its Wing," *Philadelphia Inquirer*, December 27, 1915.

106. "Kaiser's Pacific Agents Indicted," "Teuton U-Boat Fires on Flag of Uncle Sam," and "Plotters," all in the *Gazette Times*, December 5, 1915.

107. See Roosevelt's critique, published December 6, 1915, *Gazette Times*; A. E. Hartzell, "Germans May Arrest Ford's Peace Party," *Gazette Times*, December 6, 1915.

108. "Germans May Arrest Ford's Peace Party." See also "Roosevelt Scores Ford Peace Junket and Wilson Policy," *Philadelphia Inquirer*, December 6, 1915.

109. In *New York Times*, December 8, 1915.

110. See also "Cabinet Officers in Conference Plan to United against Plotters" and "Reichstag Begins Peace Talk Today" side by side with "Departing Pacifists Worry," *New York Times*, December 9, 1915; "Allies in Serbia May Be Outflanked," "German Women Do the Work of Men," and "Failure of British gets on 'Nerves' of Allied Nations" next to "Even Have War on Ford's Peace Ship," all in *Philadelphia Inquirer*, December 9, 1915.

111. "Peace Programme for Ford Party Announced," *Philadelphia Inquirer*, December 10, 1915, which only details the process, not the policies or substance of the peace position.

112. "Woman Held as Witness in U.S. Bomb Plot Probe," *San Francisco Chronicle*, December 10, 1915.

113. "Ford's Party Not Popular at The Hague: Will Be Permitted to Land, but Told to Move on if Activities Are Offensive," *Gazette Times*, December 12, 1915.

114. See also "Name Von Papen in Plot to Blow Munition Plants in the West," *Philadelphia Inquirer*, December 15, 1915; "Hold Ex-Employe[e] of Du Pont for Plot," beside "Britain Releases Ford's Peace Ship: Found Contraband Aboard," *New York Times*, December 17, 1915.

115. "Contraband Found Aboard Peace Ship," *Gazette Times*, December 17, 1915; "Britain Releases Ford's Peace Ship: Found Contraband Aboard," *New York Times*,

December 17, 1915; "Henry Ford's Peace Ship Released by British," *Chicago Daily Tribune*, December 18, 1915. Consider "Rubber on the Peace Ship," stating that "it is ascertained that fifty-five bags of rubber, all consigned to a well-known enemy forwarding agent in Sweden, were removed from the parcel mail on board the steamship Oscar II." *New York Times*, December 30, 1915, beside the headline "Orders Arrest of Four in Plots."

116. "British Allow Ford Party to Quite Kirkwall," *Gazette Times*, December 18, 1915, besides "Plot to Destroy Welland Canal: Hamburg-American Sleuth Under Arrest as One Conspirator" and "Probe of Bryan's Peace Propaganda Is Asked: Representative Gardener of Massachusetts Wants to Know if Former Secretary of State Is Pacifist for Pay—Uses Vigorous Language in Denouncing Enemies of Defense."

117. See also "War on Ford's Peace Ship: Want to Expel Reporters at Christiania," *Chicago Daily Tribune*, December 20, 1915, besides "American in Jail as Spy in Warsaw"; the farcical article "Squabbles Mark Peace Ark's Voyage," *Philadelphia Inquirer*, December 20, 1915, besides the following wartime coverage: "French's Goodbye to Troops Touching"; "Germany in Fear of Revolt of Poor"; "To Guard against Internal Enemies: Conference on Immigration Will Aim to Americanize Foreign-Born: Sessions to Be Held Here Will Start Movement to Lessen Labor Disturbances."

118. Beside "Ford Peace Meeting Barred by Denmark," *Philadelphia Inquirer*, December 21, 1915.

119. "Ford Finds Peace Elusive." See also "Dardanelles Campaign Not Given Up" beside "Copenhagen to Prohibit Ford Peace Meeting," *Gazette Times*, December 21, 1915.

120. "Ford Sails for U.S., Leave Peace Party in Europe," *Philadelphia Inquirer*, December 25, 1915, beside Christmas Day front-page titles: "Fighting in West with Artillery Is Reported Violent," "Half Starved Allies Taken Prisoner," and "Autos Bring Death to Two in Midst of Yuletide Joys."

121. "Ford Abdicates; Sails for Home: Leaves $270,000 Check for the Peace Party," *New York Times*, December 25, 1915, besides "No German Sea Trade, Says Britain, Till Germany Pays for Devastation"; "Japan May Join in Europe's War"; "War Fury Stifles Christmas Spirit: No Truce in West." Page 2 notes a Socialist peace project at The Hague from the *Telegraaf*, with no obvious connection to Ford.

122. "Ford Party in Dispute, Mrs. Boissevain Leave," *New York Times*, December 26, 1915, besides "7,200 Men Needed for Marine Corps;" Charles P. Stewart, "Peace Party Split Again," *Chicago Daily Tribune*, December 26, 1915, besides "Report Saloniki Attack Opens: Teutons Fire on Advanced Allied Lines" and "American Killed in War;" "Attacks Austrian Archduke with Axes: Mob Gathers before Palace and Breaks Windows as Protest against Squandering of Food" beside "First Photographs Made Aboard Ford Peace Ship," *Philadelphia Inquirer*, December 28, 1915.

123. See "Talks with Mr. Ford: A Quaint Crusader."

124. Peter Overby, "Koch Political Network Expanding 'Grass-Roots' Organizing," NPR, *It's All Politics*, October 12, 2015.

125. Jovy Chan, "Online Astroturfing: A Problem beyond Disinformation," *Philosophy and Social Criticism* (2022): 1–22.

126. Erez Manela, *The Wilsonian Moment: Self-Determination and the International Origins of Anticolonial Nationalism* (Oxford: Oxford University Press, 2007).

127. J. Michael Hogan, *Woodrow Wilson's Western Tour: Rhetoric, Public Opinion, and the League of Nations* (College Station: Texas A&M University Press, 2006).

128. See Sidney Tarrow, *War, States, and Contention: A Comparative Historical Study* (Ithaca, NY: Cornell University Press, 2015).

129. Ernest Freeberg, *Democracy's Prisoner: Eugene V. Debs, the Great War, and the Right to Dissent* (Cambridge, MA: Harvard University Press, 2008).

130. See "Thinks Henry Ford Peace Press Agent: Miss Addams Praises Him, but Disowns Expedition in Behalf of Women Pacifists," *New York Times*, January 6, 1916.

131. See Jennifer D. Keen, "Remembering the 'Forgotten War': American Historiography on World War I," *Historian* 78 (2016): 439–68.

Chapter 4

1. "Mrs. Dilling Hails Ending of Sedition Case," *Chicago Daily Tribune*, August 2, 1947.

2. "Mrs. Dilling Hails Ending of Sedition Case."

3. "Mrs. Dilling Hails Ending of Sedition Case."

4. James T. Sparrow, *Warfare State: World War II Americans and the Age of Big Government* (New York: Oxford University Press, 2011).

5. Alan Brinkley, *Voices of Protest: Huey Long, Father Coughlin, and the Great Depression* (New York: Random House, 1982).

6. Dennis Showalter, "The Great War and Its Historiography," *Historian* 68, no. 4 (2006): 713–21. See also Sidney B. Fay, *The Origins of the World War* (New York: Macmillan, 1928).

7. Nancy MacLean, *Behind the Mask of Chivalry* (New York: Oxford University Press, 1994); Linda Gordon, *The Second Coming of the KKK* (New York: W. W. Norton, 2017).

8. Philip Jenkins, *Hoods and Shirts: The Extreme Right in Pennsylvania, 1925–1950* (Chapel Hill: University of North Carolina Press, 1997).

9. Bradley W. Hart, *Hitler's American Friends: The Third Reich Supporters in the United States* (New York: St. Martin's Press, 2018), 8–22.

10. Fay, *Origins of World War*.

11. Leonard Dinnerstein, *Anti-Semitism in America* (New York: Oxford University Press, 1994); Manfred Jonas, *Isolationism in America, 1935–1941* (Ithaca, NY: Cornell University Press, 1966).

12. Mary Stuckey, "FDR, the Rhetoric of Vision, and the Creation of a National Synoptic State," *Quarterly Journal of Speech* 98, no. 3 (2012): 297–319; Amos Kiewe, "'Cautious Crusade,' Review of Franklin D. Roosevelt, American Public Opinion, and the War against Nazi Germany, by Steve Casey," *Rhetoric and Public Affairs* 5 (2002): 765–67.

13. Wayne Cole, *America First: The Battle against Intervention 1940–1941* (New York: Octagon Books, 1971; Myron Scholnick, *The New Deal and Anti-Semitism* (New York: Garland, 1990), 58, 149; Robert Michael, *A Concise History of American*

Antisemitism (New York: Rowman and Littlefield, 2005).

14. See Mike Milford, "Veiled Intervention: Anti-Semitism, Allegory, and Captain America," *Rhetoric and Public Affairs* 20, no. 4 (2017): 605–34.

15. Geoffrey R. Stone, *Perilous Times: Free Speech in Wartime* (New York: W. W. Norton, 2004), 235–307.

16. Sparrow, *Warfare State*.

17. Johan Galtung, *Peace by Peaceful Means: Peace and Conflict, Development and Civilization* (London: Sage, 1996).

18. Glen Jeansonne, *Women of the Far Right: The Mothers' Movement and World War II* (Chicago: University of Chicago Press, 1996).

19. D'Ann Campbell, *Women at War with America: Private Lives in a Patriotic Era* (Cambridge, MA: Harvard University Press, 1984); Elizabeth R. Escobedo, *From Coveralls to Zoot Suits: The Lives of Mexican American Women on the World War II Home Front* (Chapel Hill: University of North Carolina Press, 2013); Marilyn E. Hegarty, *Victory Girls, Khaki-Wackies, and Patriotutes: The Regulation of Female Sexuality during World War II* (New York: New York University Press, 2008); Melissa A. McEuen, *Making War, Making Women: Femininity and Duty on the American Home Front, 1941–1945* (Athens: University of Georgia Press, 2011).

20. For landmark work on feminism, politics, and citizenship, see Karlyn Kohrs Campbell, *Man Cannot Speak for Her: A Critical Study of Early Feminist Rhetoric* (Westport, CT: Greenwood Press, 1989); Susan Zaeske, *Signatures of Citizenship: Petitioning, Antislavery, and Women's Political Identity* (Chapel Hill: University of North Carolina Press, 2003); Belinda A. Stillion Southard, *Militant Citizenship: Rhetorical Strategies of the National Woman's Party, 1913–1920* (College Station: Texas A&M University Press, 2011); Catherine H. Palczewski, "The 1919 Prison Special: Constituting White Women's Citizenship," *Quarterly Journal of Speech* 102, no. 2 (2016): 107–32; Bonnie J. Dow and Mari Boor Tonn, "'Feminine Style' and Political Judgement in the Rhetoric of Ann Richards," *Quarterly Journal of Speech* 79, no. 3 (1993): 286; Kathleen Hall Jamieson, *Beyond the Double Bind: Women and Leadership* (Oxford: Oxford University Press, 1995); Mary Vavrus, "Working the Senate from the Outside In: The Mediated Construction of a Feminist Political Campaign," *Critical Studies in Mass Communication* 15, no. 3 (1998): 213–35; Karrin Vasby Anderson, "'Rhymes with Rich': 'Bitch' as a Tool of Containment in Contemporary American Politics," *Rhetoric and Public Affairs* 2, no. 4 (1999): 599–623; Karrin Vasby Anderson and Kristina Horn Sheeler, *Governing Codes: Gender, Metaphor, and Political Identity* (Lanham, MD: Lexington Books, 2005); Diana B. Carlin and Kelly L. Winfrey, "Have You Come a Long Way, Baby? Hillary Clinton, Sarah Palin, and Sexism in 2008 Campaign Coverage," *Communication Studies* 60, no. 4 (2009): 326–43; Lindsey Meeks, "Is She 'Man Enough'? Women Candidates, Executive Political Offices, and News Coverage," *Journal of Communication* 62, no. 1 (2012): 175–93; Kristina Horn Sheeler and Karrin Vasby Anderson, *Woman President: Confronting Postfeminist Political Culture* (College Station: Texas A&M University Press, 2013); Shawn J. Parry-Giles, *Hillary Clinton in the News: Gender and Authenticity in American Politics* (Urbana: University of Illinois Press, 2014); Barbara Biesecker, "Coming to Terms with Recent Attempts to Write

Women into the History of Rhetoric," *Philosophy and Rhetoric* 25, no. 2 (1992): 140–61; Shawn J. Parry-Giles and Trevor Parry-Giles, "Gendered Politics and Presidential Image Construction: A Reassessment of the 'Feminine Style,'" *Communication Monographs* 63, no. 4 (1996): 337–53; Sonja K. Foss and Cindy L. Griffin, "Beyond Persuasion: A Proposal for an Invitational Rhetoric," *Communication Monographs* 62, no. 1 (1995): 2–19; Nina M. Lozano-Reich and Dana L. Cloud, "The Uncivil Tongue: Invitational Rhetoric and the Problem of Inequality," *Western Journal of Communication* 73, no. 2 (2009): 220–26; Celeste Michelle Condit, "In Praise of Eloquent Diversity: Gender and Rhetoric as Public Persuasion," *Women's Studies in Communication* 20, no. 2 (1997): 91–116; Gust A. Yep, Karen Lovaas, and John P. Elia, *Queer Theory and Communication: From Disciplining Queers to Queering the Discipline(S)* (Binghamton, NY: Haworth Press, 2003); Erin J. Rand, *Reclaiming Queer: Activist and Academic Rhetorics of Resistance* (Tuscaloosa: University of Alabama Press, 2014); Alyssa A. Samek, "Pivoting between Identity Politics and Coalitional Relationships: Lesbian-Feminist Resistance to the Woman- Identified Woman," *Women's Studies in Communication* 38, no. 4 (2015): 393–420; Claire Sisco King, "American Queerer: Norman Rockwell and the Art of Queer Feminist Critique," *Women's Studies in Communication* 39, no. 2 (2016): 157–76; Kristan Poirot, *A Question of Sex: Feminism, Rhetoric, and Differences That Matter* (Amherst: University of Massachusetts Press, 2014), 5.

21. Carly S. Woods, *Debating Women: Gender, Education, and Spaces for Argument* (East Lansing: Michigan State University Press, 2018), 14.

22. See Joan B. Landes, *Women and the Public Sphere* (Ithaca, NY: Cornell University Press, 1988); Elizabeth Eger, *Women, Writing and the Public Sphere* (New York: Cambridge University Press, 2001).

23. *Women's Voice*, Women and Leadership Archives (hereafter WLA), Loyola University, Chicago, box 6, folder 2, "Women's Voice, 1944–1960, n.d. Women's Voice."

24. *Patriotic Research Bulletin* (abbreviated as *Bulletin* hereafter), Kenneth Spencer Research Library, University of Kansas, Lawrence (hereafter KSP) File RH WL D2091 (hereafter RH).

25. Albrecht Classen, "Female Epistolary Literature from Antiquity to the Present: An Introduction," *Studia Neophilologica* 60, no. 1 (1988): 3–13; Linda C. Mitchell, "Entertainment and Instruction: Women's Roles in the English Epistolary Tradition," *Huntingdon Library Quarterly* 66, no. 3/4 (2003): 331–47.

26. See *Bulletin*, November 1942, in KSP RH.

27. Elizabeth Dilling portrait in *Bulletin*, KSP RH, 1943.

28. Galtung, *Peace by Peaceful Means*.

29. Galtung, *Peace by Peaceful Means*. Dilling states that "New Deal 'Persecutor' Rogge wants to indict me with some 40 others by Christmas. He is now pumping 'evidence' at a Washington D. C. special grand jury, empaneled for the purpose October 27th, which includes nine out-and-out New Deal government payrollers." She also mentions Senator Wheeler's interest in a "smear book," *Bulletin*, KSP RH, 1943, 1.

30. *Bulletin*, 1943, KSP RH, 1–2.

31. *Bulletin*, 1943, KSP RH, 4.

32. *Bulletin*, 1943, KSP RH, 4–5.

33. *Women's Voice*, WLA, box 6, folder 2.

34. See the discussion of "invitational rhetoric" by Wendy Hayden, "From Lucifer to Jezebel: Invitational Rhetoric, Rhetorical Closure, and Safe Spaces in Feminist Sexual Discourse Communities," *Rhetoric Society Quarterly* 51, no. 2 (2021): 79–93.

35. Dilling's *Patriotic Research Bulletin* has many such examples of women writing in. See, for instance, *Bulletin*, December 1942, KSP RH, 1.

36. WLA, box 6, folder 1, "We, the Mothers, Mobilize for America, Inc., 1941–1945, n.d."

37. *Bulletin*, 1940, in KSP RH, 9.

38. See "Lend Lease Bill," *Records of the U. S. House of Representatives*, HR 77A-D13, record group 223, National Archives.

39. *Bulletin*, March 1941, in KSP RH, 1.

40. *Bulletin*, October 8, 1942, in KSP RH, 2.

41. *Bulletin*, October 8, 1942, in KSP RH, 2.

42. *Bulletin*, August 10, 1942, in KSP RH, 2–4.

43. *Bulletin*, August 10, 1942, in KSP RH, 4–5.

44. *Bulletin*, February 28, 1942, in KSP RH, 3.

45. See also *Bulletin*, February 1942, in KSP RH, 1.

46. *Bulletin*, February 1942, in KSP RH, 1–2.

47. *Bulletin*, February 1942 in KSP RH, 4.

48. WLA, box 5, folder 8, "Political Views: Documents, 1933–1972, n.d."

49. WLA, box 5, folder 8, "Political Views: Documents, 1933–1972, n.d."

50. WLA, box 5, folder 8, "Political Views: Documents, 1933–1972, n.d." Also contains the "Why Are Jews Persecuted for Their Religion?" pamphlet by American Publishing Society, Bremerton, WA, and "Zionism Rules the World" by Henry H. Klein.

51. WLA, box 5, folder 13, "Speeches and Notes, 1920–1942, n.d.," 1–2, emphasis added.

52. WLA, box 5, folder 13, "Speeches and Notes, 1920–1942, n.d.," 1–2.

53. See *Women's Voice* 4, no. 7 (February 28, 1946), WLA, box 6, folder 2: it describes "traitors" in a discussion involving references to George Washington and Abraham Lincoln.

54. Elizabeth Dilling, *The Red Network: A "Who's Who" and Handbook of Radicalism for Patriots* (Kenilworth, IL: Self-published, 1934).

55. Richard Hofstadter, *The Paranoid Style in American Politics* (New York: First Vintage Books, 2008).

56. Starting on page 101, ending on page 252 of *Red Network*, there is a list of over 460 organizations that are "Communist, Anarchist, Socialist, I. W. W., or Radical-Pacifist or infiltrated organizations and other agencies referred [to] in the 'Who's Who.'"

57. See Dilling, *Red Network*, 91–100.

58. Dilling, *The Octopus* (1940; Metarie, LA: Sons of Liberty, 1986), 154–202.

59. *The Roosevelt Red Record and Its Background* (N.p.: self-published, 1936), 87–88.

60. *Bulletin*, February 1939, KSP RH; "Lincoln," an Address Delivered by Mrs.

Elizabeth Dilling at the Rally at the Lincoln Cabin, Milton, MA, February 12, 1939.

61. *Bulletin*, February 1939 in KSP RH; "Lincoln."
62. Galtung, *Peace by Peaceful Means*.
63. Galtung, *Peace by Peaceful Means*.
64. *Bulletin*, January 22, 1941, in KSP RH, 1, 7–9.
65. *Bulletin*, January 22, 1941, in KSP RH, 7. Dilling states, "Denying all Christian fundamentals we see Christian institutions thus Judaized into Modernism while praising 'tolerance'; Fundamentalists and Catholics falsely summoned by their leaders to fleshly race worship. The exaltation of fleshly race above spiritual faith in Christ is Scripturally anti-Christian whether on the part of a 'Christian,' an Aryan, or a Jewish racist."
66. See Dilling, *Red Network*, 22; *Bulletin*, May 2, 1941, KSP RH, 17.
67. *Bulletin*, February 1942, KSP RH, 13.
68. *Bulletin*, February 1942, 13–20.
69. WLA, box 5, folder 13, undated and untitled "Address by Lyrl Clark Van Hyning."
70. WLA, box 5, folder 10, "Religious Views, 1914–1951, n.d." This reflects what Kristina Lee calls "theistnormativity," or the presumption and privilege given to certain religious belief in US politics to legitimize the exclusion of non-Christians and atheists alike. Kristina M. Lee, "Theistnormativity and the Negation of American Atheists in Presidential Inaugural Address," *Rhetoric and Public Affairs* 23, no. 2 (2020): 255–91.
71. *Bulletin*, December 1941, KSP RH, 1–2.
72. *Bulletin*, December 1941, 3.
73. *Bulletin*, December 1941.
74. *Bulletin*, December 1941, 15–16.
75. *Bulletin*, December 1942, KSP RH, 1.
76. *Bulletin*, October 8, 1942, KSP RH, 3.
77. See *Bulletin*, September 3, 1942, KSP RH, 1.
78. Dilling, *Red Network*, 16–17.
79. Dilling, *Red Network*, 51–52.
80. *Bulletin*, January 1943, KSP RH, 4.
81. *Bulletin*, January 1943, 4–5.
82. *Bulletin*, January 1943, 5–6.
83. *Bulletin*, December 1942, KSP RH, 14, 18.
84. *Bulletin*, September 3, 1942, KSP RH, 4.
85. *Bulletin*, July 4, 1941, KSP RH, 2, 13.
86. *Bulletin*, December 1940, KSP RH, 5–6.
87. *Bulletin*, December 1940, KSP RH, 12.
88. *Bulletin*, December 1940, KSP RH, 10–12.
89. Andrew Limbong, "Ye Says, 'I See Good Things about Hitler' on Conspiracy Theorist Alex Jones' Show," NPR, December 2, 2022 (podcast); Emma Green, "Why the Charlottesville Marchers Were Obsessed with Jews," *Atlantic*, August 15, 2017; "From Alt Right to Alt Lite: Naming the Hate," Anti-Defamation League (web);

Lisa Hagen, "Antisemitism Is on the Rise, and It's Not Just about Ye," NPR, *All Things Considered*, December 1, 2022.

90. *Bulletin*, August 1946, KSP RH, 19.

91. *Bulletin*, August 1946, 19.

Chapter 5

1. Andrew E. Hunt, *The Turning: A History of Vietnam Veterans against the War* (New York: New York University Press, 1999), 46–55.

2. Hunt, *Turning*, 64.

3. "Dewey Canyon III," from Vietnam Veterans against the War Records, 1967–2006 (Bulk 1967–1975), folders 12–15, box 8, Wisconsin Historical Society, Madison.

4. Hunt, *Turning*, 75.

5. Algis Kaupas et al., prod., *Winter Soldier* (Harrington Park, NJ: Milestone Films, 1971).

6. Bradford Vivian, *Commonplace Witnessing: Rhetorical Invention, Historical Remembrance and Public Culture* (New York: Oxford University Press, 2017).

7. David Barash, *Approaches to Peace: A Reader in Peace Studies* (Oxford: Oxford University Press, 2010), 2.

8. Hunt, *Turning*, 73.

9. For the political tensions within classical liberalism, I follow C. B. Macpherson in *The Political Theory of Possessive Individualism: Hobbes to Locke* (Oxford: Oxford University Press, 2011). I also follow James T. Sparrow's work on the trope of the "citizen-soldier," which he suggests places the veteran as the ideal type of citizen within a warfare state, which itself depends on an uneasy balance between individualism and collectivism. Sparrow, *Warfare State: World War II Americans and the Age of Big Government* (Oxford: Oxford University Press, 2011).

10. Johan Galtung, *Peace by Peaceful Means: Peace and Conflict, Development and Civilization* (London: Sage, 1996).

11. Barash, *Approaches*, 161.

12. See Robert L. Ivie, "Hierarchies of Equality: Positive Peace in a Democratic Idiom," in *The Handbook of Communication Ethics*, ed. George Cheney, Steve May, and Debashish Munshi (New York: Routledge, 2011), 378.

13. Geoffrey R. Stone, *Perilous Times: Free Speech in Wartime* (New York: W. W. Norton, 2004), 12.

14. James Kirkpatrick Davis, *Assault on the Left: The FBI and the Sixties Antiwar Movement* (Westport, CT: Praeger, 1997).

15. Bradford Vivian notes how witnessing is not a simple, linear act free of context, style, or creative choice. The VVAW peace script also illustrates the role of visual culture in what Vivian describes as "commonplace witnessing." By fusing tropes, images, and modalities of agency and structure to testify to—so as to *display*—the contradictions of "warfare." See *Commonplace Witnessing*.

16. W. J. T. Mitchell, "Interdisciplinarity and Visual Culture," *Art Bulletin* 77, no. 4 (1993): 540–44.

17. Jeremy Kreusch, "Violent Representation: Photographs, Soldiers and an

Ideological War," in *Mythologizing the Vietnam War: Visual Culture and Mediated Memory* (Tyne, UK: Cambridge Scholars, 2014), 11.

18. Chester J. Pach Jr., "And That's the Way It Was: The Vietnam War on the Network Nightly News," in *The Sixties: From Memory to History*, ed. David Farber (Chapel Hill: University of North Carolina Press, 1994), 90–118. Pach notes that only 3 percent of televised images showed images of actual combat or graphic battle (95).

19. Jeremy Lembcke, *The Spitting Image: Myth, Memory, and the Legacy of Vietnam* (New York: New York University Press, 1998).

20. While Macpherson does not discuss "war" at length in *Possessive Individualism* and Sparrow does not expound on classical liberal theory in *Warfare State*, I believe these two works, nevertheless, speak to each other to suggest that war in modern America—with its high demand for productivity—depends on a type of conformity and self-sacrifice that undercuts classical liberal ideals.

21. One could conceive of this visual work as a construction of new "civil imaginations." See Ariella Azoulay, *Civil Imagination: A Political Ontology of Photography* (New York: Verso, 2010).

22. Sparrow outlines this trope within the Zoot Suit Riot incident in *Warfare State*, 201–41. LeiLani Nishime analyzes the relationship of white bodies and Vietnam War representations in "Remembering Vietnam in the 1980s: White Skin, White Masks: Vietnam War Films and the Racialized Gaze," in *American Visual Cultures*, ed. David Holloway (New York: Continuum Press, 2005), 257–64.

23. Betsy A. McClane, *A New History of Documentary Film* (New York: Continuum, 2012), 255.

24. Bonnie J. Dow, "Fixing Feminism: Women's Liberation and the Rhetoric of Television Documentary," *Quarterly Journal of Speech* 90, no. 1 (2004): 53.

25. For a more contemporary analysis of the visual impact of war imagery, see Kevin McSorley, "Helmetcams, Militarized Sensation and 'Somatic War,'" *Journal of War & Culture Studies* 5, no. 1 (June 2012): 47–58.

26. Bryan C. Rindfleisch fleshes out the problematic dimensions of the "citizen-soldier" figure in "'What It Means to Be a Man': Contested Masculinity in the Early Republic and Antebellum America," *History Compass* 10, no. 11 (2012): 854.

27. Paul Achter, "Unruly Bodies: The Rhetorical Domestication of Twenty-First Century Veterans of War," *Quarterly Journal of Speech* 96, no. 1 (2010): 46–68.

28. John Kerry, "Statement before the Senate Committee on Foreign Relations," April 22, 1971, available at Voices of Democracy (web).

29. Kerry, "Vietnam Veterans against the War Statement."

30. Mr. H. Fox in Kaupas et al., *Winter Soldier*.

31. Thomas Paine, *Common Sense* (Mineola, NY: Dover, 1997).

32. *Winter Soldier*, 2:00–3:00 minute mark (time stamps are approximate).

33. *Winter Soldier*, 0:44–1:17.

34. *Winter Soldier*, 5:00.

35. *Winter Soldier*, 27:00.

36. *Winter Soldier*, 43:00.

37. *Winter Soldier*, 1:00:00, 1:17:00.

38. In visual terms, one could consider the *Winter Soldier* as a rupture of "regimes of sensation." Jacques Rancière describes such "regimes of sensible intensity" to draw critical attention to the connections of theory, political action, and sensation, in *The Politics of Aesthetics* (New York: Continuum, 2004), 39.

39. *Winter Soldier*, 55:00, 1:02:00, 1:19:00.

40. *Winter Soldier*, 3:30–5:00.

41. These images represent what Ariella Azoulay would call an instantiation of photographic political speech, wherein one is morally bound to interpret and engage the image beyond the mere superficiality of the photo. See Azoulay, *The Civil Contract of Photography* (New York: Zone Books, 2008).

42. *Winter Soldier*, 17:00.

43. *Winter Soldier*, 20:00–24:00.

44. *Winter Soldier*, 21:00.

45. Many other veterans in *Winter Soldier* describe this aspect, too, after Kamil's account. See, for instance, 27:00, 29:00, and 1:28:00.

46. *Winter Soldier*, 22:00.

47. *Winter Soldier*, 34:00.

48. Syed Haider, "The Shooting in Orlando, Terrorism or Toxic Masculinity (or Both?)" *Men and Masculinities* 19, no. 5(2016): 555–65. See also Casey R. Kelly, *Apocalypse Man: The Death Drive and the Rhetoric of White Masculine Victims* (Columbus: Ohio State University Press, 2020).

49. *Winter Soldier*, 1:05:00–1:10:00.

50. David R. Colburn and George E. Pozzetta offer an overview of the complicated racial dynamics of the New Left in "Race, Ethnicity, and the Evolution of Political Legitimacy," in *The Sixties: From Memory to History*, ed. David Farber (Chapel Hill: University of North Carolina Press, 1994), 119–48.

51. *Winter Soldier*, 1:10:00.

52. Brian Adams Ross, 1972, "World Conference on the A & H Bomb," box 19, folder 17, Vietnam Veterans against the War Records, 1967–2006 (Bulk 1967–1975), Wisconsin Historical Society.

53. John Pollock, 1973, "Combat and Political Alienation: Vietnam Veterans," box 7, folder 1, mss 370, Vietnam Veterans against the War Records, 1967–2006 (Bulk 1967–1975), Wisconsin Historical Society.

54. Daniel A. Friedman, "Statement to NYC Planning Commission, AT City Hall," June 23, 1971, mss 370, Vietnam Veterans against the War Records, 1967–2006 (Bulk 1967–1975), Wisconsin Historical Society.

55. No author, no date (with logs from October and November 1973), VVAW/WSO "Publicity" 1969–1972 Press Releases and Statements, mss 370, Vietnam Veterans against the War Records, 1967–2006 (Bulk 1967–1975), Wisconsin Historical Society.

56. Steve Hawkins, no date, box 25, folder 27, Mss 370, Vietnam Veterans against the War Records, 1967–2006(Bulk 1967–1975), Wisconsin Historical Society.

57. Steve Hawkins, no date, box 25, folder 83. See also "Indochina Day," May 4, 1973, box 23, folder 24, Vietnam Veterans against the War Records, 1967–2006 (Bulk

1967–1975), Wisconsin Historical Society; Barry Romo and Pete Zastrow at Stockholm Conference for Solidarity with Cambodia in Paris, December 27–31,1973, box 1, folder 12, Vietnam Veterans against the War Records, 1967–2006 (Bulk 1967–1975), Wisconsin Historical Society.

58. No author, "Speeches," January 25, 1975, box 23, folder 24, "Vietnam Veterans against the War Records, 1967–2006 (Bulk 1967–1975), Wisconsin Historical Society.

59. No author, 1970–1971, box 17, folder 31, "Third World Women's Alliance," Mss 370, Vietnam Veterans against the War Records, 1967–2006 (Bulk 1967–1975), Wisconsin Historical Society.

60. No author, no date, "Objectives of VVAW," mss 370, VVAW/WSO "Publicity" 1969–1972 Press Releases and Statements, Vietnam Veterans against the War Records, 1967–2006 (Bulk 1967–1975), Wisconsin Historical Society.

61. Protests on board the USS *Constellation*, USS *America*, USS *Coral*, USS *Duluth*, USS *JFK*, USS *Little Rock*, USS *Longbeach*, USS *Midway*, and the USS *Worden*, for instance, are mentioned in the VVAW documents. See "GI Conference. Background Literature," box 8, folder 42, Vietnam Veterans against the War Records, 1967–2006 (Bulk 1967–1975), Wisconsin Historical Society.

62. For a discussion on the historical legacy of such "colorblindness," see Michelle Alexander, *The New Jim Crow: Mass Incarceration in the Age of Colorblindness* (New York: New Press, 2010).

63. No author, no date, mss 370, VVAW/WSO "Publicity" 1969–1972 Press Releases and Statements, Vietnam Veterans against the War Records, 1967–2006 (Bulk 1967–1975), Wisconsin Historical Society.

64. Alan Dawson, "Donald Trump Called into a Boxing Press Conference and Said He'd KO Joe Biden if They Ever Fought," *Insider*, September 9, 2021; Veronica Stracqualursi, "Biden Says He Would 'Beat the Hell' Out of Trump if in High School," CNN, March 21, 2018; Caitlin Flanagan, "Why the Left Is So Afraid of Jordan Peterson," *Atlantic*, August 9, 2018; ADL's Center on Extremism, *When Women Are the Enemy: The Intersection of Misogyny and White Supremacy*, report, Anti-Defamation League, July 20, 2018.

65. Cecilia Saixue Watt, "Redneck Revolt: The Armed Leftwing Group That Wants to Stamp Out Fascism." *Guardian*, July 11, 2017.

66. Christian G. Appy, *American Reckoning: The Vietnam War and Our National Identity* (New York: Penguin, 2015), xvi.

67. Howard C. Olson and R. William Rae, *Determination of the Potential for Dissidence Event in the U.S. Army*, Technical Paper RAC-TP-410, McLean, VA: Research Analysis Corporation, March 1971; R. William Rae, Stephen B. Forman, and Howard C. Olson, *Future Impact of Dissident Elements within the Army*, Technical PaperRAC-TP-441, McLean, VA: Research Analysis Corporation, January 1972.

68. These are classic concerns of warfare. See Frederick the Great, *Instructions for His Generals*, trans. General Thomas R. Phillips (Mineola, NY: Dover, 2005).

69. Thomas E. Ricks, "The Widening Gap between Military and Society," *Atlantic*, July 1997.

70. See Peter Beaumont and Rod Austin, "Guantanamo Bay Branded 'a Symbol of Islamophobia of Trump Presidency,'" *Guardian*, January 11, 2019.

Conclusion

1. "Global Conflict Tracker," *Council on Foreign Relations*, accessed January 15, 2023 (web).

2. Francis Fukuyama, "The End of History?" *National Interest* 16 (1989): 3–18. See also Louis Menand, "Francis Fukuyama Postpones the End of History," *New Yorker*, August 27, 2018.

3. Johan Galtung, *Peace by Peaceful Means: Peace and Conflict, Development and Civilization* (London: Sage, 1996).

4. David Barash, *Approaches to Peace: A Reader in Peace Studies* (Oxford: Oxford University Press, 2010), 1, 4, and 161.

5. Robert Ivie, in *Dissent from War* (Bloomfield, CT: Kumarian Press, 2007).

6. For a discussion of how a presidential address at the end of war sets the conditions for future engagements, see Stephen Heidt, *Resowing the Seeds of War* (East Lansing: Michigan State University Press, 2022).

7. Richard A. Posner, *Not a Suicide Pact: The Constitution in a Time of National Emergency* (New York: Oxford University Press, 2006), 23.

8. See Richard C. Leone and Greg Anrig Jr., eds., *The War on Our Freedoms* (New York: Public Affairs Books, 2003); Joseph Margulies, *Guantanamo and the Abuse of Presidential Power* (New York: Simon and Schuster, 2006).

9. See D. L. Leal, "American Public Opinion toward the Military: Differences by Race, Gender, and Class," *Armed Forces and Society* 32 (2005): 123–38; D. W. Moore, "Gender Gap Varies in Support for War," Gallup, November 19, 2002; Jeffrey M. Jones, "Blacks, Postgraduates among Groups Most Likely to Oppose Iraq Invasion," Gallup, January 30, 2003; Jeffrey M. Jones, "War through Partisan Lenses: Divide over Iraq Not Necessarily Typical," Gallup, November 15, 2005; David E. Rohall and Morten G. Ender, "Race, Gender, and Class: Attitudes toward the War in Iraq and President Bush among Military Personnel," *Race, Gender, and Class* 14, nos. 3–4 (2007): 99–116.

10. Dana Hughes, "Bill Clinton Regrets Rwanda Now (Not So Much in 1994)," *ABC News*, February 28, 2014.

11. Laura Silver et al., "What Do Americans Know about International Affairs?" Pew Research Center, May 25, 2022.

12. Ivie, *Dissent from War*, 8.

13. Katharine Murphy, "Rising US Isolationism Means Australia Must Become More Resilient and Autonomous, Thinktank Warns," *Guardian*, March 15, 2022.

14. Mary Dudziak, *War Time: An Idea, Its History, Its Consequences* (New York: Oxford University Press, 2012).

15. See Doug McAdam, John D. McCarthy, and Mayer N. Zald, eds., *Comparative Perspectives on Social Movements: Political Opportunities, Mobilizing Structures, and Cultural Framings* (Cambridge, UK: Cambridge University Press, 1996).

16. John D. McCarthy and Mayer N. Zald, "Resource Mobilization and Social

Movements: A Partial Theory, *American Journal of Sociology* 82, no. 6 (May 1977): 1212–41.

17. Sidney Tarrow, *War, States, and Contention: A Comparative Historical Study* (Ithaca, NY: Cornell University Press, 2015); Charles Tilly, *Coercion, Capital, and European States, AD 990–1992* (Oxford: Blackwell, 1990).

18. David Armitage, *Civil Wars: A History in Ideas* (New Haven, CT: Yale University Press, 2017), 5.

19. Leah Ceccarelli, "Polysemy: Multiple Meanings in Rhetorical Criticism," *Quarterly Journal of Speech* 84, no. 4 (1998): 395–415.

20. Matthew Houdek, "Racial Sedimentation and the Common Sense of Racialized Violence: The Case of Black Church Burnings," *Quarterly Journal of Speech* 104, no. 3 (2018): 279–306. See also Karma R. Chávez, "The Body: An Abstract and Actual Rhetorical Concept," *Rhetoric Society Quarterly* 48, no. 3 (2018): 242–50; Lisa A. Flores, "Between Abundance and Marginalization: The Imperative of Racial Rhetorical Criticism," *Review of Communication* 16, no. 1 (2016): 4–24; Kirt Wilson, "The Racial Politics of Imitation in the Nineteenth Century," *Quarterly Journal of Speech* 89, no. 2 (2003): 89–108; Paul Elliot Johnson, "The Art of Masculine Victimhood: Donald Trump's Demagoguery," *Women's Studies in Communication* 40, no. 3 (2017): 229–50; Casey Ryan Kelly, "The Wounded Man: Foxcatcher and the Incoherence of White Masculine Victimhood," *Communication and Critical/Cultural Studies* 15, no. 2 (2018): 161–78.

21. No author, no date (with logs from October and November 1973), VVAW/WSO "Publicity" 1969–1972 Press Releases and Statements, mss 370, Vietnam Veterans against the War Records, 1967–2006 (Bulk 1967–1975), Wisconsin Historical Society. See also Alan L. Otten, "Politics and People: For Spiro, Suspiro," *Wall Street Journal*, October 31, 1969.

22. The phenomenon resembles what Kenneth Burke described as the power of "No"—the flat-out rejection that unites people more easily than any concrete delineation of policy or principles. See Burke *The Rhetoric of Religion: Studies in Logology* (Berkeley: University of California Press, 1970).

23. Carl von Clausewitz, *On War*, trans. Michael Howard and Peter Paret (New York: Oxford University Press, 2007), 20–21, 27–29.

24. Galtung, *Peace by Peaceful Means*.

Bibliography

NEWSPAPER ENTRIES AND ARCHIVAL SOURCES FROM SPECIAL COLLECTIONS

Aked, C. F. "Into the Unknown." *Philadelphia Inquirer*, December 7, 1915.
"An American Car Maker's Antics: The Trip of 'Ford's Ark' to Europe." *North-China Herald and Supreme Court and Consular Gazette*, December 11, 1915.
"Authoritarianism and Anti-Semitism in the Anti-War Movement?" *Tikkun Magazine* 18, no. 3 (2003): 39.
Bavier, Joe. "Congo War-Driven Crisis Kills 45,000 a Month." *Reuters*, January 22, 2008.
Beaumont, Peter, and Rod Austin. "Guantanamo Bay Branded 'a Symbol of Islamophobia of Trump Presidency." *Guardian*, January 11, 2019.
Blackmore, Erin. "The U.S. Forcibly Detained Native Alaskans during World War II." *Smithsonian Magazine*, February 22, 2017.
"Cities Jammed in Worldwide Protest of War in Iraq." CNN, February 16, 2003.
"Contraband Found Aboard Peace Ship." *Gazette Times*, December 17, 1915.
"Courts May Stop Ford's Peace Mission Voyage." *Gazette Times*, November 27, 1915.
Dawson, Alan. "Donald Trump Called into a Boxing Press Conference and Said He'd KO Joe Biden If They Ever Fought." *Insider*, September 9, 2021.
"Departing Pacifists Worry." *New York Times*, December 9, 1915.
Douglas, Hilary, and Andrea Perry. "Britain on the Brink: Demonstrators Flood through London and Glasgow as Anti-War Crowds Take to Streets All Over the World to Protest at Impending War; Millions on March in a Tide of Peace." *Sunday Express*, February 16, 2003.
"Dr. Aked Ill?" *New York Times*, January 1, 1916, 3.
"Editorial Comment." *Philadelphia Inquirer*, December 16, 1915.
"England May Detain the Ford Pilgrims." *New York Times*, December 6, 1915.
"Even Have War on Ford's Peace Ship." *Philadelphia Inquirer*, December 9, 1915.
"The Expedition of the Notables." *Gazette Times*, November 26, 1915.
"Fifty Lusty Filipinos." *Omaha World-Herald*, June 25, 1899.
"First Photographs Made Aboard Ford Peace Ship." *Philadelphia Inquirer*, December 28, 1915.
Flanagan, Caitlin. "Why the Left Is So Afraid of Jordan Peterson." *Atlantic*, August 9, 2018.
"Flash! Bang! Peace Party Is Forgotten." *San Francisco Chronicle*, December 22, 1915.
"Ford Abdicates; Sails for Home: Leaves $270,000 Check for the Peace Party." *New York Times*, December 25, 1915.

"Ford Aids Peace Move by Women." *New York Times*, November 27, 1915.

"Ford Asks Bryan to Be First Mate on His Peace Ship." *New York Times*, November 26, 1915.

"Ford Defies His Critics: Issues Long Statement before Leaving Detroit for New York." *New York Times*, December 2, 1915.

"Ford Deserts Pacifists at Christiania." *Gazette Times*, December 24, 1915.

"The Ford Expedition: Being Morally Right Time Is on the Side of Those Who Strive for Peace." *San Francisco Chronicle*, December 22, 1915.

"Ford Favors Allies." *Philadelphia Inquirer*, December 7, 1915.

"Ford Favors Allies: Makes Will." *Philadelphia Inquirer*, December 4, 1915.

"Ford Finds Peace Elusive." *New York Times*, December 21, 1915.

"The Ford Fireworks." *Irish Times*, November 29, 1915.

"Ford Hires Liner in Peace Crusade." *New York Times*, November 25, 1915.

"Ford Hopes Troops Will Start a Strike: Believes Men Will Climb Out." *New York Times*, November 30, 1915.

"Ford Now Planning an Overflow Ship." *New York Times*, November 29, 1915.

"Ford Offers Party $2,000,000 Backing." *New York Times*, December 28, 1915.

"Ford Opposes Loan to Allies." *Philadelphia Inquirer*, September 25, 1915.

"Ford Pacifists Go through Germany." *Gazette Times*, January 4, 1916.

"Ford Party in Dispute, Mrs. Boissevain Leaves: Indicts Party as Having No Plans and Being Directed by an Undemocratic Few." *New York Times*, December 26, 1915.

"Ford Peace Meeting Barred by Denmark: Papers in Christiania Surprised That Manufacturer Had No Definite Plan Mapped Out." *Philadelphia Inquirer*, December 21, 1915.

"Ford Peace Mission Starts Its Voyage at a Lively Gait." *Philadelphia Inquirer*, December 5, 1915.

"Ford Sails for U.S., Leave Peace Party in Europe." *Philadelphia Inquirer*, December 25, 1915.

"Ford Seeking Congress' Aid." *Chicago Daily Tribune*, December 7, 1915.

"Ford Ship Arrives at Christiansand: Peace Party Rent by Discord on Eve of First Landing in Europe: Curfew Crusade Blocked: Reported Attempts at Espionage Also Serves to Enliven the Voyage . . . Proprietors Refuse to Reserve Rooms." *New York Times*, December 19, 1915.

"Ford Urges Wilson to Start Peace Talk." *Gazette Times*, November 24, 1915.

"Ford Will Send Ship to War." *Philadelphia Inquirer*, November 25, 1915.

"Ford's Ark." *Shanghai Times*, December 18, 1915.

"Ford's Party Not Popular at The Hague: Will Be Permitted to Land, but Told to Move On if Activities Are Offensive." *Gazette Times*, December 12, 1915.

"Ford's Peace Ship on Way to War Zone." *Gazette Times*, December 5, 1915.

"From Alt Right to Alt Lite: Naming the Hate." Anti-Defamation League. Accessed November 13, 2022. Web.

"Global Conflict Tracker." Council on Foreign Relations. Accessed January 15, 2023. Web.

Gookin, Frederick W. "A Liberty Catechism." Chicago: Central Anti-Imperialist League, October 1899. In box 1, folder: Anti-Imperialist League, Bound

Volume of Pamphlets/Tracts, 1899, Swarthmore Peace Collection, Swarthmore, Pennsylvania, United States.

"Governor Willis Undecided." *New York Times*, November 26, 1915.

"Grannie Joins Global Anti-War Protests." *Guardian* (Charlottetown, Prince Edward Island), February 15, 2003.

Green, Emma. "Why the Charlottesville Marchers Were Obsessed with Jews." *Atlantic*, August 15, 2017.

"Grotesque." *New York Times*, December 1, 1915.

Haass, Richard. "The Pandemic Will Accelerate History Rather Than Reshape It." *Foreign Affairs*, April 7, 2020.

Hartzel, A. E. "Ford Party Is Split Over Resolution: Nine Pilgrims Object to Condemning Wilson's Message on Preparedness: Appeal to Rulers." *Gazette Times*, December 14, 1915.

———. "Germans May Arrest Ford's Peace Party." *Gazette Times*, December 6, 1915.

"Henry Ford Back, Admits an Error, Denies Deserting: Disabused of Idea That the War Was Caused by Militarists or Munition Men: Now Blames the People." *New York Times*, January 3, 1916.

"Henry Ford Is Reported to Be Ill." *San Francisco Chronicle*, December 24, 1915.

"Henry Ford's Peace Ship Brings $67,500 as Junk." *Chicago Daily Tribune*, September 4, 1933.

"Henry Ford's Peace Ship Released by British." *Chicago Daily Tribune*, December 18, 1915.

H. W. J. "Pepper and Salt." *Wall Street Journal*, December 10, 1915.

King, Llewellyn. "How NIMBYism Is Strangling America." *Washington Chronicles*, August 30, 2024.

Lynch, Colum. "Exclusive: Rwanda Revisited." *Foreign Policy*, April 5, 2015.

Martin, Nick. "Give Me Capitalism or Give Me Death." *New Republic*, March 25, 2020.

Menand, Louis. "Francis Fukuyama Postpones the End of History." *New Yorker*, August 27, 2018.

"Midway Gleanings." *Omaha World-Herald*, August 31, 1898.

"Mrs. Dilling Hails Ending of Sedition Case." *Chicago Daily Tribune*, August 2, 1947.

"Mrs. Ford Disputes Rumors of Ford Falling Ill, Which Ironically Would Have Made His Decision Seem More Reasonable." *New York Times*, December 25, 1915.

Murphy, Katharine. "Rising US Isolationism Means Australia Must Become More Resilient and Autonomous, Thinktank Warns." *Guardian*, March 15, 2022.

"Newspaper Specials." *Wall Street Journal*, August 24, 1915.

"Newspaper Specials." *Wall Street Journal*, September 21, 1915.

"1948 Presidential Election." 270toWin. Accessed December 27, 2024. Web.

"1926 Ford Model T Roadster." National Museum of American History, Behring Center.

"Opposition to Syrian Airstrikes Surges." Pew Research Center, September 9, 2013.

Otten, Ian L. "Politics and People: For Spiro, Suspiro." *Wall Street Journal*, October 31, 1969.

Papers from the Society for the Diffusion of Political Knowledge. New York: Society for the Diffusion of Political Knowledge, 1863–1864.

Patriotic Research Bulletin. Kenneth Spencer Research Library, University of Kansas, Lawrence, KS (KSP). File RH WL D2091 (RH).

"Patriotism and Imperialism." In *Liberty Tracts*, no. 2. Chicago: Central Anti-Imperialist League, Tacoma Building, 1899.

"Peace Ark Starts." *New York Times*, December 5, 1915.

"Peace Cries Ring; Millions in U.S., around World Protest a War in Iraq." *San Diego Union-Tribune*, February 16, 2003.

"Peace Party to Cross Germany in Locked Cars." *Chicago Daily Tribune*, January 4, 1916.

"Peace Programme for Ford Party Announced." *Philadelphia Inquirer*, December 10, 1915.

Perrigo, Billy. "White Supremacist Groups Are Recruiting with Help from Coronavirus—and a Popular Messaging App." *Time*, April 8, 2020.

Pierce, Edward C. "The 'Single Tribe': Fiction, Liberty Tracts no. 14." Chicago: American Anti-Imperialist League. Folder Anti-Imperialist League, Chicago, 1899–1901, Swarthmore Peace Collection, Swarthmore, Pennsylvania, United States.

"Platform of the American Anti-Imperialist League." In *Speeches, Correspondence, and Political Papers of Carl Schurz*. Vol. 6, edited by Frederick Bancroft. New York: G. P. Putnam's Sons, 1913.

"Proclamation on Declaring a National Emergency Concerning the Novel Coronavirus Disease (COVID-19) Outbreak." White House, March 13, 2020. Web.

"Roosevelt Likens Ford to Old Fashioned Chinaman." *Chicago Daily Tribune*, October 21, 1915.

"Roosevelt Scores Ford Peace Junket and Wilson Policy." *Philadelphia Inquirer*, December 6, 1915.

"Row on Ford Ship over Expulsions." *New York Times*, December 20, 1915.

"Sad State of Affairs." *Gazette Times*, December 22, 1915.

"Ship of Fools." *Spectator*, December 11, 1915.

"Some Topics of the Week." *Philadelphia Inquirer*, December 19, 1915.

"Squabbles Mark Peace Ark's Voyage." *Philadelphia Inquirer*, December 20, 1915.

Stewart, Charles P. "Peace Party Split Again." *Chicago Daily Tribune*, December 26, 1915.

"Talks with Mr. Ford: A Quaint Crusader." *Times of India*, January 3, 1916.

"Thinks Henry Ford Peace Press Agent: Miss Addams Praises Him, but Disowns Expedition in Behalf of Women Pacifists." *New York Times*, January 6, 1916.

Tharoor, Ishaan. "Why Was the Biggest Protest in World History Ignored?" *Time*, February 15, 2013.

Timberg, Craig, and Allyson Chiu. "As the Coronavirus Spreads, So Does Online Racism Targeting Asians, New Research Shows." *Washington Post*, April 8, 2020.

Tisdall, Simon. "Trump Is Playing a Deadly Game in Deflecting Covid-19 Blame to China." *Guardian*, April 19, 2020.

Vietnam Veterans against the War Records, 1967–2006 (Bulk 1967–1975). Folders 12–15, box 8. Wisconsin Historical Society, Madison.

Vietnam Veterans against the War/Winter Soldier Organization. VVAW/WSO Publicity 1969–1972 press releases and statements. mss 370, Vietnam Veterans against the War Records, 1967–2006 (Bulk 1967–1975), Wisconsin Historical Society.

"Wanamaker Is Skeptical." *New York Times*, December 1, 1915.

"Wanamaker May Go on Ford Peace Trip." *Philadelphia Inquirer*, November 26, 1915.

Watt, Cecilia Saixue. "Redneck Revolt: The Armed Leftwing Group That Wants to Stamp Out Fascism." *Guardian*, July 11, 2017.

Wilson, Carolyn. "War on Ford's Peace Ship: Want to Expel Reporters at Christiania." *Chicago Daily Tribune*, December 20, 1915.

"Winter Soldier: The Film." Winter Soldier. Last modified 2006. Web.

"Woman Held as Witness in U.S. Bomb Plot Probe." *San Francisco Chronicle*, December 10, 1915.

"Women Stage Anti-War Protest outside US Embassy in Guyana." BBC Summary of World Broadcasts, February 16, 2003.

Women's Voice. Women and Leadership Archives (WLA), Loyola University, Chicago, box 6, folder 2, "Women's Voice, 1944–1960, n.d. Women's Voice."

OTHER WORKS

Achter, Paul. "Rhetoric and the Permanent War." *Quarterly Journal of Speech* 102, no. 1 (2016): 79–94.

———. "Unruly Bodies: The Rhetorical Domestication of Twenty-First Century Veterans of War." *Quarterly Journal of Speech* 96, no. 1 (2010): 46–68.

Adams, Charles Francis. *"Imperialism" and "The Tracks of Our Forefathers": A Paper Read by Charles Francis Adams before the Lexington, Massachusetts, Historical Society, Tuesday, December 20, 1898"*. Boston: Dana Estes, 1899.

Addams, Jane. "Democracy or Militarism." In *The Chicago Liberty Meeting, Liberty Tract no. 1*, 35–39. Chicago: Central Anti-Imperialist League, 1899.

ADL's Center on Extremism. "When Women Are the Enemy: The Intersection of Misogyny and White Supremacy." Anti-Defamation League, July 20, 2018.

Agamben, Giorgio. *State of Exception*. Chicago: University of Chicago Press, 2005.

Alexander, Michelle. *The New Jim Crow: Mass Incarceration in the Age of Colorblindness*. New York: New Press, 2010.

Anbinder, Tyler. *Nativism and Slavery: The Northern Know Nothings and the Politics of the 1850s*. New York: Oxford University Press, 1992.

Anderson, Karrin Vasby. "'Rhymes with Rich': 'Bitch' as a Tool of Containment in Contemporary American Politics." *Rhetoric and Public Affairs* 2, no. 4 (1999): 599–623.

Anderson, Karrin Vasby, and Kristina Horn Sheeler. *Governing Codes: Gender, Metaphor, and Political Identity*. Lanham, MD: Lexington Books, 2005.

Appy, Christian G. *American Reckoning: The Vietnam War and Our National Identity*. New York: Penguin Books, 2015.

Arendt, Hannah. *The Human Condition*. New York: Harcourt Brace Jovanovich, 1951.

Aristotle, *Rhetoric*. Translated by W. Rhys Roberts. Mineola, NY: Dover Thrift Editions, 2004.

Armitage, David. *Civil Wars: A History in Ideas*. New Haven, CT: Yale University Press, 2017.
Asen, Robert, and Daniel C. Brouwer, eds. *Counterpublics and the State*. Albany: State University of New York Press, 2001.
Atkinson, Edward. "The Cost of an Anglo-American War." *American Periodicals*, March 1896, 74–88.
———. *The Cost of a National Crime*. Boston: Rockwell & Churchill Press, 1898.
Austin, Allan W. *Quaker Brotherhood: Interracial Activism and the American Friends Service Committee, 1917–1950*. Urbana: University of Illinois Press, 2012.
Axelrod, Alan. *Selling the Great War: The Making of American Propaganda*. New York: St. Martin's Press, 2009.
Azoulay, Ariella. *The Civil Contract of Photography*. New York: Zone Books, 2008.
———. *Civil Imagination: A Political Ontology of Photography*. New York: Verso, 2010.
———. *Civil Imagination: A Political Ontology of Photography*. Translated by Louise Bethlehem. London: Verso, 2015.
Bancroft, Frederic, and William A. Dunning, eds. *The Reminiscences of Carl Schurz*. Vol. 3, *1863–1869*. New York: McClure, 1908.
Barash, David. *Approaches to Peace: A Reader in Peace Studies*. Oxford: Oxford University Press, 2010.
Barney, Timothy. "The Sight and Site of North Korea: Citizen Cartography's Rhetoric of Resolution in the Satellite Imagery of Labor Camps." *Quarterly Journal of Speech* 105, no. 1 (2019): 1–24
Bennett, David H. *The Party of Fear: The American Far Right from Nativism to the Militia Movement*. Chapel Hill: University of North Carolina Press, 1995.
Benson, Thomas W. *Posters for Peace: Visual Rhetoric and Civic Action*. University Park: Pennsylvania State University Press, 2016.
Biesecker, Barbara. "Coming to Terms with Recent Attempts to Write Women into the History of Rhetoric." *Philosophy and Rhetoric* 25, no. 2 (Spring 1992): 140–61.
———. "No Time for Mourning: The Rhetorical Production of the Melancholic Citizen-Subject in the War on Terror." *Philosophy and Rhetoric* 40, no. 1 (2007): 147–69.
Black, Jason Edward. "Native Authenticity, Rhetorical Circulation, and Neocolonial Decay: The Case of Chief Seattle's Controversial Speech." *Rhetoric and Public Affairs* 15 (2012): 635–45.
———. "Native Resistive Rhetoric and the Decolonization of American Indian Removal Discourse." *Quarterly Journal of Speech* 95 (2009): 66–88.
———. "Plenary Rhetoric in Indian Country: The Lone Wolf v. Hitchcock Case and the Codification of a Weakened Native Character." *Advances in the History of Rhetoric* 11/12 (2008): 59–80.
———. "Remembrances of Removal: Native Resistance to Allotment and the Unmasking of Paternal Benevolence." *Southern Communication Journal* 72 (2007): 185–203.
Blair, William A. *With Malice toward Some: Treason and Loyalty in the Civil War Era*. Chapel Hill: University of North Carolina Press, 2014.

Blight, David W. *Race and Reunion: The Civil War in American Memory.* Cambridge, MA: Harvard University Press, 2001.
Blodgett, Geoffrey. *The Gentle Reformers: Massachusetts Democrats in the Cleveland Era.* Cambridge, MA: Harvard University Press, 1966.
Bloss, G. M. D. *Life and Speeches of George H. Pendleton.* Cincinnati: Miami Printing, 1868.
Bonilla-Silva, Eduardo. *Racism without Racists: Colorblind Racism and the Persistence of Inequality in America.* 4th ed. New York: Rowman & Littlefield, 2014.
Bordogna, Francesca. *William James at the Boundaries: Philosophy, Science and the Geography of Knowledge.* Chicago: University of Chicago Press, 2008.
Boutwell, George S. *Address to the Laboring and Producing Classes of the United States.* Chicago: American Anti-Imperialist League, 1900.
———. *Bryan or Imperialism: Address by the Hon. George S. Boutwell, Delivered at the National Congress of Anti-Imperialists at Indianapolis, Ind., August 15–16, 1900.* Boston: New England Anti-Imperialist League, 1900.
———. *The Enslavement of American Labor.* Boston: New England Anti-Imperialist League, 1902.
———. *Imperialists or Republicans?: Mr. Boutwell's Speech before the Essex Institute, Salem, January 9, 1899.* Washington, DC: Anti-Imperialist League, 1899.
———. *The President's Policy: War and Conquest Abroad, Degradation of Labor at Home.* Chicago: American Anti-Imperialist League, 1900.
———. *Republic or Empire.* Boston: New England Anti-Imperialist League, 1900.
———. *The Supreme Court and the Dependencies by George S. Boutwell.* Boston: Anti-Imperialist League, 1901.
Brands, H. W. *American Colossus: The Triumph of Capitalism, 1865–1900.* New York: Anchor Books, 2011.
Brinkley, Alan. "Richard Hofstadter's *The Age of Reform*: A Reconsideration." *Reviews in American History* 13, no. 3 (1985): 462–80.
———. *Voices of Protest: Huey Long, Father Coughlin, and the Great Depression.* New York: Random House, 1982.
Brouwer, Daniel C., and Robert Asen, eds. *Public Modalities: Rhetoric, Culture, Media, and the Shape of Public Life.* Tuscaloosa: University of Alabama Press, 2010.
Browne, Stephen H. *The Ides of War: George Washington and the Newburgh Crisis.* Columbia: University of South Carolina Press, 2016.
Bryan, William Jennings. "America's Mission." In *Speeches of William Jennings Bryan*, vol. 2, 9–16. New York: Funk and Wagnalls, 1913.
———. "Imperialism." Delivered August 8, 1900. Available at Voices of Democracy. Web.
———. *Republic or Empire? The Philippine Question.* Boston: New England Anti-Imperialist League, 1900.
Buenker, John D. "Moral Reform Movements." In *Encyclopedia of American Social Movements*, edited by Immanuel Ness, 843–920. New York: Routledge, 2004.
Buescher, Derek T., and Kent A. Ono. "Civilized Colonialism: Pocahontas as Neocolonial Rhetoric." *Women's Studies in Communication* 19 (1996): 127–53.
Burke, Kenneth. *A Grammar of Motives.* Berkeley: University of California Press, 1945.

———. "Literature as Equipment for Living." In *The Philosophy of Literary Form: Studies in Symbolic Action*, 293–304. Berkeley: University of California Press, 1973.

———. "The Rhetoric of Hitler's Battle." *Southern Review* 5 (1939): 1–21.

———. *A Rhetoric of Motives*. Berkeley: University of California Press, 1969.

———. *The Rhetoric of Religion: Studies in Logology*. Berkeley: University of California Press, 1970.

———. "War and Cultural Life." *American Journal of Sociology* 48, no. 3 (1942): 404–10.

Bush, George W. "Address to a Joint Session of Congress and the American People." September 20, 2001.

Butler, Judith. *Frames of War: When Is Life Grievable?* London: Verso, 2009.

———. *Precarious Life: The Powers of Mourning and Violence*. New York: Verso, 2006.

Campbell, D'Ann. *Women at War with America: Private Lives in a Patriotic Era*. Cambridge, MA: Harvard University Press, 1984.

Campbell, David. *Writing Security: United States Foreign Policy and the Politics of Identity*. Rev. ed. Manchester: Manchester University Press, 1998.

Campbell, Karlyn Kohrs. *Man Cannot Speak for Her: A Critical Study of Early Feminist Rhetoric*. Westport, CT: Greenwood Press, 1989.

Carlin, Diana B., and Kelly L. Winfrey. "Have You Come a Long Way, Baby? Hillary Clinton, Sarah Palin, and Sexism in 2008 Campaign Coverage." *Communication Studies* 60, no. 4 (2009): 326–43.

Carnegie, Andrew. "Americanism versus Imperialism: II." *North American Review* 168, no. 508 (1899): 362–72.

———. *Endowment for International Peace, A Manual of the Public Benefactions of Andrew Carnegie*. N.d.: Washington, DC, 1919.

Carver, Ron, David Cortright, and Barbara Doherty, eds. *Waging Peace in Vietnam: US Soldiers and Veterans Who Opposed the War*. New York: New Village Press, 2019.

Cathcart, Robert S. "Movements: Confrontation as Rhetorical Form." *Southern Speech Communication Journal* 43, no. 3 (1978): 233–47.

Ceccarelli, Leah. "Polysemy: Multiple Meanings in Rhetorical Criticism." *Quarterly Journal of Speech* 84, no. 4 (1998): 395–415.

Chan, Jovy. "Online Astroturfing: A Problem beyond Disinformation." *Philosophy and Social Criticism* (2022): 1–22.

Chávez, Karma R. "Beyond Inclusion: Rethinking Rhetoric's Historical Narrative." *Quarterly Journal of Speech* 101 (2015): 162–72.

———. "The Body: An Abstract and Actual Rhetorical Concept." *Rhetoric Society Quarterly* 48, no. 3 (2018): 242–50.

———. "Counter-Public Enclaves and Understanding the Function of Rhetoric in Social Movement Coalition-Building." *Communication Quarterly* 59, no. 1 (2011): 1–18.

Chávez, Karma R., and Cindy L. Griffin, eds. *Standing in the Intersection: Feminist Voices, Feminist Practices in Communication Studies*. Albany: SUNY Press, 2012.

Childers, Jay P. "Transforming Violence into a Focusing Event: A Reception Study of the 1946 Georgia Lynching." *Rhetoric and Public Affairs* 19, no. 4 (2016): 571–600.

"China Responsible for 'Serious Human Rights Violations' in Xinjian Province." *UN Human Rights Report*, August 31, 2022.

Churchill, Robert H. *To Shake Their Guns in the Tyrant's Face: Libertarian Political Violence and the Origins of the Militia Movement*. Ann Arbor: University of Michigan Press, 2012.

Classen, Albrecht. "Female Epistolary Literature from Antiquity to the Present: An Introduction." *Studia Neophilologica* 60, no. 1 (1988): 3–13.

Clausewitz, Carl von. *On War*. Translated by Michael Howard and Peter Paret. New York: Oxford University Press, 2007.

Cleveland, Grover. "Founder's Day Address." In *Addresses, State Papers and Letters*, edited by Albert Ellery Bergh, 403–4. New York: Sun Dial Classics, 1909.

Colburn, David R., and George E. Pozzetta. "Race, Ethnicity, and the Evolution of Political Legitimacy." In *The Sixties: From Memory to History*, edited by David Farber, 119–48. Chapel Hill: University of North Carolina Press, 1994.

Cole, Wayne. *America First: The Battle against Intervention 1940–1941*. New York: Octagon Books, 1971.

Collins, Patricia Hill. "Intersectionality's Definitional Dilemmas." *Annual Review of Sociology* 41, no. 1 (2015): 1–20.

Condit, Celeste Michelle. "In Praise of Eloquent Diversity: Gender and Rhetoric as Public Persuasion." *Women's Studies in Communication* 20, no. 2 (1997): 91–116.

Cooper, John Milton, Jr. *The Warrior and the Priest: Woodrow Wilson and Theodore Roosevelt*. Cambridge, MA: Harvard University Press, 1985.

Copperhead Conspiracy in the Northwest: An Exposé on the Treasonable Order of the "Sons of Liberty": Vallandigham, Supreme Commander. New York: John A. Gray and Green, 1864.

Corrigan, Lisa M. *Black Feelings: Race and Affect in the Long Sixties*. Jackson: University of Mississippi Press, 2020.

———. "On Rhetorical Criticism, Performativity, and White Fragility." *Review of Communication* 16, no. 1 (2016): 86–88.

Craig, John M. "The Woman's Peace Party and Questions of Gender Separatism." *Peace and Change* 19, no. 4 (1994): 373–98.

Crary, Jonathan. "Modernity and the Problem of the Observer." In *Techniques of the Observer: On Vision and Modernity in the Nineteenth Century*, 1–24. Cambridge: MIT Press, 1990.

Creighton, Margaret. *The Electrifying Fall of Rainbow City: Spectacle and Assassination at the 1901 World's Fair*. New York: W. W. Norton, 2016.

Crenshaw, Kimberlé. "Demarginalizing the Intersection of Race and Sex: A Black Feminist Critique of Antidiscrimination Doctrine, Feminist Theory and Antiracist Politics." *University of Chicago Legal Forum* 1 (1989): 139–67.

Crick, Nathan, ed. *The Rhetoric of Social Movements: Networks, Power, and New Media*. London: Routledge, 2020.

Crooker, Joseph Henry. "The Menace to America." Chicago: American Anti-Imperialist League newsletter, 1900, 3–4.

Cross, Gary. *A Social History of Leisure since 1600*. State College, PA: Venture, 1990.

Cullinane, Michael Patrick. *Liberty and American Anti-Imperialism, 1898–1909*. New York: Palgrave Macmillan, 2012.
Danbom, David B. "'Agricultural History' Roundtable on Populism." *Agricultural History* 82, no. 1 (2008): 1–35.
Davis, Allen F. "The Progressives, Once More, with Conviction." *Reviews in American History* 11, no. 3 (1983): 404–8.
Davis, James Kirkpatrick. *Assault on the Left: The FBI and the Sixties Antiwar Movement*. Westport, CT: Praeger, 1997.
De Benedetti, Charles. "Peace History, in the American Manner." *History Teacher* 18, no. 1 (1984): 94–95.
Debord, Guy. *Society of the Spectacle*. Translated by Fredy Perlman and Jon Supak. Detroit: Black and Red, 1970.
Delgado, Richard, and Jean Stefancic. *Critical Race Theory*. 2nd ed. New York: New York University Press, 2012.
Dew, Charles B. *Apostles of Disunion: Southern Secession Commissioners and the Causes of the Civil War*. Charlottesville: University of Virginia Press, 2001.
DiAngelo, Robin. "White Fragility." *International Journal of Critical Pedagogy* 3, no. 3 (2011): 54–70.
Dilling, Elizabeth. *The Octopus*. 1940; Metarie, LA: Sons of Liberty, 1986.
———. *The Red Network: A "Who's Who" and Handbook of Radicalism for Patriots*. Kenilworth, IL: Self-published, 1934.
———. *The Roosevelt Red Record and Its Background*. N.d.: Self-published, 1936.
Dinnerstein, Leonard. *Anti-Semitism in America*. New York: Oxford University Press, 1994.
Dow, Bonnie J. "Fixing Feminism: Women's Liberation and the Rhetoric of Television Documentary." *Quarterly Journal of Speech* 90, no. 1 (2004): 53–80.
Dow, Bonnie J., and Mari Boor Tonn. "'Feminine Style' and Political Judgment in the Rhetoric of Ann Richards." *Quarterly Journal of Speech* 79, no. 3 (1993): 286–302.
Drescher, Seymour. *Abolition: A History of Slavery and Antislavery*. Cambridge, UK: Cambridge University Press, 2009.
Dubisar, Abby M. "Embodying and Disrupting Antiwar Activism: Disrupting YouTube's 'Mothers Day for Peace'." *Rhetoric Review* 34, no. 1 (2015): 56–73.
Du Bois, W. E. B. *Black Reconstruction*. London: Routledge, 2017.
Dudziak, Mary L. *War Time: An Idea, Its History, Its Consequences*. New York: Oxford University Press, 2012.
Dunbar-Ortiz, Roxanne. *An Indigenous People's History of the United States*. Boston: Beacon Press, 2014.
Earle, Jonathan, and Diane Mutti Burke, eds. *Bleeding Kansas, Bleeding Missouri: The Long Civil War on the Border*. Lawrence: University Press of Kansas, 2013.
Edelman, Murray. *Constructing the Political Spectacle*. Chicago: University of Chicago Press, 1988.
Edmunds, George F. "The Insular Cases." *North American Review* 173, no. 537 (1901): 145–53.
Eger, Elizabeth. *Women, Writing and the Public Sphere*. New York: Cambridge University Press, 2001.

Enck-Wanzer, Darrel. "Decolonizing Imaginaries: Rethinking 'the People' in the Young Lords' Church Offensive." *Quarterly Journal of Speech* 98 (2012): 1–23.

———. "Trashing the System: Social Movement, Intersectional Rhetoric, and Collective Agency in the Young Lords Organization's Garbage Offensive." *Quarterly Journal of Speech* 92, no. 2 (2006): 174–201.

Endres, Danielle. "The Rhetoric of Nuclear Colonialism: Rhetorical Exclusion of American Indian Arguments in the Yucca Mountain Nuclear Waste Siting Decision." *Communication and Critical/Cultural Studies* 6 (2009): 39–60.

Engels, Jeremy. *Enemyship: Democracy and Counter-Revolution in the Early Republic.* East Lansing: Michigan State University Press, 2010.

———. "Forum: The Violence of Rhetoric." *Quarterly Journal of Speech* 99, no. 2 (2013): 180–81.

Engels, Jeremy, and William O. Saas. "On Acquiescence and Ends-Less War: An Inquiry into the New War Rhetoric." *Quarterly Journal of Speech* 99, no. 2 (2013): 225–32.

Escobedo, Elizabeth R. *From Coveralls to Zoot Suits: The Lives of Mexican American Women on the World War II Home Front.* Chapel Hill: University of North Carolina Press, 2013.

Faust, Drew Gilpin. *This Republic of Suffering: Death and the American Civil War.* New York: Vintage, 2008.

Fay, Sidney B. *The Origins of the World War.* New York: Macmillan, 1928.

Flores, Lisa A. "Between Abundance and Marginalization: The Imperative of Racial Rhetorical Criticism." *Review of Communication* 16, no. 1 (2016): 4–24.

Foley, Megan. "Of Violence and Rhetoric: An Ethical Aporia." *Quarterly Journal of Speech* 99, no. 2 (2013): 191–99.

Foner, Eric. *Give the Liberty! An American History.* New York: W. W. Norton, 2008.

Foote, Lorien. *The Gentlemen and the Roughs: Violence, Honor, and Manhood in the Union Army.* New York: New York University Press, 2010.

Ford Motor Company. "The Model T: A Timeless Legacy." Accessed November 16, 2024. Web.

Foss, Sonja K., and Cindy L. Griffin. "Beyond Persuasion: A Proposal for an Invitational Rhetoric." *Communication Monographs* 62, no. 1 (1995): 2–19.

Foust, Christina R. Amy Pason, and Kate Zittlow Rogness, eds. *What Democracy Looks Like: The Rhetoric of Social Movements and Counterpublics.* Tuscaloosa: University of Alabama Press, 2017.

Frederick the Great. *Instructions for His Generals.* Translated by General Thomas R. Phillips. Mineola, NY: Dover, 2005.

Freeberg, Ernest. *Democracy's Prisoner: Eugene V. Debs, the Great War, and the Right to Dissent.* Cambridge, MA: Harvard University Press, 2008.

Fukuyama, Francis. "The End of History?" *National Interest* 16 (1989): 3–18.

Galtung, Johan. *Peace by Peaceful Means: Peace and Conflict, Development and Civilization.* London: Sage, 1996.

Giddens, Anthony. *The Consequences of Modernity.* Stanford, CA: Stanford University Press, 1990.

Gilbert, Christopher J. "The Press of War Imagery." *Rhetoric Society Quarterly* 47, no. 2 (2017): 206–14.

Ginger, Ray. *Age of Excess: The United States from 1877 to 1914*. New York: Macmillan, 1975.

Glickstein, Jonathan A. *American Exceptionalism, American Anxiety: Wages, Competition, and Degraded Labor in the Antebellum United States*. Charlottesville: University of Virginia Press, 2002.

Gompers, Samuel. "Imperialism—Its Dangers and Wrongs: A Speech by Samuel Gompers, President of the American Federation of Labor." Delivered October 18, 1898. Available at Thirteen.org. Web.

Gordon, John Steele. *An Empire of Wealth: The Epic History of American Power*. New York: Harper Perennial, 2004.

Gordon, Linda. *The Second Coming of the KKK*. New York: W. W. Norton, 2017.

Gorsevski, Ellen W. *Peaceful Persuasion: The Geopolitics of Nonviolent Rhetoric*. Albany: State University of New York Press, 2004.

Grandin, Greg. *Fordlandia: The Rise and Fall of Henry Ford's Forgotten Jungle City*. New York: Metropolitan Books, 2009.

Green, Martin. *The Vernon Street Warrens: A Boston Story, 1860–1910*. New York: Charles Scribner's Sons, 1989.

Greenberg, Amy S. *Manifest Manhood and the Antebellum American Empire*. New York: Cambridge University Press, 2005.

———. *A Wicked War: Polk, Clay, Lincoln, and the 1846 U. S. Invasion of Mexico*. New York: Vintage, 2012.

Gribble, Richard. "The Immigration Restriction Debate, 1917–1929." *Journal of Church and State* 60, no. 3 (2018): 398–425.

Hagen, Lisa. "Antisemitism Is on the Rise, and It's Not Just about Ye." NPR, *All Things Considered*, December 1, 2022.

Haider, Syed. "The Shooting in Orlando, Terrorism or Toxic Masculinity (or Both?)." *Men and Masculinities* 19, no. 5 (2016): 555–65.

Haines, Herbert H. "Radical Flank Effects." In *The Wiley-Blackwell Encyclopedia of Social and Political Movements*, December 15, 2022. Web.

Halbwachs, Maurice. *On Collective Memory*. Translated by Lewis A. Coser. Chicago: University of Chicago Press, 1992.

Hall, Peter Dobkin. "Social Darwinism and the Poor." Social Welfare History Project, February 10, 2014. Web.

Harcourt, Felix. *Ku Klux Kulture: America and the Klan in the 1920s*. Chicago: University of Chicago Press, 2017.

Hariman, Robert. *Political Style: The Artistry of Power*. Chicago: University of Chicago Press, 1995.

Hariman, Robert, and John Louis Lucaites. *The Public Image: Photography and Civic Spectatorship*. Chicago: University of Chicago Press, 2016.

Harmon, Mark D. "This Is Not Goldfish Swallowing: Newsreels Encounter Protests against the Vietnam War." *Visual Communication Quarterly* 17, no. 4 (2010): 200–212.

Hart, Bradley W. *Hitler's American Friends: The Third Reich Supporters in the United States*. New York: St. Martin's Press, 2018.

Hayden, Wendy. "From Lucifer to Jezebel: Invitational Rhetoric, Rhetorical Closure, and Safe Spaces in Feminist Sexual Discourse Communities." *Rhetoric Society Quarterly* 51, no. 2 (2021): 79–93.

Hegarty, Marilyn E. *Victory Girls, Khaki-Wackies, and Patriotutes: The Regulation of Female Sexuality during World War II.* New York: New York University Press, 2008.

Heidt, Stephen J. "Presidential Power and National Violence: James K. Polk's Rhetorical Transfer of Savagery." *Rhetoric and Public Affairs* 19, no. 3 (2016): 265–396.

———. *Resowing the Seeds of War: Presidential Peace Rhetoric since 1945.* East Lansing: Michigan State University Press, 2022.

Hershey, Burnet. *The Odyssey of Henry Ford and the Great Peace Ship.* New York: Taplinger, 1967.

Hilfrich, Fabian. *Debating American Exceptionalism: Empire and Democracy in the Wake of the Spanish-American War.* Basingstoke, UK: Palgrave Macmillan, 2012.

Hofstadter, Richard. *The Paranoid Style in American Politics.* New York: First Vintage Books, 2008.

———. *Social Darwinism in American Thought.* Boston: Beacon Press, 1944.

Hogan, J. Michael, ed. *Rhetoric and Reform in the Progressive Era: Rhetorical History of the United States.* Vol. 6. East Lansing: Michigan State University Press, 2002.

———. *Woodrow Wilson's Western Tour: Rhetoric, Public Opinion, and the League of Nations.* College Station: Texas A&M University Press, 2006.

Houdek, Matthew. "Racial Sedimentation and the Common Sense of Racialized Violence: The Case of Black Church Burnings." *Quarterly Journal of Speech* 104, no. 3 (2018): 279–306.

Hughes, Dana. "Bill Clinton Regrets Rwanda Now (Not So Much in 1994)." *ABC News*, February 28, 2014.

Hunt, Andrew E. *The Turning: A History of Vietnam Veterans against the War.* New York: New York University Press, 1999.

Immerwahr, Daniel. *How to Hide an Empire.* New York: Farrar, Straus and Giroux, 2019.

Irons, Charles F. *The Origins of Proslavery Christianity: White and Black Evangelicals in Colonial and Antebellum Virginia.* Chapel Hill: University of North Carolina Press, 2008.

Ivie, Robert L. *Democracy and America's War on Terror.* Tuscaloosa: University of Alabama Press, 2006.

———. "Democratic Dissent and the Trick of Rhetorical Critique." *Critical Studies, Critical Methodologies* 5, no. 3 (2005): 278.

———. *Dissent from War.* Bloomfield, CT: Kumarian Press, 2007.

———. "Hegemony, Instabilities, and Interventions: A Special Issue on Discourses of War and Peace." *Journal of Multicultural Discourses* 11, no. 2 (2016): 125–34.

———. "Hierarchies of Equality: Positive Peace in a Democratic Idiom." In *The Handbook of Communication Ethics*, edited by George Cheney, Steve May, and Debashish Munshi, 374–86. New York: Routledge, 2011.

Ivie, Robert, and Oscar Giner. *Hunt the Devil: A Demonology of US War Culture.* Tuscaloosa: University of Alabama Press, 2015.

———. "Hunting the Devil: Democracy's Rhetorical Impulse to War." *Presidential Studies Quarterly* 37, no. 4 (2007): 580–98.

———. "Waging Peace: Transformations of the Warrior Myth by US Military Veterans." *Journal of Multicultural Discourse* 11, no. 2 (2016): 199–213.
Jackson, Matthew. "The Enthymematic Hegemony of Whiteness." *JAC* 26, no. 3 (2006): 601–41.
James, Pearl. *Picture This: World War I Posters and Visual Culture*. Lincoln: University of Nebraska Press, 2009.
Jamieson, Kathleen Hall. *Beyond the Double Bind: Women and Leadership*. New York: Oxford University Press, 1995.
Janney, Caroline E. *Remembering the Civil War: Reunion and the Limits of Reconciliation*. Chapel Hill: University of North Carolina Press, 2013.
Jasper, James M. *The Art of Moral Protest: Culture, Biography, and Creativity in Social Movements*. Chicago: University of Chicago Press, 1997.
Jeansonne, Glen. *Women of the Far Right: The Mothers' Movement and World War II*. Chicago: University of Chicago Press, 1996.
Jefferson, Thomas, et al. "Declaration of Independence." July 4, 1776.
Jenkins, Philip. *Hoods and Shirts: The Extreme Right in Pennsylvania, 1925–1950*. Chapel Hill: University of North Carolina Press, 1997.
Johnson, Jenell. "The Limits of Persuasion: Rhetoric and Resistance in the Last Battle of the Korean War." *Quarterly Journal of Speech* 100, no. 3 (2014): 323–47.
Johnson, Paul Elliot. "The Art of Masculine Victimhood: Donald Trump's Demagoguery." *Women's Studies in Communication* 40, no. 3 (2017): 229–50.
Johnson, Robert David. "Anti-Imperialism and Good Neighbour Policy: Ernest Gruening and Puerto Rican Affairs, 1934–1939." *Journal of Latin American Studies* 29, no. 1 (1997): 89–110.
Johnston, Robert D. "The Possibilities of Politics: Democracy in America, 1877 to 1917." In *American History Now*, edited by Eric Foner and Lisa McGirr, 96–124. Philadelphia: Temple University Press, 2011.
Jonas, Manfred. *Isolationism in America, 1935–1941*. Ithaca, NY: Cornell University Press, 1966.
Jones, Jeffrey M. "Blacks, Postgraduates among Groups Most Likely to Oppose Iraq Invasion." Gallup, January 30, 2003.
———. "War through Partisan Lenses: Divide over Iraq Not Necessarily Typical." Gallup, November 15, 2005.
Jordan, David Starr. "The Question of the Philippines: An Address Delivered before the Graduate Club of Leland Stanford Junior University on February 14, 1899." Palo Alto, CA: John J. Valentine, Esq., 1899.
Kaestle, Carl F., Helen Damon-Moore, Lawrence C. Stedman, Katherine Tinsley, and William Vance Trollinger Jr. *Literacy in the United States: Readers and Reading since 1880*. New Haven, CT: Yale University Press, 1991.
Kahan, Paul. *The Homestead Strike: Labor, Violence, and American Industry*. New York: Routledge, 2014.
Kant, Immanuel. *Perpetual Peace: A Philosophical Treatise*. Translated by Mary Campbell Smith. Project Gutenberg, January 14, 2016. Web.
Kaupas, Algis, Barbara Jarvis, Barbara Kopple, Benay Rubinstein, and David Gilles, prod. *Winter Soldier*. Harrington Park, NJ: Milestone Films, 1971.

Kazin, Michael. *War against War: The American Fight for Peace, 1914–1918.* New York: Simon and Schuster, 2017.
Keen, Jennifer D. "Remembering the 'Forgotten War': American Historiography on World War I." *Historian* 78 (2016): 439–68.
Kelly, Casey R. *Apocalypse Man: The Death Drive and the Rhetoric of White Masculine Victims.* Columbus: Ohio State University Press, 2020.
———. "The Wounded Man: Foxcatcher and the Incoherence of White Masculine Victimhood." *Communication and Critical/Cultural Studies* 15, no. 2 (2018): 161–78.
Kelman, Ari. *A Misplaced Massacre: Struggling over the Memory of Sand Creek.* Cambridge, MA: Harvard University Press, 2013.
Kerry, John. "Statement Before the Senate Committee on Foreign Relations." April 22, 1971. Available at Voices of Democracy: The US Oratory Project. Web.
Kiewe, Amos. "Cautious Crusade." Review of *Franklin D. Roosevelt, American Public Opinion, and the War Against Nazi Germany*, by Steve Casey. *Rhetoric and Public Affairs* 5 (2002): 765–67.
King, Claire Sisco. "American Queerer: Norman Rockwell and the Art of Queer Feminist Critique." *Women's Studies in Communication* 39, no. 2 (2016): 157–76.
———. "It Cuts Both Ways: *Fight Club*, White Masculinity, and Abject Hegemony." *Communication and Critical/Cultural Studies* 6, no. 4 (2009): 366–85.
King, Claire Sisco, and Joshua Gunn. "On a Violence Unseen: The Womanly Object and Sacrificed Man." *Quarterly Journal of Speech* 99, no. 2 (2013): 200–208.
King, Martin Luther, Jr. "Beyond Vietnam." Speech delivered on April 4, 1967, at Manhattan's Riverside Church. Available from the University of Hawaii. Web.
———. "Letter from Birmingham Jail." April 16, 1963. Available at King Institute, Stanford University. Web.
Kinzer, Stephen. *The True Flag: Theodore Roosevelt, Mark Twain, and the Birth of American Empire.* New York: Henry Holt, 2017.
Klement, Frank L. *Copperheads in the Middle West.* Chicago: University of Chicago Press, 1960.
———. *Dark Lanterns: Secret Political Societies, Conspiracies, and Treason Trials in the Civil War.* Baton Rouge: Louisiana State University Press, 1984.
———. *The Limits of Dissent: Clement L. Vallandigham and the Civil War.* New York: Fordham University Press, 1998.
———. *Lincoln's Critics: The Copperheads of the North.* Shippensburg, PA: White Mane Books, 1999.
Kraft, Barbara S. *The Peace Ship: Henry Ford's Pacifist Adventure in the First World War.* New York: Macmillan, 1978.
Kreusch, Jeremy. "Violent Representation: Photographs, Soldiers and an Ideological War." In *Mythologizing the Vietnam War: Visual Culture and Mediated Memory*, edited by Jennifer Good, Paul Low, Brigitte Lardinois, and Val Williams, 3–21. Tyne, UK: Cambridge Scholars, 2014.
LaFeber, Walter. *The New Empire: An Interpretation of American Expansion, 1860–1898.* Ithaca, NY: Cornell University Press, 1998.

Landes, Joan B. *Women and the Public Sphere*. Ithaca: Cornell University Press, 1988.
Laughlin, J. Laurence. "Patriotism and Imperialism." In *Liberty Tracts*, no. 2, 1–16. Chicago: Central Anti-Imperialist League, 1899.
———. "The Philippine War." In *Liberty Tracts*, no. 1, the Chicago liberty meeting, held at Central Music Hall, April 30, 1899, 14–23. Chicago, Central Antiimperialist League, 1899.
Leal, D. L. "American Public Opinion toward the Military: Differences by Race, Gender, and Class." *Armed Forces and Society* 32 (2005): 123–38.
Lears, Jackson. *Rebirth of a Nation: The Making of Modern America, 1877–1920*. New York: Harper Perennial, 2009.
Lee, Charles T. *Ingenious Citizenship: Recrafting Democracy for Social Change*. Durham, NC: Duke University Press, 2016.
Lee, Kristina M. "Theistnormativity and the Negation of American Atheists in Presidential Inaugural Address." *Rhetoric and Public Affairs* 23, no. 2 (2020): 255–91.
Leiner, Frederick C. *The End of Barbary Terror*. New York: Oxford University Press, 2006.
Lembcke, Jeremy. *The Spitting Image: Myth, Memory, and the Legacy of Vietnam*. New York: New York University Press, 1998.
Leone, Richard C., and Greg Anrig Jr., eds. *The War on Our Freedoms*. New York: PublicAffairs Books, 2003.
Limbong, Andrew. "Ye Says, 'I See Good Things about Hitler' on Conspiracy Theorist Alex Jones' Show." NPR, December 2, 2022. Podcast.
Love, Eric T. L. *Race over Empire: Racism and U.S. Imperialism, 1865–1900*. Chapel Hill: University of North Carolina Press, 2004.
Lozano-Reich, Nina M., and Dana L. Cloud. "The Uncivil Tongue: Invitational Rhetoric and the Problem of Inequality." *Western Journal of Communication* 73, no. 2 (2009): 220–26.
Lynn, Joshua A. "A Manly Doughface: James Buchanan and the Sectional Politics of Gender." *Journal of the Civil War History* 8, no. 4 (2018): 591–620.
MacLean, Nancy. *Behind the Mask of Chivalry*. New York: Oxford University Press, 1994.
Macpherson, C. B. *The Political Theory of Possessive Individualism: Hobbes to Locke*. Oxford: Oxford University Press, 2011.
Manela, Erez. *The Wilsonian Moment: Self-Determination and the International Origins of Anticolonial Nationalism*. Oxford: Oxford University Press, 2007.
Manthey, Dominic. 2020. "A Violent Peace and America's Copperhead Legacy." *Rhetoric Society Quarterly* 50 (1): 3–18.
———. "A Vision of Violence in General Orders No. 100." *Rhetoric and Public Affairs* 23, no. 1 (2020): 47–76.
Marchand, C. Roland. *The American Peace Movement and Social Reform, 1889–1918*. Princeton, NJ: Princeton University Press, 1972.
Margulies, Joseph. *Guantanamo and the Abuse of Presidential Power*. New York: Simon and Schuster, 2006.
Mbembe, Achille. "Necropolitics." *Public Culture* 15, no. 1 (2003): 11–40.
McAdam, Doug, John D. McCarthy, and Mayer N. Zald, eds. *Comparative*

Perspectives on Social Movements: Political Opportunities, Mobilizing Structures, and Cultural Framings. Cambridge, UK: Cambridge University Press, 1996.

McCarthy, John D., and Mayer N. Zald. "Resource Mobilization and Social Movements: A Partial Theory." *American Journal of Sociology* 82, no. 6 (1977): 1212–41.

McClane, Betsy A. *A New History of Documentary Film*. New York: Continuum, 2012.

McCoy, Alfred W. *Policing America's Empire: The United States, the Philippines, and the Rise of the Surveillance State*. Madison: University of Wisconsin Press, 2009.

McEuen, Melissa A. *Making War, Making Women: Femininity and Duty on the American Home Front, 1941–1945*. Athens: University of Georgia Press, 2011.

McGarry, Molly. *Ghosts of Futures Past: Spiritualism and the Cultural Politics of Nineteenth-Century America*. Berkeley: University of California Press, 2008.

McPhail, Clark. *The Myth of the Madding Crowd*. London: Routledge, 1991.

McSorley, Kevin. "Helmetcams, Militarized Sensation and 'Somatic War.'" *Journal of War and Culture Studies* 5, no. 1 (2012): 47–58.

Meeks, Lindsey. "Is She 'Man Enough'? Women Candidates, Executive Political Offices, and News Coverage." *Journal of Communication* 62, no. 1 (2012): 175–93.

Melucci, Alberto. *Challenging Codes*. Cambridge, UK: Cambridge University Press, 1996.

Michael, Robert. *A Concise History of American Antisemitism*. New York: Rowman and Littlefield, 2005.

Milford, Mike. "Veiled Intervention: Anti-Semitism, Allegory, and Captain America." *Rhetoric and Public Affairs* 20, no. 4 (2017): 605–34.

Miller, Bonnie M. "The Incoherencies of Empire: The 'Imperial' Image of the Indian at the Omaha World's Fairs of 1898–1899." *American Studies* 49, nos. 3–4 (2008): 39–62.

Mills, Charles W. *Black Rights/White Wrongs: The Critique of Racial Liberalism*. Oxford: Oxford University Press, 2017.

Mitchell, Linda C. "Entertainment and Instruction: Women's Roles in the English Epistolary Tradition." *Huntingdon Library Quarterly* 66, no. 3/4 (2003): 331–47.

Mitchell, W. J. T. "Interdisciplinarity and Visual Culture." *Art Bulletin* 77, no. 4 (1993): 540–44.

Molina, Natalia. *How Race Is Made in America: Immigration, Citizenship, and the Historical Power of Racial Scripts*. Berkeley: University of California Press, 2014.

Moore, D. W. "Gender Gap Varies in Support for War." Special report, Gallup Organization, November 19, 2002.

Murray, Billie. "For What Noble Cause: Cindy Sheehan and the Politics of Grief in Public Spheres of Argument." *Argumentation and Advocacy* 49, no. 1 (2012): 1–15.

Musicant, Ivan. *Empire by Default: The Spanish-American War and the Dawn of the American Century*. New York: Henry Holt, 1998.

Nakayama, Thomas K., and Robert L. Krizek. "Whiteness: A Strategic Rhetoric." *Quarterly Journal of Speech* 81, no. 3 (1995): 291–309.

Neely, Mark E. *Lincoln and the Democrats.* Cambridge, UK: Cambridge University Press, 2017.

Neiberg, Michael S. *The Path to War: How the First World War Created Modern America.* New York: Oxford University Press, 2016.

Nishime, LeiLani. "Remembering Vietnam in the 1980s: White Skin, White Masks: Vietnam War Films and the Racialized Gaze." In *American Visual Cultures*, edited by David Holloway, 257–64. New York: Continuum, 2005.

Obama, Barack. "Afghanistan Strategy Speech." December 1, 2009. Available on BBC. Web.

———. "Remarks by the President on the Way Forward in Afghanistan." June 22, 2011. Available at White House Archives. Web.

Ohl, Jessy J. "In Pursuit of Light War in Libya: Kairotic Justifications of War That Just Happened." *Rhetoric and Public Affairs* 20, no. 2 (2017): 195–222.

Olson, Alison. "The Pamphlet War over the Paxton Boy." *Pennsylvania Magazine of History and Biography* 123, no. 1/2 (1999): 31–56.

Olson, Howard C., and R. William Rae. *Determination of the Potential for Dissidence Event in the U.S. Army, Technical Paper RAC-TP-410.* Report. McLean, VA: Research Analysis Corporation, March 1971.

Ore, Ersula J. *Lynching: Violence, Rhetoric, and American Identity.* Jackson: University of Mississippi Press, 2019.

Overby, Peter. "Koch Political Network Expanding 'Grass-Roots' Organizing." NPR, *It's All Politics*, October 12, 2015.

Pach, Chester J., Jr. "And That's the Way It Was: The Vietnam War on the Network Nightly News." In *The Sixties: From Memory to History*, edited by David Farber, 90–118. Chapel Hill: University of North Carolina Press, 1994.

Paine, Thomas. *Common Sense.* Mineola, NY: Dover, 1997.

Palczewski, Catherine H. "The 1919 Prison Special: Constituting White Women's Citizenship." *Quarterly Journal of Speech* 102, no. 2 (2016): 107–32.

Parry-Giles, Shawn J. *Hillary Clinton in the News: Gender and Authenticity in American Politics.* Urbana: University of Illinois Press, 2014.

Parry-Giles, Shawn J., and Trevor Parry-Giles. "Gendered Politics and Presidential Image Construction: A Reassessment of the 'Feminine Style.'" *Communication Monographs* 63, no. 4 (1996): 337–53.

Perez, Louis A., Jr. *The War of 1898: The United States and Cuba in History and Historiography.* Chapel Hill: University of North Carolina Press, 1998.

Poirot, Kristan. "Gendered Geographies of Memory: Place, Violence, and Exigency at the Birmingham Civil Rights Institute." *Rhetoric and Public Affairs* 18, no. 4 (2015): 621–47.

———. *A Question of Sex: Feminism, Rhetoric, and Differences That Matter.* Amherst: University of Massachusetts Press, 2014.

Posner, Richard A. *Not a Suicide Pact: The Constitution in a Time of National Emergency.* New York: Oxford University Press, 2006.

Possner, Roger. *The Rise of Militarism in the Progressive Era, 1900–1914.* London: McFarland, 2009.

Prasch, Allison M. "Maternal Bodies in Militant Protest: Leymah Gbowee and the Rhetorical Agency of African Motherhood." *Women's Studies in Communication* 38, no. 2 (2015): 187–205.

Rae, R. William, Stephen B. Forman, and Howard C. Olson. *Future Impact of Dissident Elements within the Army, Technical Paper RAC-TP-441*. Report. McLean, VA: Research Analysis Corporation, January 1972.

Rancière, Jacques. *The Emancipated Spectator*. Translated by Gregory Elliot. London: Verso, 2009.

———. *The Politics of Aesthetics*. New York: Continuum, 2004.

Rand, Erin J. *Reclaiming Queer: Activist and Academic Rhetorics of Resistance*. Tuscaloosa: University of Alabama Press, 2014.

Ratcliffe, Krista. "In Search of the Unstated." *JAC* 27, no. 1 (2007): 275–90.

Rauchway, Eric. "Willard Straight and the Paradox of Liberal Imperialism." *Pacific Historical Review* 66, no. 3 (1997): 363–97.

Ricks, Thomas E. "The Widening Gap between Military and Society." *Atlantic*, July 1997.

Rindfleisch, Bryan C. "'What It Means to Be a Man': Contested Masculinity in the Early Republic and Antebellum America." *History Compass* 10, no. 11 (2012): 852–65.

Roberts-Miller, Patricia. *Rhetoric and Demagoguery*. Carbondale: Southern Illinois University Press, 2019.

Rodgers, Daniel T. *Age of Fracture*. Cambridge, MA: Harvard University Press, 2011.

———. *Atlantic Crossings: Social Politics in a Progressive Age*. Cambridge, MA: Harvard University Press, 1998.

Rohall, David E., and Morten G. Ender. "Race, Gender, and Class: Attitudes toward the War in Iraq and President Bush among Military Personnel." *Race, Gender, and Class* 14, nos. 3–4 (2007): 99–116.

Rotundo, E. Anthony. *American Manhood: Transformations in Masculinity from the Revolution to the Modern Era*. New York: Basic Books, 1993.

Rousseau, Jean-Jacques. *The Social Contract and Other Later Political Writings*. Edited and translated by Victor Gourevitch. Cambridge, UK: Cambridge University Press, 1997.

Samek, Alyssa A. "Pivoting between Identity Politics and Coalitional Relationships: Lesbian-Feminist Resistance to the Woman-Identified Woman." *Women's Studies in Communication* 38, no. 4 (2015): 393–420.

———. "Violence and Identity Politics: 1970s Lesbian-Feminist Discourse and Robin Morgan's 1973 West Coast Lesbian Conference Keynote Address." *Communication and Critical/Cultural Studies* 13, no. 3 (2016): 232–49.

Scheppele, Kim Lane. "Law in a Time of Emergency: States of Exception and the Temptations of 9/11." *Journal of Constitutional Law* 6, no. 5 (2004): 1001–83.

———. "The Rise of Authoritarian Democracies." Center on National Security, March 12, 2020.

Scholnick, Myron. *The New Deal and Anti-Semitism*. New York: Garland, 1990.

Schurz, Carl. "For the Republic of Washington and Lincoln." In Bancroft, *Speeches, Correspondence, and Political Papers*, vol. 6, 150–89.

———. "For Truth, Justice and Liberty." In Bancroft, *Speeches, Correspondence, and Political Papers*, vol. 6, 215–50.

———. "The Issue of Imperialism." In *Speeches, Correspondence, and Political Papers of Carl Schurz*, vol. 6, 1–34. New York: Knickerbocker Press, 1913.

———. "Militarism and Democracy." *Annals of the American Academy of Political and Social Science* 13, no. 12 (1899): 77–103.

———. "National Honor." In Bancroft, *Speeches, Correspondence, and Political Papers*, vol. 5, 453–54.

———. "Our Future Foreign Policy." Address at Saratoga, NY, August 19, 1898. In *Speeches, Correspondence and Political Papers of Carl Schurz*, vol. 5, edited by Frederic Bancroft, 477–93. New York: Knickerbocker Press, 1913.

———. "The Policy of Imperialism." In Bancroft, *Speeches, Correspondence, and Political Papers*, vol. 6, 77–119.

———. "Thoughts on American Imperialism," in Bancroft, *Speeches, Correspondence, and Political Papers*, vol. 5, 494–512.

———. "To Charles Francis Adams, Jr. New York, Jan. 1, 1899." Introduction to Bancroft, *Speeches, Correspondence, and Political Papers*, vol. 6.

Sharp, Gene. "198 Methods of Nonviolent Action." Brandeis University. Web.

———. *The Politics of Nonviolent Action*. Boston: Porter Sargent, 1973.

Shaw, Angel Velasco, and Luis H. Francia, eds. *Vestiges of War: The Philippine-American War and the Aftermath of an Imperial Dream, 1899–1999*. New York: New York University Press, 2002.

Sheeler, Kristina Horn, and Karrin Vasby Anderson. *Woman President: Confronting Postfeminist Political Culture*. College Station: Texas A&M University Press, 2013.

Shome, Raka. "Postcolonial Interventions in the Rhetorical Canon: An 'Other' View." *Communication Theory* 6, no. 1 (1996): 40–59.

Showalter, Dennis. "The Great War and Its Historiography." *Historian* 68, no. 4 (2006): 713–21.

Silbey, David J. *A War of Frontier and Empire: The Philippine-American War, 1899–1902*. New York: Hill and Wang, 2007.

Silver, Laura, Christine Huang, Laura Clancy, Aidan Connaughton, and Sneha Gubbala. "What Do Americans Know about International Affairs?" Pew Research Center, May 25, 2022. Web.

Silver, Peter. *Our Savage Neighbors: How the Indian War Transformed Early America*. New York: W. W. Norton, 2008.

Simpson, Curtis C., III. "The Logan Act of 1799: May It Rest in Peace." *California Western International Law Journal* 10, no. 2 (1980): 369–70.

Smith, Gary Scott. *Religion in the Oval Office: The Religious Lives of American Presidents*. New York: Oxford University Press, 2015.

Smith, Tony. *America's Mission: The United States and the Worldwide Struggle for Democracy in the Twentieth Century*. Princeton, NJ: Princeton University Press, 1994.

Snow, David A., E. Burke Rochford, Jr., Steven K. Worden and Robert D. Benford. "Frame Alignment Processes, Micromobilization, and Movement Participation." *American Sociological Review* 51 (1986): 464–81.

"Soldier's Letters." In *The Anti-Imperialist Reader: A Documentary History of Anti-Imperialism in the United States*, vol. 1, edited by Philip S. Foner and Richard Winchester, 316–23. New York: Holmes and Meier, 1984.

Southard, Belinda A. Stillion. *Militant Citizenship: Rhetorical Strategies of the National Woman's Party, 1913–1920*. College Station: Texas A&M University Press, 2011.

Sparrow, James T. *Warfare State: World War II Americans and the Age of Big Government.* New York: Oxford University Press, 2011.

Stahl, Roger. "A Clockwork War: Rhetorics of Time in a Time of Terror." *Quarterly Journal of Speech* 94, no. 1 (2008): 73–99.

———. *Militainment, Inc.: War, Media, and Culture.* New York: Routledge, 2010.

Stob, Paul. "Sacred Symbols, Public Memory, and the Great Agnostic: Robert Ingersoll Remembers the Civil War." *Rhetoric and Public Affairs* 19, no. 2 (2016): 275–305.

Stoltzfuls, Duane C. S. *Pacifists in Chains: The Persecution of Hutterites during the Great War.* Baltimore: John Hopkins University Press, 2013.

Stone, Geoffrey R. *Perilous Times: Free Speech in Wartime.* New York: W. W. Norton, 2004.

Storey, Moorfield. "The Neutralization of the Philippines as a Peace Measure." *Advocate of Peace* 70, no. 1 (1908): 19–20.

———. "Statement of Hon. Moorfield Storey, of Boston, Mass., before the Committee of Insular Affairs, House of Representatives (888A)." April 6, 1906. Available at the Library of Congress. Web.

———. *What Shall We Do with Our Dependencies? The Annual Address before the Bar Association of South Carolina.* Boston: Geo. H. Ellis, 1903.

Stormer, Nathan. "On the Origins of Violence and Language." *Quarterly Journal of Speech* 99, no. 2 (2013): 182–90.

Stracqualursi, Veronica. "Biden Says He Would 'Beat the Hell' Out of Trump if in High School." CNN, March 21, 2018.

Strong, Josiah. "On Anglo-Saxon Predominance, 1891." In *The New Era: Or, The Coming Kingdom.* New York: Baker and Taylor, 1893.

Stuckey, Mary. "FDR, the Rhetoric of Vision, and the Creation of a National Synoptic State." *Quarterly Journal of Speech* 98, no. 3 (2012): 297–319.

Stuckey, Mary E., and John M. Murphy. "By Any Other Name: Rhetorical Colonialism in North America." *American Indian Culture and Research Journal* 25, no. 4 (2001): 73–98.

Sumner, William Graham. "The Conquest of the United States by Spain." In *On Liberty, Society, and Politics: The Essential Essays of William Graham Sumner*, edited by Robert C. Bannister, 272–97. Carmel, IN: Liberty Fund, 1992.

Tarrow, Sidney. *Power in Movement: Social Movements and Contentious Politics.* 3rd ed. Cambridge, UK: Cambridge University Press, 2011.

———. *War, States, and Contention: A Comparative Historical Study.* Ithaca, NY: Cornell University Press, 2015.

The Record of Hon. C. L. Vallandigham on Abolition, the Union, and the Civil War. Cincinnati: J. Walter, 1863.

Tilly, Charles. *Coercion, Capital, and European States, AD 990–1992.* Oxford: Blackwell, 1992.

———. *The Formation of National States in Western Europe.* Princeton, NJ: Princeton University Press, 1975.

Tise, Larry E. *Proslavery: A History of the Defense of Slavery in America, 1701–1840.* Athens: University of Georgia Press, 1987.

Tompkins, E. Berkeley. *Anti-Imperialism in the United States: The Great Debate, 1890–1920.* Philadelphia: University of Pennsylvania Press, 1970.

Trask, David F. *The War with Spain in 1898*. New York: Free Press, 1981.
Tucker, David M. *Mugwumps: Public Moralists of the Gilded Age*. Columbia: University of Missouri Press, 1998.
Vail, Mark. "The 'Integrative' Rhetoric of Martin Luther King, Jr.'s 'I Have a Dream' Speech." *Rhetoric and Public Affairs* 9 (2006): 51–78.
Vallandigham, Clement L. *Speeches, Arguments, Addresses, and Letters of Clement L. Vallandigham*. New York: J. Walter, 1864.
Vallandigham, James. *A Life of Clement L. Vallandigham*. Baltimore: Turnbull Brothers, 1872.
Vavrus, Mary. "Working the Senate from the Outside In: The Mediated Construction of a Feminist Political Campaign." *Critical Studies in Mass Communication* 15, no. 3 (1998): 213–35.
Vitolo-Haddad, C. V. "The Blood of Patriots: Symbolic Violence and 'the West.'" *Rhetoric Society Quarterly* 49, no. 3 (2019): 280–96.
Vivian, Bradford. *Commonplace Witnessing: Rhetorical Invention, Historical Remembrance and Public Culture*. New York: Oxford University Press, 2017.
Volo, James M. *A History of War Resistance in America*. Santa Barbara, CA: Greenwood, 2010.
Voorhees, Daniel W. *Speeches of Daniel W. Voorhees of Indiana: Embracing His Most Prominent Forensic, Political, Occasional, and Literary Address*. Edited by Charles S. Voorhees. Cincinnati: Robert Clarke, 1875.
Wang, Keren. *Legal and Rhetorical Foundations of Economic Globalization: An Atlas of Ritual Sacrifice in Late-Capitalism*. New York: Routledge, 2020.
Wanzer, Darrel Allan. "Delinking Rhetoric, or Revisiting McGee's Fragmentation Thesis through Decoloniality." *Rhetoric and Public Affairs* 15 (2012): 647–57.
Warner, Michael. *Publics and Counterpublics*. Brooklyn: Zone Books, 2002.
Watts, Steven. *The People's Tycoon: Henry Ford and the American Century*. New York: First Vintage Books, 2005.
Weber, Jennifer L. *Copperheads: The Rise and Fall of Lincoln's Opponents in the North*. Oxford: Oxford University Press, 2006.
Weber, Max. "The Nature of Charismatic Authority and Its Routinization." In *Theory of Social and Economic Organization*. Translated by A. R. Anderson and Talcott Parsons. New York: Free Press, 1947.
Weheliye, Alexander G. *Habeas Viscus: Racializing Assemblages, Biopolitics, and Black Feminist Theories of the Human*. Durham, NC: Duke University Press, 2014.
White, Jonathan W. "Copperheads." Essential Civil War Curriculum. Accessed April 3, 2018. Web.
White, Richard. *The Republic for Which It Stands: The United States during Reconstruction and the Gilded Age, 1865–1896*. Oxford: Oxford University Press, 2017.
Whitlock, Craig. *The Afghanistan Papers: A Secret History of the War*. New York: Simon & Schuster, 2021.
Wiebe, Robert H. *The Search for Order, 1877–1920*. New York: Hill and Wang, 1967.
Wilentz, Sean. *No Property in Man: Slavery and Anti-Slavery at the Nation's Founding*. Cambridge, MA: Harvard University Press, 2018.
Williams, William Appleman. *The Tragedy of American Diplomacy*. New York: Norton, 1988.

Wilson, Kirt H. "Interpreting the Discursive Field of the Montgomery Bus Boycott: Martin Luther King Jr.'s Holt Street Address." *Rhetoric and Public Affairs* 8, no. 2 (2005): 299–326.

———. "The Racial Politics of Imitation in the Nineteenth Century." *Quarterly Journal of Speech* 89, no. 2 (2003): 89–108.

———. *The Reconstruction Desegregation Debate: The Politics of Equality and the Rhetoric of Place, 1870–1875*. East Lansing: Michigan State University Press, 2002.

Wilson, Woodrow. "Joint Address to Congress Leading to a Declaration of War against Germany (1917)." Available at National Archives. Web.

———. "State of the Union Address (December 7, 1915)." Available at the American Presidency Project. Web.

Woods, Carly S. *Debating Women: Gender, Education, and Spaces for Argument*. East Lansing: Michigan State University Press, 2018.

Yep, Gust A., Karen Lovaas, and John P. Elia. *Queer Theory and Communication: From Disciplining Queers to Queering the Discipline(S)*. Binghamton, NY: Haworth Press, 2003.

Young, Robert. *White Mythologies*. London: Routledge, 1990.

Zaeske, Susan. *Signatures of Citizenship: Petitioning, Antislavery, and Women's Political Identity*. Chapel Hill: University of North Carolina Press, 2003.

———. "'The South Arose as One Man': Gender and Sectionalism in Antislavery Petition Debates, 1835–1845." *Rhetoric and Public Affairs* 12, no. 3 (2009): 341–68.

Zarefsky, David. "Consistency and Change in Lincoln's Rhetoric About Equality." *Rhetoric and Public Affairs* 1, no. 1 (1998): 21–44.

Zupancic, Alena. *The Odd One In: On Comedy*. Cambridge: MIT Press, 2008.

Zwick, Jim. *Mark Twain's Weapons of Satire*. Malden, MA: Blackwell, 1992.

Index

Page numbers in italics refer to figures

Adams, Jr., Charles Francis, 57–58, 64, 67, 69
Addams, Jane, 21, 73, 78, 84, 85, 89, 93, 98, 118
Afghanistan War, 5, 143
Agamben, Giorgio, 13
Agnew, Spiro, 149, 151
Aguinaldo, Emilio, *55*
Aked, Charles F., 89, 90–92
Alien and Sedition Acts of 1798, 28
American exceptionalism, 47–48, 54, 68–72, 73, 166, 140, 168n9, 174–75n132, 175n140
Anbinder, Tyler, 163n37
anti-Asian rhetoric, 48, 50, 53, 57, 62, 63–64, 65–66, 67
Anti-Defamation League, 118
Anti-Imperialist League, 4, 12, 21–22, 24, 47–49, 52, 56–74
anti-Semitism, 1, 23, 101, 102, 103, 104, 105, 108, 112–13, 115, 116, 117–20, 187n65
Appy, Christian, 140
Arendt, Hannah, 155n35
Aristotle, 11
Armitage, David, 146–47
"astroturfing," 22, 97
Atkinson, Edward, 65, 173n103
atomic bomb, 121
Azoulay, Ariella, 134, 189n21, 190n41

Barash, David, 5, 124, 143
Benson, Thomas W., 16
Biden, Joseph, 140, 145
Biesecker, Barbara, 15
Blair, William A., 161n10, 162n28
Boissevain, Inez, 77, 92

Boutwell, George, 52, 59–61, 65–66, 67, 70
Brown, John, 26
Bryan, William Jennings, 62, 66–67, 85, 90, 93, 96, 175n140, 179n70
Burke, Edmund, 43
Burke, Kenneth, 153n7, 154n14, 158n77, 193n22

capitalism, 48, 69, 72–73, 121, 132, 159n91, 168n8, 176n5; laissez-faire, 53, 63–64, 73
Carnegie, Andrew, 52, 53, 67, 71–72, 79, 177n21
Cathcart, Robert S., 16
Chávez, Karma R., 16, 18
Churchill, Robert H., 164n82, 166n126
Churchill, Winston, 112
citizen-soldier, 23, 124–27, 128–33, 137, 138, 141, 188n9, 189n26
civil liberties, 3, 13, 20, 27, 28, 76, 78, 97, 98, 103–4, 117–18, 144, 160n95
Civil War. *See* US Civil War
Civil War Amendments, 60
class, 2, 3, 4, 6, 8, 12, 15, 20, 72, 77, 168n8; Peace Scripts, 14, 18–19, 22–23, 24, 27, 47, 49, 52, 68, 75, 76, 78, 87, 88, 94, 97, 98, 101, 104, 107, 108, 114, 116, 124–25, 127, 138–39, 141, 144, 145, 147, 148–51
Clausewitz, Carl von, 149
Cleveland, Grover, 66, 72
Clinton, Bill, 144
Cold War, 102, 120–21, 125, 133, 140
Confederacy, 29, 46, 67
conspiratorial style, 101, 102, 105, 112–13, 114, 118, 120
constitutionalism, 20, 33, 44, 116

Copperheads, 12–13, 19, 21, 22, 24–25, 26–46, 53, 61, 74, 76, 106, 119, 140, 144, 150, 161nn6–7, 162n35, 163n38, 166n118, 166n126, 166n145, 170n36. *See also* Pendleton, George; Vallandigham, Clement; Voorhees, Daniel
Corrigan, Lisa, 17
Coughlin, Charles ("Father Coughlin"), 102, 103, 107, 119
COVID-19 (the coronavirus [SARS-CoV-2] pandemic), 72
Crenshaw, Kimberlé, 18
Crosby, Edward N., 36
Cullinane, Michael Patrick, 171n45

Debord, Guy, 176n5
Debs, Eugene, 49, 98
demagoguery, 3, 15, 35, 98, 101–5, 154n13
democracy, 1, 3, 6, 9, 14, 47, 52, 103, 109, 115, 121, 125, 126, 128, 140, 143, 146
Democratic Party, 30, 32, 38, 44, 45, 49, 112
Dilling, Elizabeth, 100–121, 185n29, 186n35, 187n65
disloyalty, 3, 13, 30, 78, 94–96; sabotage, 81, 94, 96; sedition, 100, 117; traitor, 149; treason, 26
documentary film, 127–28. *See also Winter Soldier*
Dow, Bonnie J., 127
Dudziak, Mary L., 13, 49–50

Edison, Thomas, 82–83
Edmunds, George F., 70
education, 94, 108; treatises, 52; used to further "peace script," 38, 52, 109
emancipation, 26, 31, 40, 41–42, 43, 44, 53, 60–62, 65, 68, 112, 166n118. *See also* slavery
"emergency context," 7, 11, 17, 27, 28, 49–50, 52, 72, 78, 103–4, 125–26, 141–42, 144, 145, 146–47, 149; war script, 7, 13–15, 20
empire: colonialism, 45–47; imperialism, 56–74. *See also* Philippine-American War; Spanish-American War

enemyship, 15, 34
Engels, Jeremy, 13
enthymeme, 78, 119
epistolary style, 107–9
eugenics, 18, 67, 177n21

First Amendment, 3. *See also* civil liberties; "emergency context"
First and Second Congo Wars, 8, 144
Flores, Lisa, 17
Ford, Henry, 19, 22–23, 75–99, *80*, 103, 147, 176n3, 178n32, 178n40, 179n51, 179n70, 180n89, 182n121; Model T, 79, *80*. *See also* Henry Ford Peace Expedition
Foust, Christina, R., 16
Frankfurter, Felix, 117
Franklin, Benjamin, 36, 112
Fukuyama, Francis, 143

Galtung, Johan, 4, 7, 16, 104; positive and negative peace, 4, 5, 6–11, 16, 24–25, 40, 57, 68–69, 73, 84, 87, 97, 104, 107, 111, 116, 124, 130, 135, 141, 147, 150
Garland, Anna, 85, 87
gender, 50, 76, 77, 133; feminist movements, 104–5; femininity, 23, 101, 104–5, 105–11; inequalities, 2, 3, 8, 12, 14; masculinity, 17–18, 29–36, 45, 110, 128, 136–40, 148; "martial manhood," 30, 131; peace scripts, 4, 6, 12, 14, 15, 16, 17–19, 20, 21, 24, 27, 28, 40, 41, 42, 76, 78, 89, 92, 93, 102, 103, 114, 115–16, 120, 124, 125, 127, 131, 141, 144, 147, 148, 150, 151; roles, 32, 101, 102, 103, 110, 115, 121, 137
German Bund, 103
Giddens, Anthony, 159n91
Gilded Age, 52–53, 66, 68, 170n32
Gompers, Samuel, 62
Gorsevski, Ellen, 10–11
Great Depression, 75, 102; New Deal, 108, 110, 111, 116, 117, 185n29
Greater American Exposition of 1899, 50, *51*
Greenberg, Amy, 20, 30

Griffin, Cindy L., 18
Gruening, Ernest: 4–6; Alaska, 6; Ponce Massacre, 5; Vietnam War, 6

Hamilton, Alexander, 36, 112
Hanna, Louis B., 89
Hayden, Wendy, 186n34
Heidt, Stephen, 15, 192n6
Henry Ford Peace Expedition, 19, 22, 75–99, *88*, 150, 176n3, 178n32, 178n40, 179n51, 179n70, 180n89, 182n121
Hinduism, 117
Hogan, J. Michael, 98

Ickes, Harold, 108
indigenous wars, 19, 45, 66, 159n86
intersectionality, 18–19
intervention debates, 49, 53, 56, 67, 70, 81, 100, 103, 121, 145, 178n29
interwar years, 101–5
Iraq War, 1, 144
Islam, 1, 117
isolationism, 6, 8, 10, 22, 23, 69, 100, 101, 103, 104, 107, 138, 145
Ivie, Robert, 3, 11, 14, 15–16, 52, 155n42, 157n66

Jackson, Andrew, 21, 29, 30, 37, 38, 112
Jackson, Matthew, 78
James, Pearl, 79, 176n4
James, William, 22, 47
Janney, Caroline, 54
Jeansonne, Glen, 104
Jefferson, Thomas, 36, 70, 112
Jim Crow, 48, 53, 64, 65, 66, 118
John Birch Society, 23, 121
Jordan, David Starr, 53, 63, 67–68, 69, 177n21

Kazin, Michael, 81
Keller, Helen, 85
Kelly, Casey Ryan, 17–18
Kerry, John, 129, 141
King Jr., Martin Luther, 1, 3–4
King, Claire Sisco, 18
Klement, Frank, 31

Know Nothing Party, 30, 163n37
Koch Brothers, 97
Korean War, 19
Krizek, Robert L., 18
Ku Klux Klan, 1, 45, 102, 103

League of Nations, 98
Lears, Jackson, 168n8, 168n20, 169n28
Lee, Kristina M., 187n70
Lembcke, Jeremy, 126
Lend-Lease Act of 1941, 110, 115, 117
liberalism, 49, 53, 121, 124, 127, 132, 135
Lincoln, Abraham: emergency measures, 28–29, 161n14; memory appeals, 57–58, 59–62, 68, 69, 70, 71, 112, 114, 174n126; opponents, 20, 31, 35, 42, 53, 166n118, 186n53
Lindbergh, Charles, 100, 103, 107
Long, Huey, 102
Lost Cause, 21, 44–45

Macpherson, C. B., 188n9, 189n20
Madison, James, 36
Maloney, William Power, 110–11, 118
Manela, Erez, 98, 176n152
Marchand, C. Roland, 49–50, 52, 79–81, 177n21, 178n40
Marxism, 100, 103, 116, 117, 176n5; communism, 108, 113, 117, 118, 121
Mason, Charles, 41–42
Mbembe, Achille, 47
McClane, Betsy, A., 127
McKinley, William, 47, 49, 58
Melucci, Alberto, 157n70
Mexican-American War, 20
Molina, Natalia, 17
Morgan, J. P., 79
Morse, Samuel, 41, 166n124
Mothers' Movement, 12, 23, 100–121. *See also* Dilling, Elizabeth; Van Hyning, Lyrl
Mugwumps, 53, 170nn33–34
Musicant, Ivan, 167n1
My Lai Massacre, 126

Nakayama, Thomas K., 18

Nazism, 119
New Deal. *See* Great Depression: New Deal
New Left, 125
New Right, 121
Nishime, LeiLani, 189n22
Nixon, Richard, 139

Order of the Sons of Liberty, 29
Ore, Ersula, 17

Pach, Chester J., Jr., 126, 189n18
Paine, Thomas, 129
Pason, Amy, 16
Patriot Act, 144
Patriotic Research Bulletin, 106. *See also* Dilling, Elizabeth
peace movements: definitions, 9–10, 19–21
Peace Script: approach, 2, 11–13, 24–25, 143–51; class, 18–19, 138–39, 145–46; gender, 17–18, 148; race, 17–18, 147. *See also* Galtung, Johan
peace ship. *See* Henry Ford Peace Expedition
peace: definitions and debates, 1–25; disparities, 6; myths, 2, 7–11, 30–31, 32, 101, 106, 108, 115, 125, 126, 143, 145–46, 149, 151
Pearl Harbor, 23, 102
Pendleton, George, 21, 27, 33–34, 39–40, 43, 165n111
Perez, Louis A., Jr., 169n29
Peterson, Jordan, 140
Philippine-American War, 20, 21–22, 45, 54, 55, 56. *See also* Anti-Imperialist League
Pierce, Edward C., 59
Powell, Colin, 1
Progressive Era, 22, 50, 52, 78–79, 82, 98, 168n8, 169n21, 177n22
Protocols of Zion, The, 112. *See also* anti-Semitism
public memory, 147, 176n3, 178n31; Civil War and Reconstruction, 53, 57–58, 59–61, 64, 65; generational memory, 21, 27, 36–40, 114; paranoid memory, 23, 101, 102, 111–15; Philippine-American War, 22, 53; Vietnam, 122, 126

Quakers, 2

race: Copperheads, 40–44; Henry Ford, 78, 87; Mothers' Movement, 101, 115–20; peace scripts, 17–18, 147, 150, 151; Philippines, 52, 56–63, 67, 72; Vietnam Veterans against the War, 136–39; white supremacy, 40–44, 46
"radical flank effect," 50
Rancière, Jacques, 190n38
Ratcliffe, Krista, 78
Rauchway, Eric, 168n10
Reconstruction, 27, 29, 44–45, 54, 59–60, 65
religion: atheism, 103; Christianity, 23, 47, 54, 100–121; Hinduism, 117; Islam, 117; Judaism, 101, 103. *See also* anti-Semitism
Republican Party, 31–33, 34, 35, 36, 39, 40, 41, 53
Revolutionary War, 19, 54, 110
rhetoric: method and approach, 9, 12, 16, 19–21, 146–48; platforming hateful rhetoric, 20–21; war, 15–17
Rindfleisch, Bryan C., 189n26
Roberts-Miller, Patricia, 154n13
Rockefeller, John D., 79; Rockefeller family, 119
Rogness, Kate Zittlow, 16
Roosevelt, Franklin Delano, 4, 103, 108, 112, 113, 117
Roosevelt, Theodore, 83, 90, 95
Rwanda, 8, 144

Saas, William, 13
scapegoating, 3, 10, 12, 73, 87, 92–93, 102, 104, 116–19, 124, 125, 127, 130, 141, 143–44; dehumanization, 3, 10, 11, 12, 104, 117, 124; rehumanization, 10, 12, 15–16

Index

Scheppele, Kim Lane, 13. *See also* "emergency context"
Schurz, Carl, 47, 52, 61–62, 66, 67, 70–71
Schwimmer, Rosika, 77, 82, 83, 84–85, 89, 92, 93
Sharp, Gene, 9
slavery, 21, 24, 26–37, 40–45, 60, 61, 63, 64, 66, 112, 114, 162–63nn35–37, 164n74, 166n126
social movements: failures and success, 3, 24–25, 150; rhetoric, 11, 16–17, 145–46
Society for Diffusion of Political Knowledge, 27, 35–36, 36–37, 39, 41–42
Spanish-American War, 13, 18, 20, 21–22, 45, 48–49, 54–56; policing, 13, 168n12
Sparrow, James T., 104, 188n9, 189n20, 189n22
spectacle, 22, 75–98, 124, 176n5, 176n7
Stahl, Roger, 15
Stone, Geoffrey R., 125
Storey, Moorfield, 53, 62, 71, 174–75n132
Strong, Josiah, 167n4
Syria, 6, 144

Tarrow, Sidney, 14–15, 155n38, 156n57, 169n21
Tilden, Samuel J., 35–36
Tilly, Charles, 155n38
Trask, David, 167n1
Trump, Donald J., 72, 140, 145
Twain, Mark, 21, 68, 174n111, 177n21

U-boat, 81, 94
Ukraine-Russia, 6, 8, 144
US Civil War, 20, 26–46; civil liberties, 13, 28
Uyghurs, 8, 144

Vail, Mark, 15
Vallandigham, Clement, 21, 26–29, 32–33, 34–35, 36–39, 42–43, 44–45, 61, 147, 161n5, 163–64n51, 164n74, 164n76, 164n83, 165n100, 165m102, 166n145, 170n36
Van Hyning, Lyrl, 100, 101, 102, 104, 105, 106, 108–9, 112, 116
Vietnam Veterans Against the War, 23, 24, 122–42
Vietnam War, 20, 23, 6, 122–42
violence: definitions and theories, 5, 17–19, 24–25, 143, 150
visual culture, 79–80, *123*, 126–27, 131
Vivian, Bradford, 188n15
Voorhees, Daniel, 21, 27, 34, 40, 43, 165n115, 166n137

Wanamaker, John, 85
war: critical approaches, 15–19; definitions, 19–20
war on terror, 17, 141–42, 144
Warren, Fiske, 52
Washington, George, 36, 69, 70, 71, 108, 112, 113, 115
Watts, Eric King, 17
Weber, Jennifer, 21, 31, 161n6, 163n38
Weber, Max, 84
White, Jonathan W., 31
White, Richard, 168n8, 171n52
Wilson, Kirt H., 16, 17
Wilson, Woodrow, 4, 13, 78, 80, 81, 84, 95, 96, 97, 98, 102, 103–4, 176n152, 178n31
Winter Soldier, 23, 122–24, 127, 128–42
witnessing, 123, 126, 130–33, 135, 139, 188n15
Woman's Peace Party, 2, 78
Women's International Peace Party, 93, 160n95
Women's Voice, 106, 109. *See also* Van Hyning, Lyrl
Woods, Carly, 105
World War I: 13, 20, 22–21; Paris Peace Conference, 102; peace congress, 84. *See also* Henry Ford Peace Expedition
World War II, 20, 23, 100–121

Zaeske, Susan, 30
Žižek, Slavoj, 160n102